CASHFLOW FINANCE

ROBIN CLARKE

With legal materials by
EDWARD WILDE LLB, LLM
Solicitor

Asset Based Finance Association Ltd
Boston House
The Little Green
Richmond
Surrey
TW9 1QE

www.abfa.org.uk

The publishers believe that the sources of information upon which this book is based are reliable and have made every effort to ensure complete accuracy of the text. However the publishers, the authors or any contributor cannot accept any legal responsibility whatsoever for consequences that may arise from errors or omissions or any opinion or advice given.

In accordance with the Copyright, Designs and Patents Act 1988, Robin Clarke asserts the moral right to be identified as the author of this work, except as to those parts dealing with legal matters to which Edward Wilde asserts the moral right to be identified as the author.

Typeset by Origination, Tel 020 8560 9300, www.origination.uk.com

Printed by Jameson Press, Tel 01992 633662

A catalogue record for this book is available from the British Library

ISBN-10: 0-9552012-0-9
ISBN-13: 978-0-9552012-0-2

Disclaimer

This workbook, so far as it deals with legal issues, is designed to give a broad understanding of legal issues which might be encountered under English law. It does not cover any special provisions or changes needed under the laws of Scotland, Northern Ireland or any other jurisdiction in the British Isles or overseas, nor does it cover every situation or all the law on a particular topic. If you come across legal problems or companies established outside England and Wales, you should seek professional advice using your company's established procedures.

Foreword

The Asset Based Finance Association (ABFA) is a UK based trade association representing an industry with forty years of experience in supplying much needed liquidity to UK businesses. Our members provide invoice finance and in many cases additionally provide finance against other assets such as stock.

ABFA's members comprise invoice finance companies in the UK and Ireland which are owned by Clearing Banks, International companies or are privately owned. Together, these are responsible for over 95 percent of the turnover in this sector. Members provide financing to over 48,000 businesses (serving primarily the manufacturing, distribution, transport and service sectors) and transact over £192 billion of clients' invoices each year.

In 2007, the advances provided from the invoice finance industry exceeded £15.8 billion.

The ABFA provides the following activities on behalf of its members: education and training, events, industry news and statistics, lobbying, members' guidelines, professional standards, public relations and industry statistics.

Within "education and training" the ABFA runs: a range of industry specialist day courses targeted at the invoice finance industry; be-spoke and customized training courses; and a Distance Learning Programme. The latter offers members and non-members the opportunity to study for up to three, progressively challenging courses. These are the Foundation Course, the Certificate Course and the Diploma course. This book was specifically produced to support the Diploma Course; however it is also intended to be of value to all practitioners operating in or associated with the invoice finance industry.

This book is written to a syllabus drawn up by industry experts, including many senior professionals and replaces its predecessor, "Asset Based Working Capital Finance". The book has been renamed to reflect the additional content about the financing of stock and other assets, which in turn reflects the progressive nature of the industry and its practitioners.

To learn more about the activities of the ABFA and to keep abreast of industry developments please visit the website at the following address: www.abfa.org.uk

The Author

Robin Clarke

Robin Clarke has been in the invoice finance industry since 1974 when he joined the then market leader, International Factors (now GMAC Commercial Finance). In 1977 Robin attended and passed the very first examination course for the invoice finance industry run by the Association of British Factors (ABF), the predecessor of the current Asset Based Finance Association (ABFA). His experience in credit, account management, sales and international trade led to him becoming a main board director of International Factors, in 1988 where he continued for 10 years, firstly as the Sales and Marketing Director and latterly as the Client Relations Director. A spell as Associate Director at NMB Heller (now GE Commercial Finance) preceded a period of freelance consultancy within the industry. He was Chief Executive of the Factors and Discounters Association and Chairman of the Governors of the FDA Educational Foundation until 2003. He has frequently lectured on a wide variety of subjects relating to invoice finance at courses run by the ABFA.

Author of legal materials

Edward Wilde

Edward Wilde is the author of the legal topics covered by this book. He is a solicitor of the Supreme Court with a post-graduate law degree from Cambridge University. He has over 30 years of commercial law experience in advising UK and overseas asset-based financiers on all aspects of their businesses, including documentation, collections, contested litigations and mergers. For 22 years he was the senior partner of a London law firm. Currently a member of the Finance Law Team at Hammonds, Solicitors, he is also the Secretary and Honorary Legal Advisor to the Asset Based Finance Association and a Governor of the ABFA Educational Foundation. His international work includes chairing the influential Legal Committee of the International Factors Group of 65 independent companies financing export business.

Acknowledgments

The Asset Based Finance Association also wishes to record its grateful thanks to the following for their help and assistance in the production of this book:

Tony Flynn of Grant Thornton for his contribution to the insolvency sections of this book.

Richard Hawkins and **Robin Peers**, co-authors of Asset Based Working Capital Finance, the first ABFA workbook produced specifically for the ABFA Diploma Course, for permission to use extracts from their training materials.

Paul Hancock of J P Morgan, **Paul Beveridge** of Venture Finance plc and **Philip Underhill** of GE Commercial Distribution Finance Ltd for their expertise and advice regarding their specialist areas of asset finance.

The ABFA's Monitoring Group for ensuring adherence to the syllabus of the ABFA Diploma and the quality of this book's content. The Group consisted of **Edward Wilde** of Hammonds, **Mike Watson** of Arbuthnot Commercial Finance, **Kate Sharp** CEO of the ABFA and **Rachel Illidge**, the ABFA's Distance Learning Manager.

Contents

Chapter 1: An Introduction to Cashflow Finance

An overview of cashflow finance, its market and size   1
The rationale behind cashflow finance   2
    Invoice Finance – the rationale   3
    Funding against stock – the rationale   4
Other types of funding that can include some element of cashflow finance   5
    An overview of other assets which can be financed   5
    Plant and Machinery   5
    Property   6
    Intellectual Property   6
    Brand Names   6
Types of additional funding which can be used in a cashflow finance package   7
    Bank Overdrafts and Loans   7
    Venture Capital   7
    Mezzanine finance   8
    Government Loans   8

Chapter 2: Invoice Finance

Introduction   9
    The Purchase of Debts   9
    Assignment   10
    The Master Agreement   10
    Notice of Assignment   12
    Creating Availability   13
Factoring   15
    Recourse factoring   16
    Non-recourse factoring   17
Invoice Discounting   17
International Invoice Finance   19
    International Trade   20
    International Factoring   23
Other Invoice Finance Products   27
    Agency / Bulk Discounting   27
    CHOCC (Client Handles Own Credit Control)   28
    Confidential Factoring/Shadow Ledger Confidential Invoice Discounting   28
    Maturity Factoring   29
    Selective Invoice Finance   29

Chapter 3: Stock Finance

Introduction   31
   Methodology   32
   Categories of stock to be financed   33
   The type of goods to be financed   34
   Client record keeping   35
   Potential claims   36
Floor Planning   36
Trade Finance   39
The combination of financing stock and invoices   40

Chapter 4: Negotiating the Deal

Introduction   41
New Business Generation   41
   Marketing   41
Deal structuring to meet clients' needs and obtain an appropriate return on risk   48
   The process   48
   Understanding the prospect's needs   50
   Principles of pricing   52
   Pricing a cashflow finance product   53
   Aspects of risk   56
The role of other suppliers of financial services   59
   Funding implications when other financiers are involved   59
   Security issues when other financiers are involved   61

Chapter 5: Structuring the Deal

Introduction   63
Business and Corporate Risks   63
   Financial analysis   64
   Sales, profits and cashflow forecasts   64
   Sales ledger analysis   65
   Credit control procedures   67
   Cash review   69
   Bank reconciliation   70
   Contract analysis   70
   Purchase ledger analysis   71
   Stock control review   72
Evaluation of due diligence findings   73
   Financial evaluation   74
   Business plan   74
   Management quality   75

Debt evaluation 75
Stock evaluation 78
The involvement of other lenders 79
Terms and conditions of offer 80
Securing the deal 83
The Agreement 83
Warranties and guarantees 86
Plant and machinery 86
Property 86
Credit insurance 87

Chapter 6: Taking on the client

Introduction 89
The process 89
Building new relationships 89
Legal documentation 90
The agreement 90
Guarantees or Indemnities 91
Waiver 92
Fixed and Floating Charges 92
Deeds of Priority 93
Trust accounts 93
Bank mandates 93
Statutory identification of directors 93
Pre-commencement conditions 94
Verification 94
Data loading 95
Obligations of the parties 95
Procedures explained 95
Managing Expectations 96
Inter-factor handovers 96
The initial payment 97

Chapter 7: The Master Agreement

Introduction 99
Contractual Basis 99
Overview of Master Agreements 100
The Schedule of Variable Items 100
Party – Client 101
Party – Financier 101
Definitions 101

Transfer of Debts (Section 3)   103
Prepayments   104
Discounting Charge (clause 10.1)   105
Service Charge (clause 10.3)   105
Undertakings and Warranties (Sections 15 and 16)   106
Disputes with Customers (Section 8)   106
Recourse/Repurchase   106
Customer Credit Balances (Clause 9.6.1)   107
Collection of Debts (Section 13)   108
Client's Accounts (Clause 17.2)   108
Power of Attorney (Section 20)   108
Partnership and sole trader clients   108
Commencement and Termination (Clauses 2.1 and 18)   108
Termination with a Period of Notice (Clause 2(1))   109
Termination Event (Clause 18.1)   109
Effect of Termination   110
Applicable Law (Clause 20)   111
Exclusion of Other Terms (Clause 21.1)   111
Special Conditions and Pre-funding Conditions (Paragraphs 17 and 18 of the Schedule)   111
Execution of Agreement   111
Non-Recourse Agreement   112
Reassignment and Value Added Tax   112
Receipts (Clause 13.4)   112
Invoice Discounting   112
Supplementary Documents   112
Waiver   113
Deed of Priority (including consent to factoring)   113

Chapter 8: Change

Introduction   115
Where change can occur   115
Sales ledger profile   115
Stock profile   116
Management and corporate profile   118
Market   123
Underlying security   124
Mechanisms to identify change   125
Economic and market information   125
Client relationship   125
Audits   127
Statistics and trends   131
Internal Reporting   131

Client Reviews   132
External sources   133
Responding to positive change   134
Review limits   134
Switching to another product   135
Lifting constraints   135
Pricing   135
Outgrowing the need for cashflow finance   136

Chapter 9: Managing Risk

Introduction   137
Contractual provisions for protecting the funds   137
The invoice finance agreement   138
Guarantors and indemnifiers   141
Charges   142
Negative trading indicators   142
Increasing demand for additional funding   142
Deteriorating sales ledger performance   144
Deteriorating stock profile   145
Deteriorating financial performance   146
Fraud   148
Invoice finance fraud   148
Stock finance fraud   151
Responding to negative changes   152
Review limits   152
Changes to the review and visit functions   153
Increased financier vigilance   154
Prepayment percentage   155
Debtor spread restriction   155
Stock revaluations   157
Increased security   157
Pricing   159
Involvement of other financiers   160

Chapter 10: Determining and Managing an Exit Strategy

Introduction   161
Identifying circumstances requiring action   161
Client ceases to trade or threatens to cease trading   161
Serious breach   162
Accumulated non-conformance   163
Insufficient reward for effort and risk   164

Changes to third party situations   164
Assessing the situation   165
    Importance of timing   165
    Negotiation   165
    Role of audit in exit strategy   166
Client enters into a formal insolvency procedure   167
    Company Voluntary Arrangement   167
    Administration   168
    Administrative Receivership   169
    Liquidation   170
Matching exit strategies to the circumstances   170
    Legal provision for protecting the funding   170
    Collect-out   170
    Inter-factor transfer   174
    Return to bank finance   175
    No further funding requirements   175
    Business closure/run down   176

Epilogue   177

Appendix 1
Waiver by a bank (or other secured lender) with a prior charge over book debts (floating or fixed)   179

Appendix 2
Example of priority deed and consent to factoring   181

Appendix 3
Guarantee and indemnity   187

Appendix 4
Basic contract law for financiers   193

Appendix 5
Basic law of the sale of goods and services for financiers   203

Appendix 6
Example of non-recourse factoring agreement   215
    Annexe of definitions   232
    The schedule   237

Appendix 7
Basic insolvency procedures   241
    Fixed and Floating Charges   244
    Administration   245
    Administrative Receivership   247
    Liquidation   249
    Glossary of Insolvency Terms   254
    Administration and Administrative Receivership   255

Glossary   259

Index   265

An Introduction to Cashflow Finance

An overview of cashflow finance, its market and size

Every business needs capital. Initially, of course, there is equity capital put into the business by the shareholders. This capital is usually a fixed amount and remains in the business for the long term. Then there are long-term loans which range from quasi-equity put in by venture capitalists and others, to mortgages secured against fixed assets such as a property. Again these are usually fixed amounts and are repaid over an agreed period of time. Finally, there is working capital.

Working capital is required to fund the day-to-day needs of a business. Strictly speaking, it finances the changes in current assets and liabilities that occur in any business as it trades. Even for a business which buys everything for cash and sells everything for cash, there is nearly always a gap between buying and selling, therefore working capital is needed to plug that gap. However, most businesses buy on trade credit terms and may also sell on credit which further adds to the need for working capital. This constant movement is generally referred to as the "cashflow" of a business.

So, the amount of finance needed for working capital will fluctuate daily, as and when the cashflow demands. It is thus much more dynamic than either equity capital or long-term loans and the providers of this type of capital have become more dynamic in their approach. There has been a significant movement away from providing a fixed amount of working capital to cover all cashflow needs over an extended period, to one based more on the movement of specific assets.

In accounting terminology, assets are usually divided into two distinct categories. The first are referred to as "fixed" because they largely remain static, such as buildings and machinery. These assets are in the business for longer and would take longer to turn into cash. The other category is described as "current" and the actual assets turn over fairly quickly although other similar items will take their place almost immediately. Apart from cash itself, the two most common forms of current assets are debtor balances (unpaid invoices) and stock. The value of each of these categories will move up and down rapidly, usually on a daily basis. With debtor balances, the amount will increase as new invoices are raised and go down when debtors pay. Stock will similarly fluctuate as stock is bought and sold. Thus "cashflow finance" has been developed in order to address this constant fluctuation in working capital needs.

In the United Kingdom the most common form of cashflow finance is "invoice finance", which provides cash against unpaid invoices. Invoice finance, in the shape of its first product offering, factoring, has been in existence in the UK since 1960 but has its roots in America, more particularly in the textile industry based in New York. Sellers of cloth to the many clothing manufacturers would need certainty of payment, and finance to cover the often long periods of credit they had to offer. The certainty of payment was offered by companies which looked at each order to decide whether or not they could guarantee payment by the debtor to the supplier. If they could, the next logical progression was to offer to finance a certain proportion of the ultimate invoice. This offering was called "non-recourse factoring".

While some finance companies in the UK had offered similar ad hoc arrangements in the 1950s, it was not until 1960 that the first company was set up solely to provide non-recourse factoring. Unlike in America, where factoring remains largely geared towards the textile industry, factoring in the UK started to appeal to other industries and the demand for the cash became stronger than the offer of guaranteed payment. The 1960s saw many new entrants into the factoring market and by the 1970s the major banks had bought small factoring operations or started their own. Factoring, whether recourse (no guaranteed payment) or non-recourse, grew tremendously in the 1970s but by then the demand for finance was outstripping the other benefits of factoring. Thus invoice discounting (basically a finance-only product) grew at around £7 billion per annum during the 1980s, compared with £3 billion per annum for factoring.

Although the 1980s started and ended with recessions, the intervening years were very successful and generally profitable. Technology was introduced to provide electronic links with clients which overcame the potential clients' fear of losing touch with their ledgers. It also enabled clients to send invoice details to the factor electronically, saving the factor the expensive and damagingly repetitive task of data-punching.

In the 1990s factors and discounters introduced flexible finance against other assets such as stock, and plant and machinery, encouraged by new entrants from the USA and Europe. Most funding against stock or other working capital assets is in addition to an invoice finance arrangement although there are some niche players offering specialist funding solely against assets other than debtor balances.

In 1996 three trade associations representing most of the providers of asset-based working capital finance merged to form the Factors and Discounters Association (FDA), now known as the Asset Based Finance Association (ABFA). Their aim was to provide education and training, publicity, legal and technical support, and to establish professional standards. It now has around 43 members based in the UK and the Republic of Ireland and has links with the Commercial Finance Association (CFA) in the USA, International Factors Group and Factors Chain International. The latter two act as umbrella organisations for factoring companies worldwide wishing to undertake reciprocal business.

In 2007 the invoice finance market represented a total volume of £192 billion, with total advances of £15.8 billion to over 48,000 clients. Invoice discounting represented 88% of the volume, yet factoring, (combining domestic, export and import), represented 52% of the total number of clients.

Whilst the majority of ABFA volume is put through financiers owned by the clearing banks, there are several large American-owned players as well as some owned by European financial institutions, and many smaller providers.

As the market has developed within the UK many phrases have been introduced to describe the products and services offered within the industry in order to differentiate them from factoring. The term "invoice financing" is now seen as a collective term incorporating all types of factoring and invoice discounting. Financiers who have extended their product range to include the funding of all kinds of assets are frequently referred to as "asset- based lenders". However, this book is principally about the funding of invoices and stock and so the phrase we shall use throughout the book to describe this is "cashflow finance".

The rationale behind cashflow finance

The rationale behind cashflow finance is that the funds made available are in direct proportion to the assets in the business which are being financed. Whilst the financial health of the business and perceived quality of the management are important considerations when offering this type of finance, they are less crucial when determining the level of funding available from day to day. The "quality" of the asset being financed is usually paramount for day to day decisions.

Stock and debtors tie up cash in a business. Debtor balances, in the form of unpaid invoices, tie up cash. Finished goods, in the form of stock, tie up cash. Paying cash to import goods which will take time being shipped before being invoiced to the debtor has a negative impact on cashflow. Thus the rationale behind funding specific current assets is that cash is released from exactly the right place – i.e. wherever the cash blockage is most acute.

It therefore follows that if the level of unpaid invoices is increasing due to business growth, then invoice finance might be appropriate. If the business is required to hold a high level of relatively fast moving finished goods, then stock finance may be appropriate and so on.

If the overall rationale is to release cash from where it is being most tied up, let us explore in more depth, the range of services available to release cash from current assets.

Invoice Finance – the rationale

The phrase "invoice finance" is generally used to describe the range of products which releases cash from unpaid invoices. These unpaid invoices make up the debtor balances of a company and the phrases "debt finance" or "debtor finance" are sometimes used. Some finance companies providing these services are American-owned and therefore tend to refer to these products as "receivables finance". However, for the sake of clarity throughout this book, the phrase "invoice finance" will be used to describe the range of products and services which provide funding against unpaid invoices. Also for clarity's sake, the word "client" will be used throughout the book to refer to the business which is being financed i.e. the client of the financier. Finally, the word "debtor" will be used throughout the book to refer to the debtor of the client i.e. they are a debtor in that they owe the debt created by the invoice.

The prime products within this group are as follows:

- **Factoring.** This offers businesses the availability of cash against unpaid invoices but it is disclosed to the debtor. The factor runs the sales ledger and operates a credit control function including chasing overdue debts.

- **Invoice Discounting.** This offers businesses cash against unpaid invoices and is usually undisclosed to the debtor. The client retains control of the sales ledger management. This product is suitable for large, more established businesses.

Each of these products is available for domestic and export debts although there are usually restrictions concerning which export markets can be financed. Recourse (where the risk of the debtor failing lies with the business receiving the finance) and Non-Recourse (where the same risk lies with the financier) are alternatives offered for each of the two main products and are described in more detail later on.

Invoice finance is most appropriate when a business is selling to other businesses on short to medium trade credit terms. Typically a business might offer 30 days credit and has to wait until that period is up before the debt is due. Even then, many businesses will have to wait further whilst their debtor processes the invoice or deliberately delays payment in order to help their own cashflow. Thus the original 30 days credit granted could turn into a wait of 60 days or more for many businesses. A typical 'debt turn' (the average number of days a business's invoices take to be paid) in the UK could be 60, 75 or 90 days, depending on the industry or the competitive environment.

So, a business with an annual turnover of, say, £600,000 could have a sixth of that figure (based on a 60 day debt turn) tied up in unpaid invoices. That is £100,000 in unpaid invoices at any point in time. An invoice finance facility unlocks that cash by making available a certain percentage of the debtor balances. Put simply, invoice finance works by providing a certain proportion (typically 80% to 85%) of the invoice value as soon as it is raised. The balance is paid once the debtor has paid the invoice. In this scenario, a figure of between £80,000 and £85,000 would be injected into the business in the form of working capital.

Invoice finance is particularly useful in a business that is growing. As sales grow, the debtor balances rise and so too does the need for cash. Thus the amount of funds generated through invoice finance is in direct proportion to the growth in sales. Businesses with a low capital base or where the debtor balances are an unusually significant proportion of the total assets are also prime candidates for invoice finance. Examples of the latter category include Management Buy-Outs (MBOs) or takeovers.

The mechanics of how the funding is provided, the cost structure and the risks to the financier are discussed in the next chapter.

Funding against stock – the rationale

The same rationale is continued in this group of services, in that it is funding geared to a specific type of current asset. As the name suggests, this type of finance unlocks cash held up in stock owned by a business. There are principally three product offerings involving the funding of stock:

Stock Finance
This term will be used throughout the book to aid clarity although it should be noted that financiers with American parentage refer to this as "inventory finance". In much the same way as invoice finance, a certain proportion of the value of a pre-determined type of stock will be made available to the client by the financier. This type of funding is particularly useful where stocks are built up for a seasonal sales period or where there is a consistent hard core of easily saleable stock. A floating charge in favour of the financier is the usual security.

Floor Planning
One of the facilities offered by finance houses to businesses that are suppliers of goods (typically cars), that may be the subject of instalment credit agreements, is the finance of stock. Such facilities are often referred to as 'floor planning'. The techniques by which this is done vary considerably. The underlying essence in all cases is that the finance house puts up the money so that the dealer may, for example, take a car into its showroom at no immediate cost to the dealer, on condition that the finance house is repaid after a specified period, or when the car is sold, whichever is sooner. The security for the loans, and who has title to the car whilst it is on the showroom floor are considerations that vary according to the arrangements in each case and are discussed in later chapters.

Trade Finance

A facility to meet the cashflow gap created when a company is purchasing goods for onward sale. The trade financier will raise a Letter of Credit in favour of the supplier in order to purchase the goods on behalf of their client. To protect their investment the trade financier will hold title to the goods until such time as their facility is repaid. Once the goods are delivered, the client will sell the goods, effectively acting as an agent for the trade financier. As there is a time delay between the trade financier having to pay the supplier and their client receiving payment for the goods sold, the trade financier will usually draw a bill of exchange on their client for payment to be made by an agreed date. By the time the payment is due, the goods should have been sold and the debtor payments collected, so providing the client with the funds to settle the debt.

Other types of funding that can include some element of cashflow finance

An overview of other assets which can be financed

As in any financial package, it may well be that the level of funding available, using some of the methods already described, is still insufficient. It may be that a financier will look to fund assets other than invoices or stock. The funding of these other assets will not be covered in detail in this book but the following gives an overview:

Plant and Machinery

Finance against plant and machinery can be provided by way of leasing, hire purchase or specific loans, usually secured by a fixed charge. However, plant and machinery can often be included as another asset to be included by a financier already offering invoice finance.

The prime consideration of a financier in deciding whether or not to fund plant and machinery and at what level is: 'How will I recoup my investment if the business itself fails?' To try to find an answer to this, the financier needs to try to gauge how saleable the equipment is and will consider the following:

- The more common the type of equipment, the better.
- The less likely it is to date, the better.
- Is it reliant on bespoke software and if so, what are the licensing issues?
- Can it easily be moved from the premises, or can a landlord make this difficult?

Most of these questions will be answered by the financier obtaining a valuation. A professional valuation will give a 'market value' and the financier will use this to consider the level of funding. Typically, funding will be up to 80% and repaid over a period of three to five years. Usually a fixed charge will be taken as security over each specific item of equipment.

Perhaps most importantly of all, the financier will wish to be assured that the business will generate sufficient cash to enable it to repay the loan. The forecasts need to be credible and a prudent financier will monitor the cashflow forecasts regularly and perhaps use a model that changes the forecasts in light of actual performance.

Property

Again, there are companies which will provide long term finance against commercial property for anything up to 25 years. However, a cashflow financier might look to add property funding to a package which already includes invoice finance. Normally the financier would be looking at a secured loan against property of between five and seven years.

The financier will be looking at similar issues to those associated with funding plant and machinery. They will look at the ability of the business to repay the loan, the saleability of the property in a forced sale, and the valuation.

Commercial property is not as easy to sell as residential property, nor do prices increase at similar rates. Therefore the financier will be more cautious in its approach to property than it is to plant and machinery and will typically advance only up to 70% of the valuation.

Intellectual Property

Businesses can own their creativity and innovation in the same way as they own other assets. These usually take the form of copyrights, designs, patents and trade marks. Collectively, they are referred to as 'intellectual property' and are usually described as 'intangible assets' on the balance sheet. As with any other asset, intellectual property can be used as security for the finance provided. This is a specialist field but some cashflow finance providers will offer funding against intellectual property in addition to the funding it provides against current assets.

The key is to determine how much the intellectual property which is being funded will be worth if the business ceases to trade and the financier has to enforce its security. Many will be worthless but others may have a value because they can be sold on. A professional valuation is absolutely essential in determining how much finance could reasonably be provided.

Brand Names

Technically, a brand name is a form of intellectual property. Many famous brand names have been bought from failed companies and a few have attracted large sums of money. However, many more brand names simply die with the business, probably because they have become associated with failure. So, funding a brand name is risky. There are specialists who will put a value on a brand name and there are one or two cashflow providers who will finance a brand name as part of a larger package.

Types of additional funding which can be used in a cashflow finance package

There are other types of funding open to a provider of cashflow finance, although the following options would never be offered in isolation, but as part of a package including an invoice financing arrangement.

Bank Overdrafts and Loans

One of the reasons behind the huge growth of invoice finance, and other types of cashflow finance, is that banks have been unwilling or unable to move away from offering lending based on fixed ratios secured by fixed and floating charges. As we have already seen, banks lend against assets based on their historical value and are therefore more cautious in the amount they will fund. However, when a bank and a cashflow financier put together a joint package, they can usually offer more to a business than if they made offers independently.

Venture Capital

Venture capital is the provision of equity funding whereby the funder takes an equity stake in a business with an option to exit from the arrangement at a later date. The advantage to the funder is that they could reap the rewards of a business that has significantly increased in value – but the risks are high. This type of finance is usually provided by venture capitalists which specialise in equity finance, and is outside the scope of this workbook.

However, some cashflow financiers provide venture capital as part of their package. This is normally when they are funding an MBO or similar restructuring. A feature of restructured deals is that whilst the assets are high, the amount of equity is usually low in comparison to the funding required. It is not uncommon to have the shareholders putting up, say, £250,000 in equity and yet having to borrow £5 million to finance their business. These deals are referred to as "highly leveraged" arrangements.

Following this example of a £5 million funding requirement, it may be that a financier, having looked at each of the specific assets, can only muster £4.75 million. To make the deal work, there is a shortfall of £250,000. The financier still wishes to support the client and one way to make up this shortfall is to provide venture finance.

The financier will take a fixed and floating charge over all the assets and probably look for a term of between two and five years to recoup its investment.

It is worth pointing out that deals involving venture capital put up by cashflow financiers are still infrequent, and each deal will have its own bespoke terms and conditions. It will only be offered as part of a package involving invoice finance. Nevertheless, venture capital can play a part in a package involving cashflow finance. It could make the difference between clinching the deal or not, and will probably give the financier a much closer insight into the progress of the business it is financing.

Mezzanine finance

Strictly speaking, mezzanine finance refers to funding that ranks below 'senior' debt (secured against specific assets) and above equity funding. Again, this is a specialised subject outside the scope of this workbook and usually occurs with larger corporate deals.

However, like venture capital, a form of mezzanine finance can be used as part of a package offered by cashflow financiers.

Let us take the same example of the funding requirement of £5 million and the financier being able to muster £4.75 million, leaving a shortfall of £250,000. Again, the financier wants to back the client and acknowledges that it only works with the full £5 million. An option will be to provide a loan of £250,000 over, say, six to eighteen months if the forecasts show that there will be sufficient cash generated to pay back this amount at the end of the term. Hence this type of finance will sometimes be referred to as a 'cashflow loan'.

The financier will usually be secured by a fixed and floating charge and will only offer this type of funding as an addition to an invoice finance package.

Government Loans

Government grants and larger loans businesses which are governed by European Union rules, are outside the scope of this book. However, there is a government scheme which will guarantee loans which include cash for working capital.

The *Small Firms Loan Guarantee scheme* (SFLG) makes it possible for small businesses with a workable business proposal but lacking security, to borrow money from approved lenders. The SFLG is a joint venture between the DTI and approved lenders and is administered by the Small Business Service, an agency of the DTI. The loan decisions and the finance are provided by the lenders, but in the event of default by the borrowers, the government will pay – currently 75% of the outstanding amount. The SFLG is strictly for businesses which are unable to obtain a normal commercial loan, and with no more than 200 employees or £5 million turnover, if they are a manufacturer, or £3 million turnover for all other types of businesses.

Loans of between £5,000 and £100,000 are available (for businesses less than two years old) or £250,000 for more mature companies, and must not be used for buying shares or replacing an existing loan or overdraft. The length of each loan is between two and ten years. Some lenders can grant loans of £30,000 or less without first referring them to the Small Business Service and this is called the Small Loans Arrangement.

It is important to recognise that it is the lenders themselves who will structure the loan and provide the finance. Thus some lenders could use the SFLG as part of a cashflow finance arrangement. A list of approved lenders can be found on the DTI website and will include some invoice financiers.

So, we have seen that working capital is needed to fund the daily changes in the current assets and liabilities of a business and that finance can be geared to specific types of current asset. The two most common forms of cashflow finance are invoice finance and stock finance and in the next two chapters, we will examine these areas in more detail.

Invoice Finance

Introduction

Having briefly looked at the rationale behind current asset finance, this chapter now goes into more detail about how invoice finance works.

The main reason for the tremendous growth in popularity of invoice finance in the UK in recent years is its ability to provide more cash against debtor balances than a traditional bank overdraft. The amount of cash available through a bank overdraft will generally be determined by historical debtor balances drawn from audited accounts and perhaps updated by later management accounts. As this information is historical and produced at arm's length, the percentage of cash availability against these debtor balances by a bank is lower than that offered by invoice finance companies.

The main reason that an invoice financier can provide more cash against total debtor balances than a bank overdraft is that the debts are actually purchased by the financier. That way, the financier has title to the debts from the start and will keep up-to-date and accurate records of the actual total debtor balances outstanding.

The Purchase of Debts

We have already seen that there is a significant difference between traditional lending, where the lender usually takes a charge over the asset, and invoice finance, where the debts are actually purchased. This is a fundamental principle of both factoring and invoice discounting. The procedure is that the client transfers ownership of the debt in return for the payment of a purchase price. This transfer is called an "assignment" and we shall look at this subject in greater depth shortly.

We must distinguish at this early stage between the "purchase" of debts and taking debts as "security". The first is an outright sale and the second is lending. A bank is more likely to lend on the security of book debts. If a financier were to take debts as security for loans it would need to register a charge at Companies House. Without this registered charge the financier would lose the debts to a receiver or a liquidator in the event of the client's insolvency. Thus it is important to remember that invoice financiers do not make loans against debtor balances. It is also important that the invoice financier does nothing to contradict its purchase through any communication it has with the client, debtor or any other party. Words such as "loan", "interest", "security" or "advance" should never be used when talking about the purchase of debts. The purchase of debts has certain advantages:

- An invoice financier collects purchased debts without appointing a receiver;
- Discount is payable without deduction of tax. Interest on a loan may be payable net of tax to a non-bank lender.

The problem of confusing a purchase with a secured loan may disappear if the Law Commission's proposals in 2005 become law. It proposes that notice of every factoring and invoice discounting agreement will be given to Companies House. This will give priority over all subsequent charges and assignments of debts.

As we have seen, the invoice financier is the owner of the unpaid invoices and in the event of the demise of the client company. The invoice financier seeks to recoup the money it has provided to its client from the client's debtors.

As the debts are purchased rather than used as security, there is no "lending", nor is there an "advance", or and no "interest". The debts are purchased "at a discount" calculated against the amount of each prepayment of the purchase price. The amount charged in respect of discount is similar to or better than the interest rate on an overdraft. The percentage available against each unpaid invoice is the "prepayment" percentage. Thus an invoice financier would agree to purchase a debt of, say, £100, payable upon receipt by the debtor. However, a prepayment of up to, say, 80% of that debt could be made available at a discount rate of, say, 2% over base rate. The invoice financier will also normally charge a fee dependant on the level of service offered within each facility. This fee may be expressed as a percentage of debts purchased, or perhaps as a flat monthly or annual charge.

Assignment

The method by which the debts are transferred to the financier as part of the sale process is called an "assignment". There are two types of assignment:

1. A legal (or statutory) assignment. In this case the assignment of a whole debt must be absolute and not by way of security, in writing, signed by the client and notice must be given to the debtor. The effect is to transfer to the financier as the assignee (i) the legal ownership of the debt (ii) all legal and other remedies for the debt (iii) the power to give a good discharge for the debt without the concurrence of the assignor client. This means that the invoice financier can issue legal proceedings to collect the debt without involving the client.

2. An equitable assignment. This refers to any other assignment which fails to comply with the requirements of a legal assignment. The only disadvantage for the invoice financier is that, strictly speaking, the client needs to be a party to any legal proceedings to collect a debt. In practice the client is left out until the debtor demands the client becomes a party, and this is rare.

Provided there are no matters having priority (such as a debtor's rights of set-off or third party priority claims) the assignment gives the invoice financier what he needs, namely the unencumbered sole right to collect from the debtor.

The Master Agreement

When signed and exchanged between the financier and its client, this creates a legally enforceable contract. It describes in detail what the invoice financier can do and what the client must do. It sets out a lot of detail in order that disputes with the client are avoided. It also ensures that debts are purchased and not taken as security.

The agreement may consist of one long document or comprise several. If it is in several documents it may include some or all of:

- Short Agreement
- Standard Conditions
- Letter of Offer
- Supplementary Agreements for
  - Electronic Notification of Debts
  - Export Debts
  - Partnerships
  - Foreign Currencies
- Procedures Manual
- Computer User's Guide

Each will normally state whether it is intended to be a contractual document.

The purpose of the agreement is to establish mechanisms so that outright and absolute ownership of the debts is given to the invoice financier. The two most common mechanisms rely on equitable assignments of debts. The master agreements containing them are described as either a "facultative agreement" or a "whole turnover agreement".

The Facultative Agreement

This agreement usually requires the client to offer all debts (within specified categories e.g. UK debts or export debts) for sale to the invoice financier. The invoice financier then has the right to accept or reject these debts. In law it does not have to accept all the debts offered to it, but in practice will usually do so. Some agreements state that if the invoice financier does not reject the offer it is taken that they have accepted it. Others state that entering the debt in the records of the invoice financier constitutes acceptance of the offer. Now that stamp duty is no longer levied, facultative agreements strictly will only be needed with partnerships and sole trader clients, where the financier does not wish to register the agreement at the Bills of Sale Registry (see below).

Disadvantages of a Facultative Agreement

The main disadvantage is that not all the client's debts automatically belong to the invoice financier, even though there is usually an obligation to offer them. The client can choose not to offer certain debts. Those not offered do not then belong to the invoice financier. Although this would be in breach of the master agreement, giving rise to a claim for damages, the invoice financier will not have the financial benefit or security of such debts.

The Whole Turnover Agreement

As with a facultative agreement the categories of debts covered by the agreement are identified. These could be all debts arising in the course of the clients' business, or in a defined part of its business, or within specific categories. The key aspect of such agreements is that all future debts belong to the invoice financier, without the need for any further formality. This constitutes an effective equitable assignment of all future debts.

Such future debts which have already been transferred to the financier by the master agreement are merely "notified" to the invoice financier on notification schedules.

Advantages of a Whole Turnover Agreement

The benefit to an invoice financier in having clients assign all their future debts is:

- All the debts of the client, whether or not notified to the invoice financier, are the property of the invoice financier. This is useful in insolvency situations when the client may have sold goods without telling the financier about the debts. They are automatically the property of the invoice financier.
- There can be no claims to the debts by third party security holders who take a charge over book debts after the date of the invoice financing agreement. The ownership of all future debts was transferred to the invoice financier with effect from the commencement date. They are not available for the later security to attach to.
- It prevents the client choosing which debts it will transfer to the invoice financier and keeping back those which it believes will be easy to collect.

Disadvantages of a Whole Turnover Agreement

The principle disadvantage of such an agreement, with unlimited partnerships and sole traders with clients in England, Wales and Northern Ireland, is the need to register the agreement at the Bills of Sale Registry. This is required under the Insolvency Act 1986 to protect the invoice financier against the claims of a trustee in bankruptcy if the client goes bankrupt. Failure to register the agreement will result in the invoice financier losing its ownership of all debts outstanding at the client's bankruptcy. It would then have to claim as an unsecured creditor, against its client's bankrupt estate for its funds in use and unpaid charges. Registrations have to be renewed every five years. This is a complex and expensive procedure but does give greater security to the invoice financier. Registration can be avoided by relying on a facultative agreement. However, if the unincorporated client under a facultative agreement does not offer the debts to the financier, then ownership cannot be obtained.

Scotland

It is worth noting that Scottish law does not recognise whole turnover assignments of future debts. Where the client is incorporated or domiciled in Scotland the master agreements have to provide for the debts to be held in trust for the invoice financier. There is no Bills of Sale Registry in Scotland.

Notice of Assignment

With disclosed facilities, such as full factoring, the debtor is told of the Factor's purchase of debts by a "notice of assignment". This appears on invoices sent to the debtor, and is also repeated on statements. Typical wording may state:

"Our sales accounts are factored to X Factors Ltd to whom the benefit of this debt has been assigned and to whom all cheques should be made payable. This debt can only be discharged by payment to X Factors Ltd and not to any other party. Cheques should be sent to them at... If you prefer to pay by a bank transfer our account details are..."

This notice of assignment is important because:

- If the debtor then pays the client direct, it does not obtain a good discharge for the debt and can be made to pay the debt a second time to the financier.
- It fixes the rights of the parties.
- It avoids some secured third parties obtaining priority.
- Where two financiers claim to be the owners of a debt then priority will be given to the one which first gives notice of assignment to the debtor. This is known as the Rule in Derle v Hall. However it cannot be used where the financier taking the last assignment in time knew of the first assignment when it took its own assignment. Again this rule will be modified if the Law Commission's 2005 proposals become law. Then priority will be given to the first to register its assignment at Companies House. This is expected to be a simple on-line process.

The method of purchasing the debts which are to be funded is common throughout each of the products offered under the general heading of invoice finance. As we shall see later in this section, whilst there are key differences when comparing these products, the basic method by which availability of cash is generated, is the same across all products.

Creating Availability

We looked at an example earlier of a client turning over £600,000 per annum and an average debt turn of 60 days. This means that its outstanding debtor balances "turn" about six times a year. Thus the average debtor balance will be £100,000. At the outset, the financier and the client will agree on a certain percentage that will become available against these debtor balances. This percentage figure would be determined by the "quality" of the debtor balances (this area will be discussed fully in chapter 5) and the perception by the financier of the client's financial strength and management capability. The invoice finance market in the UK is very competitive and thus there will also be a strong pull towards offering the highest percentage figure with which the financier is comfortable.

At the commencement of an invoice finance facility, it will be agreed that certain debts (usually the vast majority) will be "approved" or "allowed" for funding purposes and that some will not. For example, inter-company sales, sale or return invoices or contra accounts may be disallowed for funding. So, continuing with the example of the £100,000 debtor balances, it may be that only, say, £95,000 are categorised as "approved" for the purpose of funding. Thus, if the agreed percentage is, say, 80%, then the amount of funding available to the client will be 80% of £95,000, which is £76,000.

Let us suppose that the client takes the whole £76,000. Some time in the future, the debtors will pay and for reasons that will become apparent shortly, these debtors will in fact pay the financier and not its client. The financier will pass on to the client, 100% of the receipts representing debts which had not been approved for funding (i.e. £5,000) and 20% of the receipts which had been approved for funding (i.e. £19,000). Thus the client takes £76,000 immediately and then a total of £24,000 as and when each debtor pays. There is, however, one vital element missing in this example: the financier will deduct its charges from these sums, as and when they are payable. There are two primary charges, a service fee and a charge for the amount of funds provided.

So far, this example has shown only what happens at the commencement of the facility. The reality is that a client will raise new invoices daily or weekly or whenever necessary. The client will send the financier new invoices, a fresh calculation will be made and more "availability" will be created. The following example assumes that the agreed percentage is 80%:

Date	New invoices	Cash received	Debtor balances	80% of debtor balances or "Gross Availability"
Brought forward			£100,000	£80,000
01 January	£10,000		£110,000	£88,000
08 January		£5,000	£105,000	£84,000
15 January	£7,000		£112,000	£89,600
22 January		£15,000	£97,000	£77,600

Taking this example one step further, let us look at what happens when the client takes some of that availability in cash:

Date	Gross availability	Cash drawn down by the client	Cash received from debtors	Actual availability
02 January	£88,000	£70,000		£18,000
08 January	£84,000		£5,000	£19,000
15 January	£89,000			£24,600

As can be seen, "gross availability" is increased by 80% of new invoices and 20% of cash received, but is offset by whatever has already been drawn down by the client company.

Without getting into too much detail at this stage, it is perhaps just worth mentioning the impact upon availability caused by credit notes. Let us assume that a client company raises an invoice for £100, receives an £80 prepayment from the invoice financier, and then needs to cancel the invoice by raising a credit note for £100. Looked at in isolation, the client company has received £80 for which the invoice finance company now has no invoice. The financier will have to immediately deduct the value of the credit note from the availability. In an on-going situation, the client will shortly be raising fresh invoices which will bring the situation back into line but nevertheless, if credit notes are issued just before or even after a client has ceased to trade, the invoice financier is at greater risk. The same risk applies when a debt is disputed because the resolution of the dispute may result in a credit note being issued. Following this theme, it can occasionally be tempting for a client to raise a fictitious invoice just to obtain the funding. These "fresh air" invoices will be worthless if the client fails and the invoice financier seeks to collect this debt from the supposed debtor. Protection against this and other types of fraud are covered in later chapters.

So far in this chapter we have looked at the mechanics of invoice finance that are the same whatever the product offering, but as we are about to see there are some fundamental differences between these products.

Factoring

Factoring was the first and, for many years, the foremost method of cashflow finance. Some people still use the word factoring as a generic term to describe all types of invoice finance. In this section we shall refer to the "factor" and in the following section may refer to the "invoice discounter" but in each case this also means the financier.

With a factoring arrangement, the factor not only provides funding against outstanding debtors, it also provides a sales ledger management service, which includes the credit control function including the collection of overdue debts. Thus the facility is disclosed to the debtor, who is given notice of this arrangement by a notice of assignment on the invoice itself and by letter or statement from the factor.

Once the client has delivered the goods or provided the service to the debtor, an invoice is raised by the client, which includes a notice of assignment stating that the debt has been assigned to the factor who is solely entitled to payment. Some factors insist that they send the original invoice to the debtor themselves but it is more common that the original is sent out by the client and that the client forwards a copy to the factor.

The factor then maintains an individual debtor account, sends statements and, if necessary, reminder letters and telephone calls to the debtor if the account becomes overdue. In providing this comprehensive credit control and sales ledger management service, the factor relieves the client of a considerable workload and in doing so charges a higher administration fee than for other invoice finance products. However, not only is there a benefit to the client in utilising a factoring service but there is an added benefit to the factor. As the arrangement is disclosed to the debtors with whom the factor is in regular contact, there is a reduced risk of fraud. The factor is thus more likely to offer factoring to a newly established or financially weak business than it would be to offer invoice discounting, which we shall see is normally undisclosed to the debtor. Diagrams 1, 2 & 3 explain the factoring process and the relationships between the client, the factor and the debtor.

Diagram 1

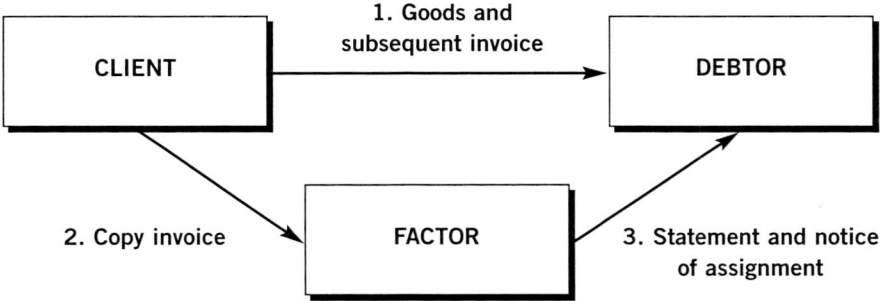

1. Client sells goods to debtor. A debt arises. Normally client sends the original invoice to the debtor with a notice of assignment.
2. Client sends copy invoice to the factor via post or e-mail. Sometimes the factor may require supporting documents such as proof of delivery.
3. Factor sends statement (or sometimes the original invoice) to debtor - the notice of assignment also appears on the statement.

Diagram 2

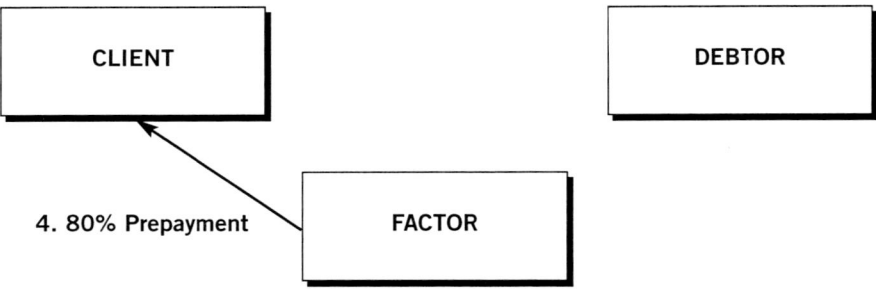

4. Factor makes, for example, an 80% prepayment to the client against the value of the invoice, less any service charges. However, before doing so, the factor may wish to verify the validity of the invoice or the credit worthiness or existence of the debtor.

Diagram 3

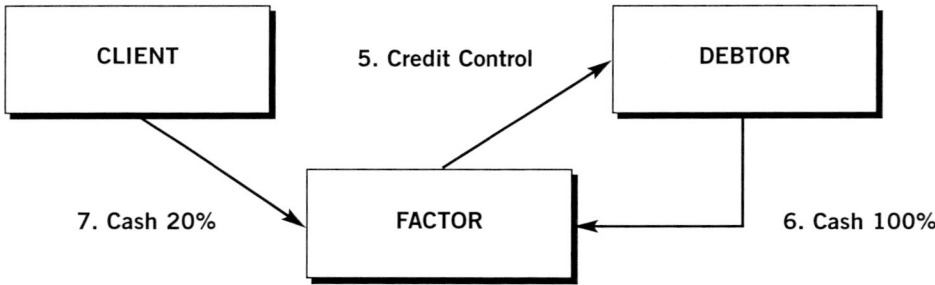

5. Factor provides sales ledger management and credit control.
6. Factor collects payment from the debtor (100%).
7. Factor remits the balance of the purchase price (20% of the debt in this example) to the client less any discounting charge.

The majority of factored debt in the UK is in respect of domestic invoices, where both client and debtor are based in the UK. However, there is a significant volume of export debt which is factored, often using different currencies. The funding operates in exactly the same way as for domestic debt, but the methods used to collect it vary and are outlined later in this chapter.

What happens when the debtor fails to pay due to its insolvency. The consequences depend upon whether the facility is on a "recourse" or "non-recourse" basis.

Recourse factoring

Under a recourse arrangement the factor will recover from the client any prepayments previously made in respect of any debts which are not collected within a given time period. This is usually between 90 and 120 days following the month of invoice, and is often referred to as the "recourse period". The legal agreement achieves this by requiring the client to guarantee that all debtors will discharge their debts within a fixed period (typically 90 days past the due date) failing which the client has to pay back the prepayments made.

Non-recourse factoring

The purchase of the debts for a prepayment operates in the same way as the recourse facility. The difference is that where a debt has been "approved for credit" by the factor, the client is protected against a loss due to a bad debt, provided that the debt remains undisputed. The protection relates only to the VAT exclusive amount of the debt. So where a prepayment is provided at 80% of the face value of a debt then the balance of 20% less VAT is paid to the client even if the debtor fails to pay. The factor therefore suffers the credit loss.

Where a debtor has gone bankrupt owing a debt which is non-recourse, the factor will pay the client the full amount of the debt less any VAT. Factors are unable to re-claim VAT on bad debts, unlike the original supplier. So, the factor will re-assign the bad debt, to enable the client to obtain VAT bad debt relief via their VAT quarterly return. Some financiers will only accept responsibility if the debtor is insolvent. Others will pay even upon protracted default (the debtor fails to pay though the company is still trading). Where goods or services giving rise to the factored debt are the subject of a dispute (usually about non-delivery or the quality of the goods) the debt will no longer be approved. In these circumstances the factor will recover any prepayment made against the debt from the client in the same way as for a recourse factoring facility.

A variation of a non-recourse facility is where the financier in partnership with a credit insurer, administers an insurance policy for the client providing cover against the risk of debtor failure. However, since 2005, the financier needs to be registered with the Financial Services Authority and comply with their regulations regarding the selling and administration of such policies. As a result of these burdens many financiers are withdrawing from offering this product.

Invoice Discounting

Invoice discounting enables a client to obtain the cashflow benefits of factoring whilst still retaining control over all sales ledger and credit control functions. It is sometimes referred to by its acronym "ID". It is the largest of the invoice finance products in terms of client turnover, and whilst it still has fewer client numbers than those that use factoring, it has for many years been the faster growing product.

Whilst factoring is more suitable for smaller businesses which can benefit from the addition of the sales ledger management service, invoice discounting suits more established businesses where the need is purely for cash rather than help with their credit control. As it often an undisclosed facility, it is perceived to be riskier for the invoice discounter, and thus they will look at financially stronger and more mature businesses with a proven administrative capability than would a factor.

As most invoice discounting is undertaken on a confidential basis, this means that no notice of assignment is shown on the invoices and the debtor is unaware of the relationship with the invoice discounter. The client retains responsibility for sales ledger management and credit control. The client will submit an "aged debtor analysis" to the discounter and report on all debts over a certain age. Once debts reach a certain age, the discounter will normally "disallow" them for funding, which in effect means they will claw back these debts from the calculation for availability. When the debtor pays, it will of course send the payment to its supplier, unaware that the debt is in fact owned by the invoice discounter. In order that these funds are received by the discounter rather than into the client's bank account, a separate trust account is set up in the name of the client but under the sole control of the discounter. Once a cheque is received at the client's premises, they are obliged to pay this directly into the trust account. Electronic receipts are paid directly into the trust account by the debtor who remains unaware that the bank account is a trust account.

It is possible to provide this product on a disclosed basis, usually when the discounter is seeking more comfort through disclosure. With a disclosed facility, the notice of assignment will be shown on the invoices and the debtor will be aware of the relationship with the invoice discounter. However the client will still undertake the sales ledger management and credit control. This is usually called a "disclosed invoice discounting" facility. The key difference between a disclosed and an undisclosed facility from the invoice discounter's perspective is that with an undisclosed facility, they cannot verify the debt with the debtor. Thus an undisclosed facility is a greater risk. To mitigate this, most invoice discounters will attempt to verify debts through other means such as using external accountants to contact the debtor under the guise of a routine audit enquiry. The master agreement will give them the ability to do this but care needs to be taken to ensure that where the debtor is an unlimited partnership or sole trader its rights under the Data Protection Act are not infringed. This is done by mentioning that information may be transferred to the financiers of the client whose details are available upon request.

The following diagrams show the process and relationships in a *confidential* facility.
Invoice discounting remains predominately a recourse facility but it is increasingly available with an added non-recourse service whereby the financier accepts the credit risk of the debtor's failure, within agreed limits.

Diagram 4

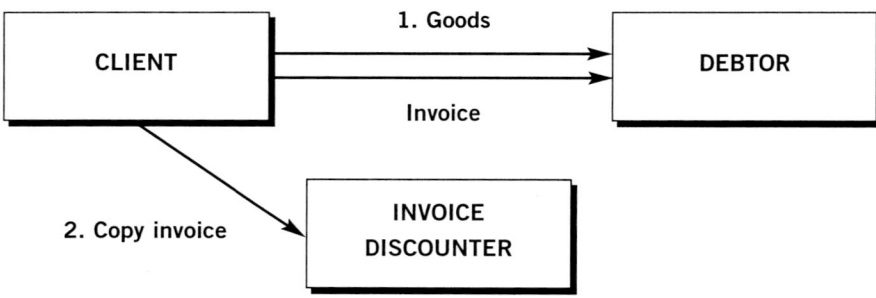

1. Client sells goods and invoices the debtor in the normal way.
2. Copy invoices sometimes sent to invoice discounter but more often a "day book" listing is sent, which gives basic details of each invoice.

Diagram 5

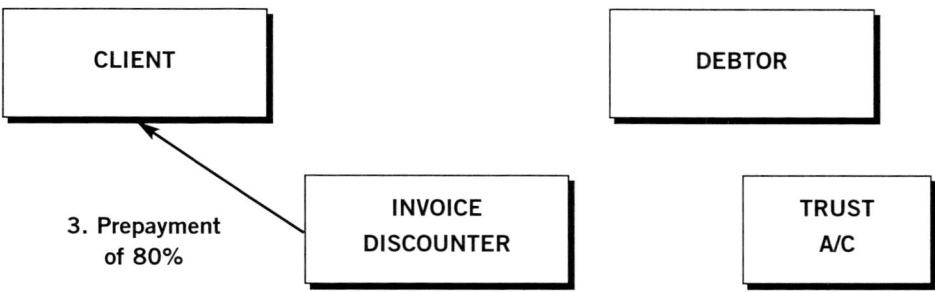

3. Invoice discounter makes, for example, an 80% prepayment to the client against the total value of the invoices less any service charges.

Diagram 6

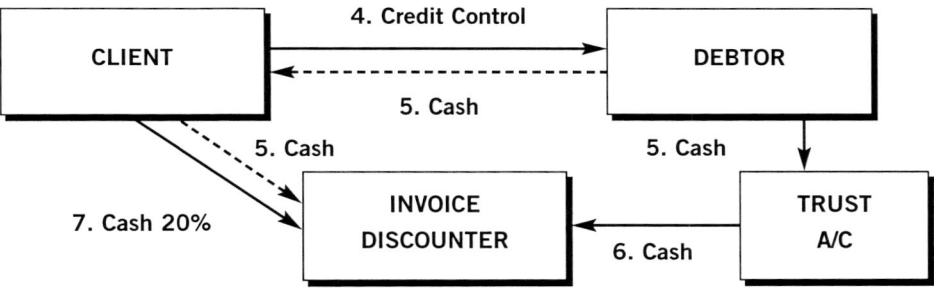

4. Client maintains sales ledger and chases debtor for payment.
5. Debtor instructed to remit payment to trust account. If debtor pays the client direct, then client will deposit payment into trust account each day.
6. Trust account receipts automatically transferred to invoice discounter daily.
7. Invoice discounter pays the balance of the purchase price (20% of the debt in this case) to the client less any discounting charges.

Invoice discounting grew by offering finance against domestic sales but there is an increasing number of financiers offering to fund export debts, although rarely in isolation, without the addition of the domestic debts.

International Invoice Finance

We have seen that when funding alone is required, some financiers will offer to finance export sales. The risks are greater but the logistics are broadly similar. However, when export *factoring* is offered, the logistics are altogether more complex.

International Trade

Before looking at the structure of international factoring we will look at some of the problems that any exporter faces and then the solutions provided by international factoring services:

Distance
When the customer is in another country, it is less easy to visit them, correspondence takes longer and when they are in a different time zone, even telephone calls need some planning. Therefore if a dispute arises or there is some difficulty about payment, then these issues become much more difficult to resolve. Also, there is an added risk that goods could perish or become lost in transit due to the longer distances involved.

Language
Selling goods or services in another language is difficult enough but collecting money or resolving a dispute often means that a customer's previous fluency in your language disappears.

National Customs/Culture
Expectations differ widely between countries with regards to speed, commercial courtesies and other cultural issues. Unless one is experienced in dealing within a particular market, offence could be caused or frustration suffered.

Credit Information
The standard and quality of credit information on debtors will vary from country to country, making it harder to make a decision about whether to deal with the potential debtor.

Local Legislation
When exporting goods, these will inevitably have to pass through customs and when the destination is outside a trade group, such as the European Union, there may be additional import restrictions and tariffs. A knowledge of these customs controls and tariffs will be essential and will inevitably produce more paperwork. This additional paperwork (or lack of it) can further complicate the process of collecting overdue invoices.

Foreign Currency
Debtors normally prefer that invoices be in their currency. This builds in a further problem, with its attendant risk of exchange loss. The main risk is one of currency fluctuation during the period between order and payment. If invoicing in currency, then the Forward Market can be used to protect the financier and client against exchange rate loss. The financier will also need to arrange special statements to cope with the different currencies.

Local Economic and Political Conditions
A UK business selling outside the major western markets needs to consider the political and economic conditions of the country into which they are selling. It is therefore vital to look at the risk to payment prospects on a 'country' basis before assessing it on a debtor basis.

Shipping Terms

When shipping goods in a domestic market, it is common for the seller to pay for the cost of the delivery. When goods are exported, however, there are often additional costs, such as insurance or duty to consider and there are various ways in which these costs are apportioned. The most common methods are as follows:

- **Ex-works.** This is where the exporter pays all the costs up to the time when the goods leave their warehouse. Thereafter, the buyer pays all the costs, including those for freight, insurance and any duties.

- **F.O.B.** This stands for "free on board" and means that the exporter pays for all the costs up to the point where the goods are loaded on board the method of transport to be used.

- **C. & F.** This stands for "cost and freight" and means that the exporter will pay for all the costs to a foreign port (usually the port in the buyer's country) although in this instance, the exporter will not pay the insurance costs.

- **C.I.F.** This stands for "cost, insurance and freight" and means that the exporter will cover all the costs, including that of any insurance, up to the point where the goods reach the foreign port.

- **Free Domicile.** This is where the exporter pays all the costs from their warehouse to that of the buyer, which will include freight, duties and insurance.

Proof of Shipment

Trade with another country usually results in much longer delivery periods and if the goods are not transported by the seller, then the following proofs of shipment will be used, depending on the mode of transport:

Bills of Lading

When goods are transported by sea, there is a standard document which confirms that the goods have been shipped, known as a Bill of Lading. This is drawn up by the shipping company and signed by the captain with a copy sent to the exporter via the shipping agent. The signed document becomes known as a negotiable Bill of Lading and is evidence of a contract of carriage. The signed Bill of Lading must be produced by the buyer in order to obtain the goods and process them through customs. It is international practice that title in the goods passes with the Bill of Lading. Thus it is general practice that Bills of Lading are not released until either payment is made or payment is promised through the acceptance of a Letter of Credit or Bill of Exchange.

Air Consignment Notes

These are issued by the airline which is transporting the goods and provide evidence of receipt of the goods for despatch by that airline. Unlike the Bill of Lading, the airline does not require a copy of the Air Consignment Note before releasing the goods because the buyer would not receive the document until long after the goods have arrived and this would negate the advantage of air transport which is to speed up delivery. Air Consignment Notes are not used in conjunction with methods of payment because there is no passing of title with this document.

Parcel Post Receipts

These receipts are issued by the Post Office as proof that the goods have been presented for delivery. Both Parcel Post Receipts and Air Consignment Notes share the shortcoming that they carry no security for the exporter. However that can be overcome by arranging for the goods to be consigned to a local bank. Once all the payment terms have been complied with, the bank can then be instructed to release the goods.

Payment Terms

In addition to COD, (cash on delivery) and open account terms, the following methods of payment are widely used in respect of international trade:

Letters of Credit

Letters of Credit offers the highest degree of security to the exporter provided that the stated conditions are fulfilled. These terms and conditions of the Letter of Credit become part of the sale contract.

A Letter of Credit is a written undertaking by the issuing bank, given to the beneficiary (usually the exporter) at the request of and in accordance with the instructions given by the applicant (the buyer), to make payment up to the stated sum of money, within a prescribed time limit and against stipulated documents. The process is as follows:

- The exporter and buyer agree a sales contract in which payment is to be by Letter of Credit.
- The buyer instructs its bank (the issuing bank) to open a Letter of Credit in favour of the exporter.
- The issuing bank asks a bank in the exporter's country (the advising bank) to advise or confirm the Letter of Credit to the exporter.
- The exporter ships the goods and submits all the required documents to the advising bank.
- The advising bank checks the documents and either pays on sight or on some future date stipulated in the terms of the Letter of Credit.
- If the advising bank has added its "confirmation" and provided the terms of the Letter of Credit have been fulfilled, then it must pay regardless of any other consideration.

Letters of Credit come in three forms:

- *Revocable.* Letters of Credit can be amended or cancelled at any time without any warning or notice. They give no more security to the exporter than a post-dated cheque and are very rare.
- *Irrevocable.* Letters of Credit can be amended only with the agreement of all parties and are thus very secure although the exporter does have to rely on the undertaking of the foreign bank. This is the most common form of Letter of Credit.
- *Confirmed.* Letters of Credit are an undertaking by the advising bank to pay without recourse and recovers its funds from the issuing bank. Although costlier, this type is even more secure.

Letters of Credit thus offer a high degree of security to the exporter if irrevocable or confirmed, although there are significant bank costs for both the exporter and buyer. The banks of course, are concerned only with the documents and have nothing to do with the actual goods. One of the main disadvantages of Letters of Credit is that they may weaken the exporter's competitive position because the buyer's credit facilities have to be tied up before payment is actually due.

Some countries do not like using Letters of Credit although others, such as China, use them frequently. Finally, it should be noted that many presentations of documents to the advising bank are faulty in some way which of course negates the security aspect which is perceived to be the main benefit of Letters of Credit.

Bills of Exchange

A Bill of Exchange is an unconditional order in writing, addressed by one party to another, signed by the party giving it, requiring the party to pay on demand or at a fixed and determinable time, a sum of money. Bills of Exchange are initiated by the supplier (unlike a post-dated cheque) and some may also contain the place of payment or other specific terms. Once the Bill has been drawn up, the supplier sends it to their bank. The bank will then ask the buyer to authorise payment (on sight) or to sign an acceptance for future payment. The instrument is then called an "accepted" Bill of Exchange and is a negotiable instrument and may be discounted by banks. In fact the accepted Bill may exchange hands many times before being presented for payment.

Some Bills may be accompanied by documents relating to that specific sale. Those without documents are called "clean" Bills. Those with documents are very useful when the goods have been sent by sea as they will not be released until the Bill of Lading is presented. The exporter sends the Bill of Lading along with the Bill of Exchange to the buyer's bank. The bank will then only release the goods once the Bill of Exchange has been signed.

Payment can only be made by the buyer's bank once it has been accepted. However, if the buyer delays signing the Bill, then it may suggest either that there is something wrong with the goods or that the buyer has some financial difficulties. However, once the Bill has been accepted, payment is due irrespective of whether the contract between the supplier and buyer has been properly executed. If an accepted Bill is not met, then it must be "protested" to the issuing bank.

International Factoring

It can be seen from the above list, that trading with debtors in another country has many added difficulties to those encountered for domestic sales. Funding these sales using invoice finance will help cashflow in the same way as for domestic sales, but using factoring in particular for export business can have many more benefits. The factoring company which specializes in export business will be able to help the supplier through all the additional difficulties of trading internationally. Factoring companies use two different methods of handling exports. The first is to use one of the "factoring chains" and the second is to do it all themselves, or "direct export factoring" and we shall now examine both methods.

Using a Factoring Chain

Over recent years the use of factoring 'chains' has grown. There are two such "chains":

International Factors Group and Factors Chain International

Both have members based around the world and use sophisticated computer communication networks to pass and track transactions between member companies on behalf of their clients. Both organisations have similar standard terms of business upon which members rely when assigning debts. These are called "General Rules of International Factoring", often shortened to "GRIF". Members of both chains agree to settle their differences by arbitration.

The chain can best be seen as a correspondent system of sub-contracted services. The aim of sub-contracting is to make arrangements for foreign debts to be handled by a factor based in the debtor's own country. This overcomes many of the export market problems that we have already seen, as the factor understands the market and all the economic complications of that market. The chain effectively turns an export debt into a domestic debt, and the relationship between client and debtor is also altered.

In a normal trading relationship, there are two parties involved. When an invoice finance facility is in place, there are three. When there is an export factoring facility which utilises a chain, there are four parties involved. Whilst this works smoothly in reality, it takes time initially to understand the paper flow and communications between the four parties. The following diagrams show an example of an invoice financier and its client which are both based in the UK and the debtor and what is known as the "import factor" each based in Italy.

A. Contractual Agreements

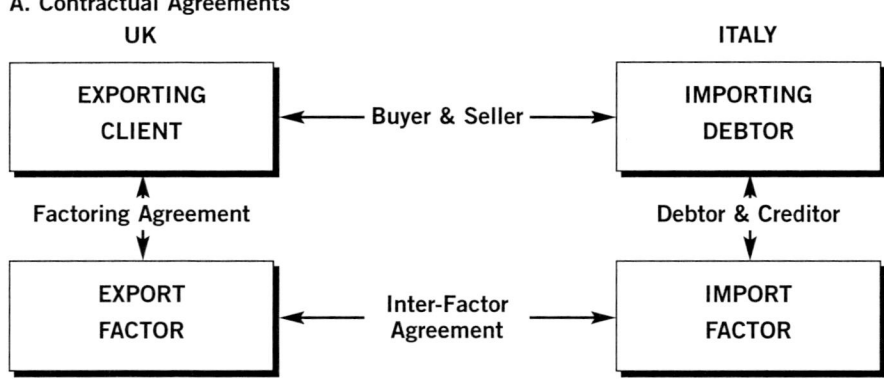

Diagram A shows the normal contractual relationship between buyer and seller and the factoring agreement between client and factor. There is an inter factor agreement between the two factoring companies by which they agree to conduct all their transactions between them in accordance with GRIF. Finally the notice of assignment stipulates that payment of the debt must be made to the import factor in Italy.

B. Transactions

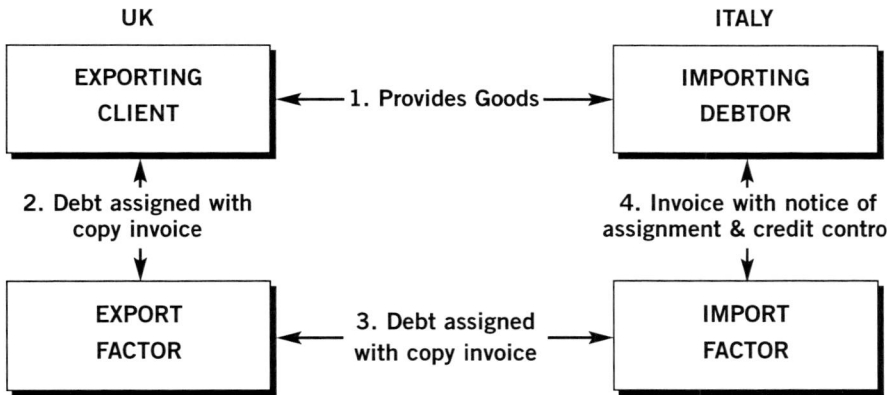

Diagram B shows the paper flow from the raising of the invoice to the sending out of a statement.

C. Payment of Invoice

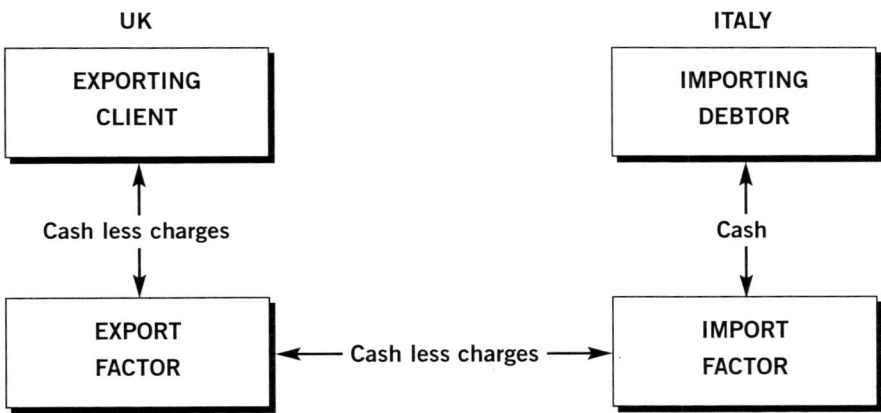

Diagram C simply shows the flow of cash from the debtor back to the client. This example does not show any prepayments taken, but that will happen between the factor in the UK and its client, in the same way as for domestic factoring.

As can be seen from these diagrams, factoring companies within each chain will perform the following two functions:

Export Factor: The export factor provides a factoring service in its own country to assist with the export business of its client.

Import Factor: The import factor in its own country provides a factoring service to an export factor in respect of exports to the import factor's country by the client of the export factor.

The Role of the Export Factor
There will be a factoring agreement between the factor and the exporting client covering the assignment of export debts. Any prepayments due under the agreement will be made by the export factor against export debts. The flow of the transactions (in this case utilising a non-recourse facility) will be as follows:
• The client requests credit cover on the overseas buyer.
• The export factor asks the import factor to assess the credit worthiness of the importer.
• Given satisfactory credit approval the client will deliver the goods.
• The client raises an invoice, which is assigned to the export factor.
• The export factor prepays against the invoice and then assigns the debt to the import factor.
• The import factor collects payment when it is due and repays the export factor which passes the balance of the prepayment to the client.

The export factor will also be responsible for:

• Monitoring the export sales ledger
• Maintaining communication with the import factor
• Assisting the import factor by resolving disputes and queries with the client
• Receiving and passing credit notes
• Accounting to the client for currency transactions

The Role of the Import Factor
The import factor needs a good assignment of the debt and a clear, precise invoice.

Ideally the invoice will set out all the terms of trade and carry the assignment notice in the debtor's own language indicating that payment is to be made to the import factor. The import factor is responsible for advising on the wording required.

The import factor will then take over all the normal credit control procedures and attempt to obtain payment of the debt. As part of a non-recourse facility, the import factor offers credit protection to the export factor. As the debt is being collected in the importer's own country the exporter can offer open account terms and compete with local suppliers on an almost level footing.

The import factor will be responsible for:

• Credit assessment and credit protection (if non-recourse)
• Credit control
• Litigation, if required, against the debtor, but usually at the export factor's cost
• All communication with the debtor
• Collection and transmission of funds to the export factor

It will be understood that the relationship between the export and import factor is vitally important. The export factor, whilst having made a prepayment to the client, is totally in the hands of the import factor. A poor performance by the import factor will undoubtedly affect the relationship between the client and export factor.

Direct Export Invoice Financing

Some factoring companies do not belong to one of the "chains" and prefer to provide all the services, including those undertaken by the import factor, themselves. Therefore the factoring company with which the client has an agreement, is responsible for overcoming all the difficulties of the export markets. This they will do either through their head office (say, in the UK) or through a network of associated companies. These associated companies may not even be factoring operations but may be part of a large group and are able to provide a credit control service in their own market. It is normal for these transactions to be linked to credit insurance either via the client's own insurance policy endorsed to the factor or via a factor's managed policy.

Direct Import Invoice Financing

In the same way that there is an alternative to the chain for the export invoice financier there is also one for the import invoice financier. In this situation the client is based in a different country to that of the invoice financier and signs a direct agreement for the client's exports to the invoice financier's own market. Whilst credit insurance and a collection service are offered under this facility, funding is not normally part of the agreement due to the difficulties of obtaining an effective assignment between parties in two different countries.

This facility helps those who wish to export to a certain market but have little knowledge or experience in that marketplace.

Other Invoice Finance Products

By far the majority of invoice finance business carried out in the UK is either factoring or invoice discounting, whether it be domestic or export sales, recourse or non-recourse. However, there are some other products on the market, albeit variations of the two main products. These include:

Agency / Bulk Discounting

Each of these names describes an infrequently used halfway house between full factoring and invoice discounting. It is similar to factoring in that a notice of assignment is attached to each invoice thus notifying the debtors that the invoice has been assigned to an invoice financier. Agency factoring is so-called because the notice of assignment states that the debtor may send their cheques to the client who is acting as the financier's "agent". The client sends batches of invoices to the invoice financier but it is there that the similarity with factoring ends.

Upon receipt of the batches of invoices, the financier processes only the total of the schedule rather than individual invoices to separate debtor accounts. In most other respects, the process is similar to invoice discounting in that the financier keeps just a control account dealing with the total of the client's sales ledger, from which they then calculate the availability of funds.

The complete credit control function is carried out by the client, including sending out statements and all collection activity. When the debtor pays, they are asked to make the cheques payable to the financier but send them to the client. The client must then pay these into the trust account in the same way as for invoice discounting. A copy of the paying-in slip is sent to the financier who will adjust the client's control account accordingly.

The monthly controls are then much the same as for invoice discounting. The client will send a monthly aged debtor analysis which the financier will reconcile with its own control account and make any adjustments for "disallowed" debt.

Apart from the subtleties of sending in copy invoices and making cheques payable to the financier, this product is almost exactly akin to disclosed invoice discounting and is rarely used these days.

CHOCC (Client Handles Own Credit Control)

As the name suggests, the client retains control over the credit control function but in all other respects this product is similar to factoring. The client raises invoices, (each carrying an assignment notice), which are then sent to the debtors. Copies are sent, or automatically notified, to the invoice financier, who processes them onto their own computer system as they would for factoring. Rather than the financier chasing overdue debts, this is undertaken by the client although the debtor statements are sent out by the financier. Some financiers take over collections after a certain period, say 60 days.

Debtor cash is sent to and banked by the financier and the availability is calculated in the same way as if it were factoring.

By allowing the client to handle their own collections, the factoring charge can be significantly reduced but the financier is at more risk in that they will be aware of disputes or fraudulent invoicing somewhat later than if they were handling the collections themselves.

Confidential Factoring/Shadow Ledger Confidential Invoice Discounting

As the names suggest, these products are not disclosed to the debtor and yet a full sales ledger is maintained by the financier. The financier in fact does everything they normally would as in factoring except that there is no notice of assignment on the invoices. When it comes to collection of overdue debt, the financier does this, but in the name of the client.
This facility gives the client the advantage of an undisclosed facility but the financier retains full control of the sales ledger and thus operates at a lower risk. The key to this facility is the use of communications technology to maintain confidentiality.

Maturity Factoring

This product is basically the same as non-recourse factoring, other than the unique way in which the financier agrees to pay the balance of the invoice not already taken as a prepayment. Normally, the financier will pay the client the full value of the invoice (less any prepayments taken and charges) once it has been paid in full by the debtor. However with maturity factoring, the financier agrees to pay this amount on a fixed date regardless of whether the debtor has actually paid or not.

At the commencement of the facility (and from time to time thereafter), the average "debt turn" is used to predict the future period between invoice and payment dates. For example, this period might be 60 days and the financier will guarantee to pay the balance of the invoice after this fixed maturity period of 60 days. Some debtors will pay before that period, in which case the financier keeps the funds until maturity. Some debtors will pay after the maturity period, by which time the financier has already paid the client.

This product was popular when factoring first started in the UK but is now rare. It is considered too risky by the invoice financiers.

Selective Invoice Finance

Most invoice finance facilities are arranged on the basis that all invoices raised by the client will be assigned to the invoice financier unless a specific agreement has been reached to exclude certain debtor accounts.

Selective Invoice Finance will allow only selected debts to be assigned. This will be anything from a small selection of large but well spread debtor accounts to a specified part of the sales ledger, for example A to L by debtor name.

This product is used when only a small amount of finance is needed and a reduction in administration can be achieved.

So we have seen in this chapter that invoice finance is the prime form of cashflow finance in the UK. The fundamental feature of invoice finance is that the assets, the unpaid invoices, are actually purchased by the financier. The two main products are factoring and invoice discounting; the former includes a sales ledger management service and the latter is usually undisclosed to the debtor.

Both domestic and export debts can be financed. With export factoring there are the added benefits of reducing the many complications and hazards of export trade.

Stock Finance

Introduction

Although not as popular in the UK as invoice finance, stock is the second most common current asset to be financed.

A definition of stock is:

"Merchandise which a company is holding for sale and/or the materials in various stages of completion which, when completed, will be the company's merchandise for sale."

The funding of stock (or "inventory" as it is referred to by American-owned companies) has three very different product offerings. They are:

Stock finance which has similarities to invoice finance.

Floor planning is specialist funding of high value items of stock for display purposes.

Trade finance is specialist funding to finance the gap between the purchase of goods (often imported) and their ultimate sale.

Let us now look at each of these products in more detail.

Stock finance is the provision of a revolving facility, not unlike invoice finance, whereby a percentage of the value of an agreed type of stock is made available as security for funding. Security is usually taken by way of a floating charge although in some cases a fixed charge over high value items which can be clearly identified, may be more appropriate. Generally a cashflow financier would offer funding against stock only when it is in addition to an invoice finance facility. However, there are those that finance the stock of retailers, which is then sold for cash. In this case no invoices are raised and, because the stock turns to cash so quickly, it is seen as being safe enough to finance on its own.

Stock finance is more common in the USA. Its introduction into the UK followed the entry into the cashflow finance market of American banks and other financial institutions in the 1990s. These American-owned cashflow financiers (or asset based lenders as many call themselves) have long recognised that stock can successfully be financed. In the USA, more often than not, cashflow facilities include an element of stock finance and in most cases the package will also include invoice finance. In the USA the same financial assessment techniques are applied to the client for whatever asset fund. However, it is also recognised that there are fundamental differences between unpaid invoices and stock. In both cases the financier will be looking at the likely value of the asset if their client becomes insolvent. Some invoices will be devalued and some will have no value at all in a collect out. Overall, most invoices (albeit perhaps by a small majority!) are likely to retain their value, even upon the demise of the company which raised them. The position with regard to stock is very different.

The value of stock to a financier is its liquidation value. Rarely is repossessed stock sold under the best circumstances. More often than not, the stock has to be sold in an unfavourable economic environment, where the number of buyers is limited and where transaction costs, including the removal of the goods and legal fees, can be substantial.

The best type of stock, from a financier's point of view, is that which has a value unconnected with the value of the company that holds it, i.e. the client. Thus low margin, commodity-type goods that have a wide market, will hold their value in the situation where the client goes out of business. Conversely, high margin, state of the art or bespoke products, will devalue steeply upon the client's demise.

However, there are some similarities in the way in which stock finance operates compared with invoice finance. Let us now compare and contrast the two products.

Invoice finance	Stock finance
The financier purchases the invoices	The financier takes a floating charge
Thus ownership of the asset is rarely challenged	There is greater potential for competing rights to the proceeds from stock
A set percentage is financed against "eligible" or "approved" invoices	A set percentage is financed against "eligible stock"
The known value (to the financier) of unpaid invoices usually changes daily	The known value (to the financier) of stock usually changes once a month
Recourse invoices become "ineligible" or "unapproved" after a certain period of time	Stock becomes "ineligible" after a certain period of time
Most invoices retain their value even in a collect out	Stock is devalued quickly in a collect out

The financier has less control over stock than over unpaid invoices and as it is not purchased there are some added risks. So the amount of funds generated by the stock figure shown in the balance sheet is often much less than the funds generated by the corresponding figure shown for debtors.

The actual methodology of how much stock is held by the client, is cruder than the way in which a financier records the value of unpaid invoices. However, the way in which a value is placed upon that stock is becoming much more sophisticated.

Methodology

At the outset, the financier will agree that certain categories of stock will be financed and that an agreed percentage of its value will be made available for the client to take by way of finance. We shall look at the various categories of stock that are likely to attract finance in a moment.

Having agreed the type of stock to be financed, the client will submit a regular (usually monthly but sometimes more frequently) stock listing to the financier. The financier will then make adjustments for any ineligible or disallowed items plus any other deductions and then apply the agreed percentage to the net figure to arrive at the "availability". Typically, the ineligible items or deductions will include:

- Any stock which might be subject to a Reservation of Title claim
- Slow moving or obsolete stock (a method of identifying such items needs to be agreed at the start of the relationship).
- The pool of unsecured creditors which, under the Enterprise Act 2002, will have priority over a floating chargeholder in the event of insolvency.
- Any third party warehousing costs such as rent
- Any packaging
- Spare parts
- Consignment stock (stock which still belongs to the supplier where the terms are, in effect, "sale or return".)

The financier must rely quite heavily on the amount of stock that the client says it is holding and therefore the financier will require regular audits and valuations to check that the amount, mix and value of stock is as stated by the client. These audits will look at how the stock is being kept, how accurate the client's record keeping is, how fast the stock is moving, identify slow moving stock and check that there is the right balance of stock. An example of this latter point would be if a shoe distributor had a lot of stock of small and large shoes in a market where the vast majority of sales were in the "medium range".

It is important to identify these ineligible items prior to commencement, but the most important decision of all is the category or type of stock to be financed.

Categories of stock to be financed

Stock progresses through three basic stages: (1) **raw materials,** (2) **work-in-progress,** and (3) **finished goods.** The value of that stock will depend on what stage the goods are in. Once again, it is important to remember that the best type of stock, from a financier's perspective, is one which will retain its value even if the client goes out of business.

As a general rule, the closer the stock is to being converted into cash, the more likely it is that a financier will want to provide funds against it. The main consideration is the ability of the financier to convert the stock into cash should the client fail. A crude example of this would be comparing a stock of standard bricks with a stock of half finished souvenirs of a Royal Wedding. Clearly, in a collect out, the bricks would be fairly easy to sell and would have devalued very little. The souvenirs, however, may already be obsolete in a collect out and would probably be worth very little. So, the golden rule in stock finance is to try to establish the likely worth of the stock in the event of a forced sale. Even having arrived at that figure the likely costs of making the goods into finished products, transporting and selling them have to be deducted to arrive at its net worth.

So, let us now look at the categories of stock and whether they are likely to be financed:

- *Finished goods* are nearest to being converted to cash and there could already be existing orders for the stock in the event of the demise of the borrower. This is the most likely category to be financed, typically between 50% and 65%.

- *Work in progress* (WIP) is not normally financed as there will be a cost involved in converting the w.i.p. into finished goods and then into cash. However, if the production period is short, some financiers may opt to fund w.i.p and in so doing, might offer to fund between 25% and 40%.

It is perhaps worth mentioning that there can be occasions where w.i.p. is worth more than the finished article. An example of this would be if "grey or unbleached cloth was used to make T shirts for a specific rock concert". The grey cloth is technically work in progress but is probably much easier to sell in a collect out than the finished T shirt which at best has a limited market and at worst may be obsolete by the time it is to be sold.

- **Raw materials** are even further away from being converted into cash and carry the additional problem of reservation of title (ROT) claims. This is where the original supplier retains ownership until the goods are paid for. Therefore the borrower may not actually own these materials. ROT is a complex issue and is discussed in more depth later in the workbook. It is thus rare for raw materials to be financed unless they are of a commodity nature and not subject to ROT.

- **Spare parts** may not be for re-sale at all but used in the manufacturing process or, for example, they may be carried around by a fleet of service engineers and difficult to track. For this reason spare parts are not usually financed.

- **Bonded goods**, consignment stock and in-transit stock are all difficult to finance because of doubts over ownership, risk of damage and costs in retrieving them before a forced sale. Bonded goods, such as alcohol or tobacco, are held in bonded warehouses and may not be removed until the duty is paid and thus a financier would have to bear that cost to retrieve them. Consignment stock is similar to goods provided on a "sale or return basis". Thus the goods remain the property of the original supplier who could reclaim them. Finally, goods in transit from the client to the debtor may be being shipped by a third party carrier. If the carrier has not been paid, they can apply a "carrier's lien" whereby their bill must be paid in order to release the goods.

The type of goods to be financed

The key question is: "how easy will it be to sell these goods should the client fail?" Thus a commodity-type product would be fine. A speculative stock of plastic bags carrying a shop's name but with no firm orders, would not. Examples of these commodity items are blank CDs, envelopes, non-patterned fabrics and standard sized timber. Less of a commodity but still acceptable to the financier would be non-fashion items of clothes, tools, fastenings and office furniture. However, examples of goods which would be difficult to sell if the client failed might be computer software or any complex product which would usually carry a warranty. The list is endless and largely common sense but it cannot be stressed enough that saleability upon the client's failure or insolvency is the key to assessing whether or not to fund stock.

For a financier, dealing in a variety of different industries, the assessment of how much any given group of stock might be worth in a collect out, is a difficult or near impossible task. If the stock is fairly basic and the amount of finance required quite modest, then the financier might be content to accept the client's own "at cost value. However, where the amount of finance is high or perhaps syndicated amongst other financiers, then a third party valuation is more appropriate. There are an increasing number of "Professional Valuers who will give an "orderly liquidation valuation" on a specific batch of stock. Such a valuation will either be "gross" i.e. before the costs of disposal or "net" which will have taken into account the transport and selling costs. It is worth mentioning that some stock is valued highly because of a brand name. Clearly "designer clothing" is worth more if the name of the designer is mentioned, than if it is not, even though the product itself is identical. In such cases, the financier may wish to take out a charge over the brand name to ensure that it can continue to be used after insolvency until the stock has been sold. Such action is rare but vital when funding stock which carries a significant premium value due to the brand name.

Client record keeping

The business being funded must be able to answer promptly and accurately where, what and how much the stock is worth. Many financiers say that the weakest record keeping of businesses is often that of stock control. Quite often the system used is a bespoke one for the product which does not integrate with the rest of the accounting system. If this happens, it is very easy to make errors and to manipulate falsely.

Ideally the stock control should be "real time". In other words, every item of stock and its value is checked in and every item, including its value, checked out. Most large retailers have such a system, but many manufacturers or distributors fall short of that. They may have a record of the type of stock they hold, but not necessarily an accurate value and certainly not a system which reduces that value if the stock is slow moving. Clearly the better the record keeping, the happier the financier will be in providing funding.

Prior to commencement of a stock finance facility, the financier needs to understand how the prospective client values its stock. Stock must be stated at the lower of cost or net realisable value and there are several pricing methods, such as FIFO (First In, First Out).

Whichever method is used, the most important consideration is its accuracy, given the type of goods and the overall administration of the business. It is also vital that the method is consistently applied. From the financier's perspective, it is important to understand the methodology and to ensure that the client does not change it without prior agreement. The biggest test of the client's own stock record keeping will be a comparison between these records and the year-end physical stock take.

The financier will have regular audits by its own auditors to test the accuracy of the client's record keeping. The audit will attempt a physical stock take and match it with the records being kept by the client. The financier may even use a third party Industry Appraiser to revalue the stock every few months if the sums involved are substantial. It is usual that the costs of the audits and of any third party valuations are at the client's expense.

If the stock is a commodity with an externally quoted value on a recognised exchange (such as copper), then the client's record keeping should reflect any change in value. Certainly the financier should be aware of any quoted values and note when these start to decline. The financier would also be well advised to keep up to date with what is happening in the client's industry. If an item is being "dumped" on the market to reduce stocks, then the financier should not rely on the client to advise them of this.

Potential claims

Since the Enterprise Act 2002, there is no crown preference which means that state institutions such as the Inland Revenue no longer rank above a floating charge holder in an insolvency. However, where there is a floating charge, an administrator must now set aside a prescribed amount of an insolvent company's assets subject to a floating charge to be distributed to unsecured creditors in preference to the charge holder. Therefore, a stock financier, holding a floating charge over the assets of a client, will usually seek to retain an amount equal to this likely value from the client's availability.

Some of the client's suppliers may have a reservation of title (ROT) clause in their terms and conditions. If it is thought that this could lead to a valid claim, then the stock will not belong to the client and therefore will not be captured by the floating charge. Not all ROT claims prove to be valid but it is a complex area and if a financier is considering funding stock that may be subject to ROT, then legal advice must be sought. The safest approach is not to fund any stock which might be subject to ROT or at least hold back a reserve sufficient to cover all potential claims.

Where stock is being held in a third party warehouse, then a reserve needs to be made in respect of any unpaid rent otherwise the stock will be very difficult to recover in the event of insolvency because of the Landlord's right of lien, i.e. to hold the goods until the rent is paid.

It is also worth noting that the financier must ensure that it is fully covered in respect of the insurance on the stock. Typically, the financier will set out in its offer letter, the fact that the stock must be fully insured, at the client's cost and with the financier as "loss" payee i.e. the party to whom claims must be paid. Proof of the cover must be provided to the financier.

So it can be seen that this type of stock finance is generally more risky than financing debtor balances. Nevertheless, it can be a useful option to an invoice financier seeking to increase the level of funding to a client. The next two products involving the finance of stock are very different and tend to be offered by specialist financiers as "stand alone" 35 products.

Floor Planning

Floor plan financing was born in the early days of the car industry in America. It remains more common in the USA than in the UK and differs from the stock finance described in the previous section in the following ways:

- It is used specifically to finance the stock that a dealer or distributor has on its "floor", i.e. its showrooms or retail outlets.
- Stock control is generally more intensive than in the stock finance just described.
- There is coordination among the three parties to the transaction: the financier, the client and the manufacturer. This means that instead of the two-way relationship which characterises traditional cashflow financing, there is a three-way relationship in floor plan facilities.

Floor plan financing is a specialised form of stock financing designed to meet the needs of businesses selling high value products such as computers, cars, motor cycles, white goods, industrial equipment, caravans and boats, which need substantial stock for display purposes. It also provides the manufacturers of such stock with guaranteed regular cashflow which they can re-invest into their business. As the products are usually high value, floor planning deals tend to be large and the financier is required to be flexible and provide a bespoke service. This means that the deal between the parties is likely to be sophisticated. Many of the benefits of invoice financing are also seen in floor planning, such as prompt payment of invoices and bad debt protection. However there is an added sales-aid dimension as the manufacturer and financier typically agree flexible terms for the dealers, designed to encourage dealers to hold stock without tying up cashflow and thus improving sales.

This situation is best illustrated by considering a private motor car dealership selling to the general public. The dealer needs to have on display a full range of cars to fill his showroom. However, the cashflow demands on the dealer of directly purchasing stock from the manufacturer would be prohibitive.

By entering into a floor plan facility the financier will purchase the cars in its own name from the manufacturer and onward sell them to the dealer on credit terms maturing in say, 60 days from delivery. This is called the "maturity date". The financier protects its position by selling with "reservation of title". This is the financier's security and is more effective than the floating charge used in stock finance, as there are no creditors with priority to take care of, such as the unsecured creditors under the Enterprise Act. This means that should the dealer become insolvent before paying the financier then the financier can repossess the vehicles as the unpaid owner, without having to appoint an insolvency practitioner. The dealer is often appointed as the financier's disclosed agent to arrange purchases from the manufacturer. He may also be the undisclosed agent of the financier to sell cars to the public.

On the maturity date the financier can either:
• Receive the sale price from the dealer
• Give the dealer more time to sell the car
• Sell the car back to the manufacturer

It is very common for floor plan deals to be instigated by the manufacturer, in order to get their products into the dealers' showrooms without any credit risk. To encourage a financier to become involved the manufacturer will usually enter into guaranteed buy–back arrangements with the financier to cover the possibility that the financier has to repossess the stock upon the client becoming insolvent or committing a breach of the facility.

This arrangement is illustrated by the following diagram:

Stage 1

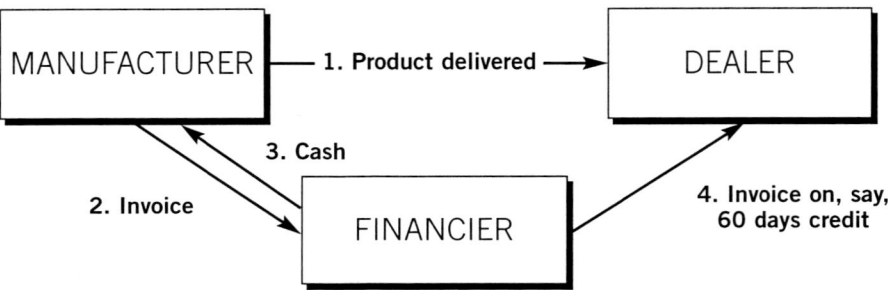

1. Manufacturer delivers product to dealer pursuant to sale contract with financier
2. Manufacturer invoices financier
3. Financier pays manufacturer on delivery or pre-delivery
4. Financier sells product to dealer on, say, 60-day credit terms plus interest and service fees and reserves ownership to the product until paid

Stage 2

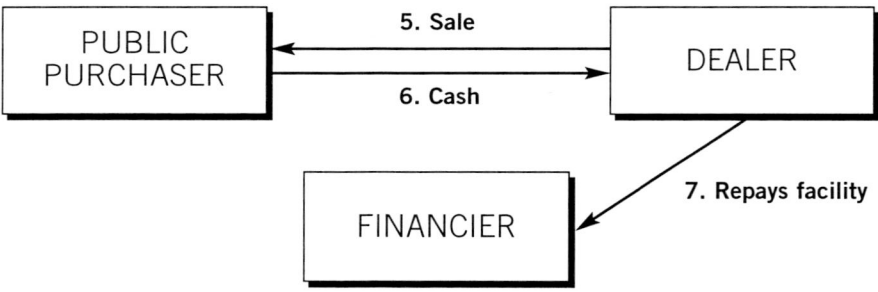

5. Dealer sells product 14 days later to public purchaser
6. Purchaser pays cash to dealer
7. Dealer pays financier invoiced price of the product, interest and fees.

Floor plan facilities are normally provided on a revolving basis against an agreed credit line so the dealer (as agent of the financier) can keep ordering new product from the manufacturer within the value of the facility. His continued right to do so is conditional upon the dealer complying with the terms of the facility, the most important of which is to repay the financier promptly upon a sale.

The financier will normally monitor the dealer's compliance with such terms by regular audits. These involve visiting the dealership and checking that each unit purchased and outstanding on the financier's ledger physically exists and is in good order.

Floor plan finance, whilst very common in the US, is relatively new in the UK. Recent developments include major manufacturers setting up captive finance companies to facilitate dealers' floor planning, plus consumer finance for the purchaser of the product. Under these arrangements the manufacturer derives profits both from financing the initial sale to the dealership and the retail credit sale by the dealer to its debtors.

Trade Finance

As we have already seen, trade finance (or "merchant finance" as it is also called) is a facility which meets the cashflow gap created when a company purchases goods for onward sale. The trade financier will raise a Letter of Credit in favour of the supplier in order to purchase the goods on behalf of their client. To protect their investment the trade financier will hold title to the goods until such time as their facility is repaid. Once the goods are delivered the client will sell the goods, effectively acting as an agent for the trade financier. As there is a time delay between the trade financier having to pay the supplier and their client receiving payment for the goods sold, the trade financier will usually draw a bill of exchange on its client for payment to be made by the client's bank by an agreed date. The way a bill of exchange works is explained in chapter two. By the time the payment is due the goods should have been sold and the debtor payments collected so providing the client with the funds to settle the debt.

The trade financier is reliant on the client selling the goods and collecting payment from their debtors. Therefore the type of goods purchased and the quality of the debtors are of vital importance. The goods should be finished products and quick-selling items. It is not a suitable form of finance for a client who purchases components which they then make into something else. The resale value of the product is then unreliable should the client be unable to complete their part of the process. A trade financier wants to know that the product that it purchases can quickly be sold at a reasonable price should their client fail and they need to recover their funds from selling the goods elsewhere.

Likewise the trade financier wants to know that once the client has the goods, they can sell them and that the debtors will pay. Often the trade financier will purchase goods only if they have evidence of confirmed orders from debtors that they view as good quality. As far as possible they are ensuring that there is a complete chain that will result in money being generated to repay their facility.

Some trade financiers will take further control over the transaction to reduce the risks by both purchasing the goods and selling them on to the debtors. In this case the trade financier rather than the client will invoice the debtor and collect the monies due. The client will receive only the profit margin on each transaction less the financiers' costs. Sometimes this sort of arrangement is referred to as merchant finance.

A similar kind of approach can be taken by linking the trade finance arrangement with the client invoice financier. In this case the client sells the goods and assigns the invoices to the invoice financier. The prepayment or a percentage of it is then made directly to the trade financier to repay their facility. All three parties will have previously entered into an agreement setting out what amounts are paid and to whom.

The combination of financing stock and invoices

Of the three stock related products we have discussed in this chapter, floor planning is usually a stand-alone facility and trade finance is sometimes stand-alone. However, a large proportion of trade finance facilities form part of a cashflow finance package and almost all stock finance is only offered in addition to an invoice finance facility.

One of the main reasons why financiers prefer to combine the financing of stock with that of funding invoices is that the latter can support the former. The creation of stock comes before the creation of an invoice. Similarly the purchase of goods for re-sale comes before the creation of an invoice to sell those goods. Therefore financing stock or the purchase of goods for immediate re-sale will ultimately be repaid by cash from debtors which have been invoiced for the goods. Thus invoice finance can be used to support the funding of stock or the funding of purchases of the type used in trade finance.

Another advantage to the financier in funding both stock and invoices is that it can gain a better overall view of the business it is financing and an additional insight into the saleability of the stock. For example, the financier will be able to gain an impression of how well the stock is being received by the debtor. The financier will also get a feel for the quality of the stock it is funding from the level of disputes and/or credit notes through its invoice finance facility.

It has thus been a natural progression for many financiers to expand their product range from a core of invoice finance, into financing other assets, particularly stock.

In this chapter we have identified ways in which stock can be financed and looked at the three main product offerings in some detail. The next chapter will begin to look at the process of how cashflow financiers find, analyse and take on their clients.

Negotiating the Deal

Introduction

The sales function in most organisations is important. Where the product is not particularly well known and the unit price perceived to be high, as in most types of cashflow finance, the sales function becomes even more important. Add to that a very competitive sector and sales become crucial.

The sales function in a cashflow finance company is thus crucial, but equally important is choosing the right type of business to achieve the financier's corporate aims. These aims will vary from one financier to another but will usually involve volume and profit growth, in conjunction with a policy on the type and spread of risk. Thus the appetite for every piece of new business will depend on the level of risk that is acceptable to the financier and for how much reward. Therefore the process of obtaining new business is a particularly complex area for cashflow financiers.

We saw in the first chapter that most cashflow arrangements in the UK contain a core invoice finance facility at its heart. When we look at how cashflow financiers examine new business, we will do so primarily, from the point of view of providing an invoice finance facility.

The process of seeking new business right up to the point of taking on a new client is so important in this industry that we are covering it over the next two chapters. In this chapter, we shall examine new business generation, the suitability of prospects, identifying client needs, pricing, types of risk and the role of other financial institutions. In later chapters we shall look at how we extract and subsequently examine the risks, the legal agreements and the process of taking on a client.

New Business Generation

In this section we shall look at how cashflow financiers generate their new business, the use of intermediaries and the suitability of prospective clients.

Marketing

The length of time that a client stays with a financier is finite. Businesses get taken over, their cash requirements change, they go out of business or they source another form of working capital. The average "client life" experienced by invoice financiers varies enormously, according to their positioning in the market but can be anywhere from three to eight years. Some businesses have been clients for much longer but if a financier's average client life is, for example, five years and they have 500 clients, then that's 100 new clients to find each year just to stand still.

The invoice finance market in the UK is particularly competitive which is why many have offered finance against other assets in order to differentiate themselves. Within the membership of the Asset Based Finance

Association (ABFA), some financiers stick to one product, and many offer factoring only or invoice discounting only. Some will specialise in non-recourse, others in international business. Most will offer the usual variations of invoice finance, but not finance against other assets. An increasing proportion will offer invoice finance coupled with finance of stock, property, plant and machinery and perhaps mezzanine loans or venture capital. A minority will specialise in a niche market such as floor planning, or financing a particular industry. Whatever their product offering, they each need to generate new business through marketing. This marketing will usually cover three areas: raising awareness, direct lead generation and indirect lead generation through intermediaries.

Raising awareness

Raising awareness of how cashflow financiers can provide working capital solutions is vital in this market, more so than in a well-established consumer market. Take a simple example of selling television sets. Everyone knows what a television set is, what it looks like and what it does. So there is little need for the television manufacturers to raise awareness of the product unless there is an innovation which needs introducing to the market. In this case almost all the marketing will be about the product range itself, their various features and of course the price.

Contrast the television manufacturing industry with the cashflow finance sector. In the latter case, most potential users of this type of finance will have only a vague notion of what is on offer. Many will not have even heard of the range of products. Worse still, some will have a false or negative impression, which will not be changed until they receive the correct information demonstrating the positive benefits. While factoring was in its infancy in the UK some of its providers took on businesses that were in terminal decline and, as a result, the product gained the label of "lender of last resort". Whilst that period ceased in the 1960s when the industry focused on providing factoring to growing businesses with a good chance of success, some of that negative image stuck for many years and required an industry-wide approach to change the perception in the market place.

So, raising awareness of cashflow finance is not only vital, it has to be in place before individual providers can even begin to market their own product range.

Membership of the ABFA will help raise awareness of the products on offer. The organisation uses public relations agents, articles in the press and other methods to raise the profile of cashflow finance.

Individual financiers will of course use their own methods to raise awareness of their own product range and how well placed they are to provide certain solutions. They may use public relations organisations or they may advertise, not just for direct leads but more to raise the profile of their company. Let us look at some of these methods in more detail:

• **Press Coverage** is a useful way of raising awareness of cashflow finance. However, newspapers and magazines need a "hook" that will make the story topical or newsworthy. The ABFA publishes its quarterly statistics but a set of figures is uninteresting unless there is a good story attached to them. The tremendous growth of cashflow finance is newsworthy in itself. However, it is useful to relate that growth to what is happening in the economy or in a particular sector or region. Individual providers may get an article published in their local press or they may target a certain sector and aim for coverage in a trade magazine.

- *Case Studies* are very useful when included in a press article because they add credibility and most businesses can relate to the importance of adequate working capital.

- *Advertising* can be used to raise awareness and attract new business leads. Attention should be given to the choice of appropriate media. Advertisements on television can be very expensive and most of the audience will not be the prime movers in small to medium sized businesses. Radio advertising has been used effectively but again most of the audience are not going to be potential users. The same can be said for press advertising although the right type of publication can aim more accurately at potential users.

- *Conferences, Exhibitions and Events* can be used to raise awareness of cashflow finance. Such events may attract potential users or intermediaries who may introduce potential users. Some financiers may choose to sponsor an event which may not only help raise awareness of the industry but also of the financier's brand.

- *Hospitality* is a vital part of building business relationships. Entertaining those who can themselves raise awareness of the industry is an approach often used by financiers and, as we shall see shortly, is even more common when applied to intermediaries who can introduce business directly.

Direct lead generation

We have already seen that advertising and press coverage can be used to raise awareness; they can also be used to generate direct leads. Individual financiers will have their own unique selling proposition. Some will promote their ability to provide a wide range of solutions to a business's working capital needs, some will focus on a high level of customer service, others on the use of technology for speed and convenience, and some will major on price. Whatever their corporate focus, they may choose advertising or one of the following methods of direct lead generation:

- *Web sites* are increasingly used as sources of direct leads. Most financiers have their own web site and can promote their range of products in much the same way as in a brochure. Some financiers will have interactive sites where a prospect can enter certain information to see how much cash they may be able to generate and at what cost. Although only useful as a guide, this technique may lead to the prospect making direct contact with the provider.

- *Direct Mail* is used by many industries to promote their services but response is usually very low. It is more effective to target specific industries, or businesses of a certain size, or use other selection criteria. Some factoring companies may even send mail shots to the debtors of their clients. The financier has the database from which to target potential users although care must be taken not to interfere with the collection process.

- *Reference publications* such as Yellow Pages are relatively cheap and may generate the occasional lead.

Intermediaries

Whilst every financier will try to market their range of services directly to the potential user, a large proportion of new business will be introduced by a third party. These intermediaries may even provide more new business than all the sources of direct lead generation.

Intermediaries will often already have a business relationship with the prospective client and will have developed a level of mutual trust. Any financial service is an intangible offering. You cannot touch it or try it out or see it in action. So prospective clients are naturally cautious about committing their business to a service of which they have had no experience. Thus recommendation by a trusted advisor or business associate is going to make the prospective client feel much more comfortable.

Introducers of new business usually fall into the following categories:

- 'Professional' introducers: accountants, brokers, insolvency practitioners
- Existing clients
- Staff
- The parent company of the financier

Each of these three can have a vested interest in offering business to a financier.

The first, the professional introducer, has both a professional interest in that they may work with the prospect on many other aspects of their business (financial accounting, auditing, insurance, capital equipment purchasing, etc.) and are keen to offer the best solution to their client's financial funding, as well as a general package of services. They are also keen to collect commissions on their introductions, and these can be substantial. If the introducer is a firm of accountants they may also be seeking reciprocal business. They might offer the financier's existing clients specialist accounting services or perhaps be appointed receivers or liquidators by the financier in the case of failure of clients.

The second category, existing clients, have less to gain in terms of increasing their own business but can gain excellent commissions. In this case the benefit is far more on the side of the financier who can gain through client introductions very good quality leads at very little cost.

The third, the financier's own staff, can be really effective. Many of them will be in contact with other businesses, within or outside work. They will understand at least the basics of what makes a suitable prospective client for their employer's business and they will usually be enthusiastic advocates of the benefits. An introductory payment is usually paid to the member of staff.

The effectiveness of the fourth, the parent company, varies depending on who the parent is. Some smaller financiers have a parent whose only involvement in financial services is as their financier so there is little opportunity for leads from this source. At the other end of the scale the bank-owned financiers have considerable scope for developing leads.

For example, a bank will have many thousands of customers funded by a traditional overdraft product. If the bank can convert these accounts into clients of their cashflow finance subsidiary, they can make the following considerable gains:

- Increased group profitability through increased lending - the financier may well be able to advance far more than the bank as they manage the asset security on a day-to-day basis;
- Improved group risk management by this improved management of the assets;
- Improved customer relations by making more money available via the financier than would be available under traditional overdraft.

There is a general move in today's industry, by bank-owned financiers to become closer to their parent companies and to adopt integrated strategies for delivering the financial service best suited to the client and the financier/bank. In the UK, introductions by the big clearing bank-owned financiers, is by far the largest source of new business generation.

Suitability of prospects

Not every business which seeks to benefit from cashflow finance will be suitable. What is a "suitable" prospect will of course vary from one financier to another but there are some key areas that will determine their suitability:

Nature of business

The nature of a prospect's business is probably the first question to be addressed. We saw in Chapter 1 that invoice finance is suitable only for businesses selling to other businesses on trade credit terms. Some niche forms of stock finance may cater for retailers but the vast majority of cashflow funding is for businesses selling to other businesses.

Most financiers are wary of "craze" products where the lifespan of the business may be very short. Some are wary of industries in sharp decline, for the same reason. Theoretically, most types of businesses are suitable provided that the nature of their invoicing is acceptable.

Collectability of the asset – Invoices

We saw in the last chapter that a cashflow financier is often able to provide more cash because it is closer to the asset. By far the most common assets to be funded are unpaid invoices and therefore we shall first look at the importance of the nature of that invoicing.

A good rule of thumb as to what is acceptable is that "each invoice is a legally enforceable debt in its own right". Examples of some of the problems that make it difficult for invoice financiers are as follows:

- *Stage payment invoicing.* Manufacturers who supply and install large machines, for example, might invoice a quarter of the contract price upon receipt of an order, a quarter when the machine is manufactured, a quarter upon delivery and a final quarter when it has been installed. The first three invoices may not be legally enforceable in their own right because they form part of a larger contract. If the client were to go out of business before completing the contract having only completed and invoiced the first stage of the contract then the customer will refuse to pay that invoice because the contract has not been completed.

- *Contra trading.* This is where the client company and its end customer are undertaking reciprocal trade. If ABC Client Ltd does some work for XYZ Debtor Ltd and then XYZ Debtor Ltd does some work for ABC Client Ltd, then both companies will raise invoices to the other. If ABC Client Ltd goes out of business being owed £500 by XYZ Debtor Ltd but owing £750 to the same company, then XYZ Debtor Ltd will clearly not be paying the £500. Thus reciprocal trading is generally to be avoided by an invoice financier unless they can be certain that the amount being owed to its client far exceeds any potential sum being owed by its client to the same company.

An example of an industry where reciprocal trade is common, is the haulage business, and certain industries, such as steel stockholding, where companies buy and sell to each other to make up a complete order for a third party.

- **Right of offset.** Similar to reciprocal trading, there may be occasions when a customer has a right to offset a sum of money from an invoice it has received. E.g. for prompt payment or retrospective quantity discounts. Even if there is no specific right, a customer could argue that goods which carry a warranty no longer have the benefit of that warranty if the supplier goes out of business.

- **Sale or return.** If an invoice is raised for goods which are allowed to be returned as part of the contract, then the debt is unenforceable.

- **Bans on assignment.** This is where the customer specifically states that the debt must not be assigned to a third party. The reasons for imposing such a ban vary and may even be lost in the mists of time but such a ban is clearly enforceable against an invoice financier. The Law commission in 2005 has considered making such bans unenforceable.

- **Invoicing in advance.** This is where a business raises an invoice prior to providing the goods or service. An example of this might be a publisher which invoices for an advertisement in its magazine which is not published for another month. If the publisher goes out of business before they produce the magazine, then the customer will not pay for an advertisement that has not appeared. Another example of pre-invoicing is when a business invoices in advance in respect of maintenance that it will provide sometime in the future.

The above list is not exhaustive and it does not mean that a business will be deemed unsuitable by a financier. If some of its invoicing fits into one of these categories. However, it is highly likely that if all of the invoices raised by a business fall into one or more of these categories, then the business will have to find an alternative source of finance.

Collectability of the asset – Stock

We have seen that an invoice can become devalued; we shall now look at how stock can become worth less than the value on which the finance was based. When deciding whether or not to finance stock and at what level, the most important question to ask is: "How much is this stock likely to be worth if the client goes out of business?" Let us examine some of the ways in which stock can be devalued by the time it comes to a "collect-out".

- **Reservation of Title.** This is where a supplier has, as a condition of sale, a clause that states that they retain title of the goods until they are paid for. It is a complex area and will be discussed in more detail in Chapter 5 but suffice to say that a financier may think it has the right to sell the client's stock in a collect-out but if the client's supplier (or sometimes even a supplier further back in the chain) has a valid claim under its Reservation of Title clause, then the stock will belong to the supplier and not the financier. Not all claims under Reservation of Title succeed, particularly if the original goods are not easy to attribute to the supplier or are now mixed in with other materials. However, unless a financier can obtain a waiver from a Reservation of Title clause, they should not finance stock that is the subject of such a clause.
- **Obsolescence.** Some slow moving stock can become obsolete quite quickly, even when a client is still trading. Thus the value of that stock will become devalued before a collect-out and therefore it should not

be funded in the first place. However, the issue of obsolescence becomes more acute once a client ceases to trade. A commodity-type product would usually be fine, but a stock of last Christmas's toy fad might not. Thus a financier needs to estimate how much the stock being financed will be worth if the client goes out of business.

- **How near is the stock to being finished?** As a general rule, most financiers would like to see the stock they are financing as near as possible to being finished goods. This is because in a collect-out situation stock that still requires some work on it before being saleable will cost the financier money to complete before it can begin to sell the stock. Thus "work in progress" is usually not financed, or if it is, it will be done so at a lower percentage. Raw materials are even further away from being finished and may also be the subject of a valid Reservation of Title claim.

Bonded goods, consignment stock and in-transit stock are all difficult to finance because of doubts over ownership or costs in retrieving them before a forced sale.

Financial performance
A financier will be looking for both a long-term relationship with its client and also to minimize its risk. Therefore the financier will be looking for a prospective client that can either show a history of profitability or can demonstrate how it will achieve future profitability and ensure the long term viability of the company.

The assessment of current and future financial performance is thus of vital importance to a financier. The methods by which the financier will make this assessment will be looked at in greater detail in the next chapter.

Management capability
A financier will expect the management of a prospective client to be capable of:
- Achieving the financial forecasts which they have set for the business;
- Adapting to changing circumstances which may upset those forecasts;
- Being honest and open in their dealings with the financier;
- Providing a satisfactory level of control with regards to the administration of the accounting function.

Assessing the capability of the management is one of the most important aspects in judging suitability of a prospective client, and yet it is one of the most difficult. Negotiations with a prospective client should always be with a director of that company, and ideally the financier should meet all the key members of the management team. In doing so, the financier is able to make a judgment as to the mix of skills which the team brings to the overall management of the business.

Clearly a long established business, run by the same management team and with a proven history of profits, largely speaks for itself. However, many prospective clients are new companies or perhaps new management in old, loss-making businesses. It may even be that a financier is asked to look at a business that has failed and is starting again with the same management. Such "phoenixes" must be examined very closely in order to be persuaded that the same mistakes will not happen again.

It is also important to ensure that the people purporting to run the business are actually the ones so doing. It has been known for undischarged bankrupts or disqualified directors to be running a business day-to-day whilst their names appear nowhere on an application form or at Companies House.

The identity of each of the directors will have to be verified, but there may also be some background checking of their professional history and personal standing, particularly if the prospect company is only recently incorporated.

Size of business

Cashflow finance is primarily aimed at small to medium sized enterprises (SMEs). The really large corporations may be able to borrow funds cheaply because of their financial strength, although some cashflow financiers target these "big ticket" deals. However, whilst the average size of an invoice finance client continues to grow, the vast majority of clients of members of the ABFA have an annual turnover of less than £10m. Normally, nothing will preclude the maximum size of a prospective client other than perhaps a limit to the size of risk that a financier wishes to take.

However, there are normally minimum turnover requirements and these will vary from one financier to another. Some factoring companies will look at new starts which forecast as little as £100,000 turnover a year. Most invoice discounters will wish to see annual turnover in excess of £1m although some will look at smaller companies. Financiers looking to put together a broad package of cashflow finance will have an even bigger minimum turnover requirement in order to make it cost effective.

Deal structuring to meet clients' needs and obtain an appropriate return on risk

Having generated a lead which on the face of it looks suitable, the next part of the process is to understand the needs of the prospective client and to obtain an appropriate return on the risk for the financier.

The process

The role of marketing continues long after a lead has been generated. A prospect needs to develop a rapport with whoever he meets from the financier in order to gain trust. Similarly, the financier needs to understand exactly what type of funding is required, how much and for what purpose.

Normally, the person entrusted with both developing the relationship and understanding the requirements is someone from the financier's sales team. This group is normally called the Business Development Team or New Business team. Theirs is usually a dual role of generating leads through intermediaries and then following the lead from its introduction through to the point where the prospect becomes a client. In almost all the structures within invoice finance companies, the role ceases at "take on" and does not extend to managing the relationship thereafter, because a different skill set is required for the two roles. The new business role requires not only selling skills but the ability to weed out unsuitable prospects at an early stage. The new business manager may also play a key role in gathering the information required by the financier and may even have authority to "underwrite" small deals himself. The account manager however, needs to have a high degree of risk management skills and be more suited to handling the day-to-day pressures of looking after a portfolio of different clients.

The process of taking an introduction onwards varies from one financier to another but broadly follows these steps, most of them carried out by the new business manager, who will hand over to others to continue the relationship once the prospect becomes a client:

Initial assessment of likely suitability

More often than not, this can be achieved by a telephone call during which the financier will try to establish the size and nature of the business, the type of invoicing and the financial performance of the business. If the prospect looks as though it meets the minimum criteria of the financier, then a meeting is usually arranged.

The new business meeting

This may be one visit to the client's premises or a series of visits. The aim is to gain an understanding of the needs of the prospect and to explain how the financier may be able to meet those needs. It is normally at this stage that a form is completed giving more detail of the nature of the business, the management team, financial performance and sales ledger data. Some factoring companies will use this information to decide whether to make an offer and on what terms. However, it is more common for this information to be used to decide whether to undertake a "survey" or a "due diligence" visit. It is, however, not uncommon for the new business manager to have discussed broad terms with the prospect or to have made a quotation "subject to survey".

Pre-survey assessment

This may be just an informal look at the information gathered so far and the points to be specifically addressed during the survey. Or it may be that a committee sits to decide whether to proceed and if so, what specific issues must be addressed at the survey.

Survey

This is a visit by a representative(s) of the financier who has experience of looking in some detail at the information required in order for the financier to fully understand the business and the asset it is being asked to finance. The new business manager may or may not attend but the outcome of the survey is that a report is put together in order for the deal to be "underwritten".

New business underwriting

The financier at some stage makes a decision as to whether to offer and on what terms. For small factoring deals, this may be undertaken by the new business manager. More often though, the business is "underwritten" by an individual or committee of individuals who are independent of the new business team. If it is more than one individual, then this is often referred to as the Credit Committee.

An offer

A written offer is made which sets out the criteria for cash to be made available, usually a limit to the amount of cash to be provided, the cost and any specific terms and conditions. The new business manager will often wish to discuss the offer face to face with the prospect, ultimately agreement will be reached and the prospect will sign a copy of the offer to confirm acceptance.

The Legal Agreement

This is the legally enforceable contract between financier and client. There may be other documents which form part of the contract.

The take-on

This is the final stage once the contract has been signed, any conditions have been met, the procedures gone through in some detail, and the initial injection of finance is made available to the client.

Understanding the prospect's needs

In general terms we have already identified why a company should come to a financier - for cash and perhaps for some added element of the financier's service package, e.g. credit control. However, this is far too broad because companies approach financiers for a whole range of reasons and it is important to understand these needs. The following are some of the most common:

Working Capital Needs

- To meet the general day-to-day cashflow needs; in particular during periods of rapid growth when sales are growing faster than working capital to support those sales.
- To take opportunities offered by obtaining large discounts from key suppliers or to purchase special 'lots' of product at reduced prices.
- To reduce creditor pressure by releasing cash tied up in debtors or in stock.
- To assist as part of a restructuring-package of financial support in MBOs and take-overs.
- To assist with the development of new product lines or markets.

Credit Control and Sales Ledger Needs

- To take pressures away from owners/managers (particularly in small companies) to enable them to direct their activities towards business generation and profit earning
- To run a more professional sales ledger operation.
- To control the debtor base.
- To cut costs.

Risk Protection Needs

- To protect against bad debt.

A prospect may have identified some or many of these needs itself. It is also possible that a prospect is unaware of some of these needs and a skilled new business manager will be able to point them out. However, it is important to identify the needs first, before jumping in with all the solutions.

The need for cash is likely to be the need that is identified most often, but it is important to establish what has caused that need. If the business is growing rapidly, with funds tied up in debtor balances, then invoice finance is probably appropriate. However if the real need for cash is because the company is losing money, then invoice finance will not return the company to profitability! However, if there is a viable rescue plan, the invoice financier may be able to help. It may be, for example, that a rescue plan will involve the business being put into administration or in some form of voluntary arrangement. Not all financiers will look at this type of situation, but many will.

Let us look at an example of a prospective client which has provided the following brief details:

ABC Prospect Ltd

Manufacturer of garden tools (mainly spades, forks and rakes). Has been established five years, has broken even for the last two years but recognises it has to go for increased sales to return to profitability. Says the market is there but just needs the cash to finance the growth.

A summary of its forecasts shows that:

Sales are budgeted at £2.5m for this year, up from £1.7m last year, 75% during February to August.

Purchasing will be year-round but increasing in the autumn and winter to build up stocks for early spring.

Stock will peak at £1m in February and decline to £100,000 in August.

Mix of customers: 50% large retail chains, 50% small independent stores.

Currently all sales are within the UK but have appointed a sales agent in Germany.

The details given are only brief and there are many more questions to ask but it appears that the needs are as follows:
- An overall need for cash to fund the anticipated growth. Invoice finance will release cash during the summer months.
- A month-by-month cashflow forecast should be seen but suffice to say that stock will peak in winter, debtors will peak in late spring and summer, and extra cash will be needed to pay creditors during the winter. So, invoice finance is probably not enough and stock finance is probably needed as well.
- Half the customers are probably credit-worthy but the other half may be less so. Perhaps there is a need for bad debt protection.
- New to exporting, they may need help in managing their export credit control. This is a very simplistic example but it does show that there are many different needs. In this case, to offer invoice finance on its own would not meet the prospect's needs unless they had another form of finance which covered the extra cash needed during the winter months.

Principles of pricing

There is a fundamental difference between costing and pricing although both contribute to the amount finally charged for a product or service. This particularly applies to establishing the amount to be charged for a cashflow finance product because it is not a commodity, it is intangible although highly competitive. The aim when arriving at the charge is to cover all the costs in providing the service, plus an element of profit. That is the costing part of the process. The pricing process is to take that costing and relate it to the market, the risks involved and the appetite of the financier for the particular business on offer.

Let us firstly examine the costing and there are two types of costs, variable and fixed.

Variable Costs

This category is described as "variable" because the costs can vary according to the known features of a particular business. If, for example, the offer was to provide factoring, then there would be a cost per debtor account, and there would be a cost for processing an invoice. Whilst these "costs per item" would be the same for all factoring clients, they would vary for each individual client depending on the number of debtor accounts and the number of invoices. Thus the variable costs for most invoice finance providers would include:
• Data processing and collection costs (factoring only)
• Credit assessment costs
• The cost of client liaison and communication
• The costs of monitoring the risk
• The commission payable to the introducer of the business

Fixed Costs

These cannot be directly related to a particular product or service. These costs will have to be incurred whether or not a specific new client is taken on. Typically they will include:
• Marketing and business development costs
• Buildings and furniture
• Rent, rates, power, insurance etc.
• Computer equipment and staff
• Personnel overheads
• General management and administration

Pricing a cashflow finance product

The first stage in pricing a cashflow finance product is to calculate these fixed and variable costs. The next step may be to add an element of risk within the price. If the product is non-recourse, then an amount will be included within the costing to reflect the debtor risk. This amount is usually expressed as a percentage of the forecast turnover of the client and will vary from 0.1% of turnover to 1% or more.

The next element of risk, common to all cashflow finance products, is that the client will fail and that the financier will not collect the funds it has provided from the underlying asset (i.e. the invoices or stock). This risk will be calculated to reflect the financial standing of the client, the industry sector it is in, the perceived probity of the client's management, the economic climate and the risk of fraud. Most financiers will reflect this risk in the cost of the money it provides. Thus a very good risk might be able to take funds as low as 1.5% over a bank's base rate, whereas a client who is perceived to be a greater risk might have to pay 4% over base. In the following example of a costing, we have assumed that the "client risk" is reflected in the cost of funds rather than the fee.

Example of a costing for the fee to be charged to ABC Client Ltd.

ABC Client Ltd – statistics
Product: Domestic non-recourse factoring
Forecast turnover: £1,000,000 p.a.
Number of "live" debtor accounts: 100
Number of invoices and credit notes per month: 100
Forecast number of credit applications per month: 10
Debtor risk: Low (Manpower) = 0.25% of turnover

Costing

Variable costs

Credit control activity - £30 per live account. £30 x 100	£ 3,000
Processing costs - £1 per invoice/credit note. £1x 100 x12	£ 1,200
Credit application costs - £5 each. £5 x 10 x 12	£ 600
Credit risk - 0.25% of turnover	£ 2,500
Total variable costs	£ 7,300
Fixed Costs (set sum per client)	£ 2,700
Total variable and fixed costs	£10,000
Profit (say 10%)	£ 1,000
Total	£11,000

There is an increasing trend to charge the fee as a fixed monthly charge, which, in this example would mean charging a twelfth of the £11,000 per month. However, it is still more usual to express the estimated annual cost as a percentage of turnover. Thus in this instance, the annual cost of £11,000 is 1.1% of turnover. Everything else being equal, the price to be charged to this client should be 1.1%. However, the final element in pricing is the highly subjective aspect of market forces. On the one hand may be the desire for the financier to maximize its income and on the other hand is the likelihood of a competitor offering a lower fee for a similar service. So, the financier has the benchmark of 1.1% to cover all its costs and achieve a 10% profit but it may then choose to actually quote less to attract this business.

It should be remembered that the costs of sales, marketing and setting up a new client are relatively high and that it will take some time before the financier can actually recoup those costs. Thus the longer a client remains on the books, the more profitable it becomes to the financier and so it is very important that clients are retained for as long as possible.

Cashflow finance charges

It is probably fair to say that the more complex or comprehensive the finance package, the more complex and diverse the charging structure. Thus there is no "typical" charging structure for these deals because they are so bespoke. Nevertheless, in almost all products offered by cashflow financiers, the charges fall into two categories:
- A fee (either expressed as a percentage of turnover value or a fixed sum) which is intended to cover the costs of administering the facility, with a small profit.
- A price for the money. This is almost always a fixed percentage above a named floating rate. In the case of invoice finance, this is called the discount charge. In the case of a loan, it is called the interest rate.

Invoice finance charges

There are two main charges and they are:

The Fee

This charge is for the administration of the facility as opposed to the charge made for the funds provided. We saw earlier an example of a factoring fee which is often charged as a percentage of factored turnover. In this situation, the fee is charged, plus VAT, on receipt of every new batch of invoices. However, there is an increasing trend to charge the fee as a fixed amount each month.

The same principle applies to invoice discounting although the fee will be smaller, reflecting the fact that less of a service is provided. Again the fee can either be expressed as a percentage of throughput or as a fixed sum charged monthly or in some cases annually.

Where the fee has been expressed as a percentage, it will have been calculated on what was expected to be the turnover for the next twelve months. In the case of fast growing clients, particularly new start companies, that forecast turnover could be quite optimistic and so the financier may wish to safeguard its income by insisting on a minimum income based on the forecast turnover. Taking the above example, the financier may offer a 1.1% fee but subject to a minimum charge of, say, £10,000. If after the first twelve months the actual income fell short of the £10,000, then a minimum income charge would be put through to cover the shortfall.

The discount charge

This will be the charge for the amount of funds used. Unlike the fee, this charge will only be levied when the client draws down funds. The charge will usually be calculated daily and charged monthly on the amount of funds "in use" in much the same way as a bank would calculate interest on an overdraft. The amount charged will usually be expressed as a percentage over a nominated bank's base rate.

In addition there may also be:

Re-Factoring Charges (factoring only)

This is an additional fee charged by some recourse factors in cases where a debt exceeds the terms and becomes "age disapproved" (often at 90 days). The charge is for the extra work involved in the collection.

Charges for additional work

Occasionally clients may request additional services, for example advancing in excess of agreed limits, renegotiating the terms of the facility or requesting extra print-outs. In such cases the factoring company will make a charge.

Rechargeable Costs

This relates to charges made for additional work requested by the client where an external organisation has made a charge. For example: solicitors fees for debtor litigation work (if the debt is with recourse), or bank fees for telegraphic transfers. Often these charges will be passed to the client on the basis of cost plus profit to cover any additional work by the financier.

In addition, there may be specific charges made for:
• Initial set up of the facility
• Renegotiating the facility
• Increasing the finance limit
• A temporary "overpayment"

Stock finance charges

Interest rate

As the funding of stock is by way of a loan rather than an outright purchase, the cost of the funds is expressed as an interest rate. Again, the actual amount will almost always be expressed as a set percentage over an agreed bank base rate.

Fee

Fees will be charged, usually monthly, to cover the management of the facility and as with invoice finance, it is common for the financier to pass on any external charges. Some financiers will charge for stock audits or for any significant changes to the agreed facility.

Aspects of risk

With well-managed trustworthy businesses, which sell good, uncomplicated products or services to good debtors who can and will pay their debts as they fall due, the financier can be reasonably confident that their funds will be safe and that a facility can be offered. At this stage, the financier's strategy for going forward should determine whether or not it can successfully recover its funds in the future; if the financier gets the assessment right the facility should be set up with suitable terms and conditions that protect the financier from loss, except where fraud occurs.

However, every financier runs the risk that the company they are financing could go out of business. They then run the risk that the asset they have been financing turns out not to be worth as much as the finance they have provided against it. In addition, invoice financiers, particularly those offering non-recourse arrangements, run the risk that the underlying debtor will also go out of business.

Let us look at a very simplistic example of a financier and its client, ABC Client Ltd:

> ABC Client Ltd raises an invoice for £1,000 to XYZ Debtor Ltd. The financier gives an 80% prepayment against this invoice in the sum of £800.

> ABC Client Ltd raises an invoice for £2,000 to Dodgy Debtor Ltd. The financier gives an 80% prepayment against this invoice in the sum of £1,600.

> ABC Client claims it has £3,000 worth of finished stock. The financier provides 50% against this, i.e. £1,500.

As a result of the above, the financier has provided the client with £3,900 but then the following happens:

- ABC Client Ltd goes out of business
- It transpires that XYZ Debtor Ltd was owed a credit note for £1,000
- XYZ Dodgy Debtor Ltd goes out of business
- It transpires that ABC Client Ltd has no finished stock

The result is that the financier is unable to recoup any of the cash it provided to ABC Client Ltd. A simplistic and extreme example of course but these things do occur, albeit not often. Whilst financiers are in the risk business, they need to minimise that risk and their prime tool is the initial assessment which will decide whether to quote for a piece of business and on what terms.

The assessment of those separate types of risk will be looked at in more depth in the next chapter but let us just look at the principles of these risks in the context of whether or not to make an offer.

The risk that the business being financed might fail

For companies that have been trading for some time, the financier will wish to see audited or certified accounts. In addition, they will probably wish to see up-to-date management accounts. They may also want to see some forecasts, especially if the business has been through a bad patch and is attempting to return to profitability.

For new companies, the financier will certainly want to see a business plan which includes some forecasts.

Each financier will have its own view of an acceptable risk. Sometimes this will be written down in a "credit policy" but more often than not it will be the judgement of experienced personnel either individually or collectively.

Not only will the judgement about the risk vary enormously between different financiers, it will vary between different products. Many that offer factoring feel that as they are very close to the asset, they could take a greater risk on the client failing. This is on the basis that they are more likely to collect their financial commitment from the outstanding debtor balances.

So there is a trade-off between the risk of the client failing and the risk that the asset will prove collectable. These two elements will be weighed against each other when deciding whether to quote and if so, on what terms. Clearly the greater the risk, the more reward should be built into the offer, but it is a truism that there is no price worth charging for a bad risk.

The risk that the asset will be worth less than the finance provided against it

This can further be divided into two categories:
• The risk that the asset will be devalued in the event of a supplier failure.
• The risk that there might not be an asset in the first place as a result of fraud by the client.

Firstly, the asset becoming devalued: the basic rule of thumb in making this assessment is to put yourself in the place of the end customer and ask: "Will I pay for this invoice if the supplier goes out of business?" If you have received all the goods or services that you have ordered, with no other obligation on behalf of the supplier, then you will be obliged to pay. However, if there is a warranty or ongoing maintenance or part of the order was not delivered and renders the delivered goods useless, then you will be inclined not to pay. Certainly you will not pay in full.

The same test can be applied in trying to sell some stock that has been financed. How much will this be worth once the supplier has gone out of business and will anyone buy it?

The historical level of credit notes will give a clue as to how often an invoice becomes devalued. An examination of the reason will give a clue as to the "collectability" of the debtor balances. In addition to this, knowledge of the prospect's industry will alert the financier to particular problems in relation to that sector. For example, in the haulage industry there is considerable reciprocal trade between companies, not always apparent in normal trading but in a "collect-out" much of the debt is uncollectable because of these contras. In another example, clients selling to large retail stores often allow annual volume rebates. If a certain volume is reached, usually in a calendar year, then the debtor will be entitled to deduct a rebate in January that will often exceed the amount of invoices still unpaid. These and many other peculiarities of certain sectors will dilute the face value of invoices in a "collect-out". However, common sense and experience of "collect-outs" are the best tools to use in assessing this risk.

The second category, i.e. fraud, is harder to predict. Criminals have been known to target invoice finance companies but the more frequent type of fraud arises as a result of desperation to keep a company going through a rough patch. We shall examine fraud in greater detail later in the book but although it is rare, it has been said that it accounts for £1 in every £1,000 of throughput. At this stage in the book, suffice to say that the risk of fraud has to be looked at in conjunction with the risk that the business will fail. Fraud does not cause a loss if the business continues to trade as normal as there will be fresh (and hopefully genuine!) invoices to re-build security to an acceptable level. So, assess the risk as to whether or not the company might fail, alongside the risk as to whether or not the individuals that run the business are trustworthy and committed.

The risk that the debtor will go out of business

It may seem unlikely but it is not uncommon for a company to fail because its main customer (or its main supplier) also fails. Thus it is possible that both your client and one or more of its debtors could fail at the same time. The invoice financier will thus have nowhere to go to recoup the funds it has provided. It therefore follows that it is very important to assess the credit worthiness of the debtors prior to making an offer.

Broadly speaking, the better the quality of the customer, the less risk there is for the financier. A good standard of customers will also mean that the product sold by the prospective client is of equally good quality.

However, there is another issue which should be looked at in conjunction with the debtor quality and that is the spread of debtors. One or more predominant debtors increases the risk to the financier because if they go out of business or have a big dispute with your client, that means that a large amount of debt may prove uncollectable. So, there is a slight trade off between debtor quality and spread. Mediocre quality debtors but good spread may be perceived as equal to, or better than, good quality debtors but poor spread. As we shall see in later chapters, there is a way to mitigate poor spread from a financier's point of view but very little that can be done about poor quality debtors.

A credit insurance policy or a non-recourse facility may be attractive to a client if the debtor base is average or above. But no financier will deliberately cover a client against a poor risk. Most financiers will tolerate one or two poorly rated debtors but if the whole book is of poor quality, they will usually decline to quote unless all other risks are very low.

Finally, a word about non-recourse finance. Financiers offering a non-recourse facility will either take the debtor risk themselves or may have their own credit insurance policy which covers them against the larger losses. A non-recourse financier will therefore look at the debtor base even more closely as they will usually stand to lose 100% of the value of the debt (net of VAT which can be claimed back from H M Revenue and Customs by the client). This means that they stand to lose if debtors go out of business even if the client continues to trade.

A recourse financier will only take a debtor loss if the client itself fails. Non-recourse facilities vary but many financiers will operate some form of "first loss", which is the client's responsibility if the debt is credit protected. Such financiers may offer clients the ability to have small discretionary limits without first checking with the financier. These options are weighed against the perceived risk of debtor bad debts, and a percentage of turnover is arrived at for inclusion in the overall fee. The percentage can be as low as 0.1% or as high as 1% and is usually included in the overall fee rate although some financiers make it a separate charge.

The role of other suppliers of financial services

Invoice finance is often taken as one element of a financial package for a company. On the simplest level this could entail the involvement of the prospect's bank providing an overdraft. For more complex deals, this could mean involving stock finance, mortgages, or loans as part of a funding package.

We have already seen that identifying the needs of a prospective client is of paramount importance. It may be that the financier can provide all the solutions to those needs although care must be taken not to barge in and take away valued business from the introducer! However, there will undoubtedly be times when involving other financial institutions will be in the best interests of the prospective client.

With management buy-outs (MBO) and other financial restructuring, it is necessary to take a holistic view of a company's financial requirements rather than try and address perhaps many different needs through one type of financial arrangement. It is therefore not uncommon for the financier to become part of a consortium of financial providers providing elements of a mixed package of financial support.

When assessing the risk we need to consider the implications for any other financial institution. These implications will include:
- The continuing role of the bankers. It will not assist the prospect if the bank completely takes all the funds released from an invoice finance facility leaving the prospect with little if any extra cash.
- The nature of charges and other securities taken by other financial providers and the impact these have on the ability of the debts to be assigned.
- The control to be exercised over the prospect company by other investors who may take equity shareholdings as part of their financial package; this may involve linking them into any legal agreements.

Funding implications when other financiers are involved

As we have seen, if a financier can provide everything to satisfy the needs of a prospective client, then all well and good. However, there will normally be some existing funding in place and the new financier needs to look at what will happen to that funding should the prospect decide to take up any new offer. So a dialogue needs to start between the existing provider of funds and, say, an invoice finance company proposing to quote. If the existing provider is, say, the parent bank of the invoice finance company, the dialogue will be very easy to start. If the existing funder is outside the invoice financier's group, the commencement of a dialogue needs to be handled with care. It may well be that the existing funder is a banking group that may wish to introduce their own invoice finance company. Even so, it is vital to establish what, if anything, the existing funder will provide, after commencement of a new finance facility and so this is probably best done through the business itself and they need to insist that they have the revised arrangement in writing.

So, let us look at an example.

ABC Client Ltd has a £500,000 overdraft secured by a fixed and floating charge over all assets, those being:

Debtors	*£700,000*
Stock (raw materials)	*£100,000*
Fixed assets (cars, IT equipment, furniture etc.)	*£200,000*

A new financier has been invited in to quote and decides they are interested in funding the debtors but not the stock or the fixed assets. On examination of the debtors, they estimate that there is £80,000 that they cannot fund, leaving £620,000 that they will fund, at 80%. This provides finance of £496,000 on current figures.

The existing bank would have to release the debtors from their charge and would thus wish to revise their overdraft arrangement. However, what if the existing bank will no longer provide any lending? The business would in fact be worse off because it would have £496,000 from the invoice finance facility and nothing from the bank, compared with the £500,000 it currently has from the bank. So it is vital in this case that the bank stays in with a reduced overdraft facility, albeit on reduced security, for this to be a viable alternative for the business.

Let us look at another example. XYZ Client Ltd already has an invoice finance arrangement that on average provides £400,000 against debtors of £600,000. It also has an overdraft of £120,000 secured on stock of £200,000 and a building valued at £150,000. The bank has calculated that the stock should generate £20,000 and the building £100,000. Along comes a new financier offering exactly the same invoice finance arrangement but 75% against finished stock. The bank stays in at £100,000, leaving just £20,000 to be made up by the proposed stock finance. However, the stock financier upon investigation realises that most of the stock is either raw materials or work in progress. Whilst the client might have expected 75% against all its stock, it will only get 75% against the finished goods and that amounts to little over £15,000. On this occasion, one could say that the bank is blindly and perhaps foolishly offering a fixed percentage against all stock without the in-depth knowledge of a stock financier. So it is always important to work out exactly how much the proposed facility will generate in new cash for the prospective client.

This raises another deal structuring issue, that of "headroom". Headroom is the concept of ensuring there is always some room within the facility being offered to cope with both "hiccups" within the plans and also allow for anticipated growth. The flexible and "open-ended" nature of providing finance against current assets has a built in expectation of headroom e.g. more invoices equal more cash. But that does not take away the fact that the financier may well wish to set some limits to their involvement and that it is almost inevitable that there will be "hiccups" to the cashflow plans of a business.

So, whenever another finance provider is involved, it is vital that they make their intentions clear, in writing, before a new financier makes an offer. It is quite normal for an offer of new finance to contain a condition which states that there must be a written undertaking of "X" amount of funding to be in place from another finance provider.

Where several finance providers are involved, such as an MBO or another type of re-structuring, then an open dialogue is essential. It is often the case that the level of funding offered by each provider is an iterative process. In other words, one financier might offer a certain amount of funds by taking assets as security but then find that another provider wishes to have some of the same security. The finance providers need to work together to come up with the best package for the business, albeit whilst trying to maximise their own income stream.

Security issues when other financiers are involved

We know that businesses offer certain assets as security in order to obtain finance. In the case of debtor balances, this particular asset has to be sold to the invoice financier in order to obtain the finance. Where finance is being provided against most other assets, the lender will take a "charge" over some or all of these assets.

Charge

A charge is a contractual right given to a creditor by his debtor to have designated assets taken and sold to satisfy the debt should the debtor break his contract. It is usually enforced by an administrator or receiver appointed by a creditor.

An administrator's duty is to use his best endeavours to rescue the company as a going concern. If that is not possible, his objective must be to achieve a better result for the creditors than would be likely in a liquidation. If these objectives are not achievable he may use his powers to realise the charged property for distribution to the secured creditors. Generally an administrative receiver will be appointed under a floating charge issued before 15 September 2003. His prime task is to collect the creditor's money through sale of the company's assets. His appointment is a debt collecting weapon.

It is normal that most banks and other lenders will insist on security to cover their advances. This security is often taken in the form of a charge over the assets of the company. Charges can be of two main types, fixed or floating. The "fixed" charge is, as it suggests, attached to a particular asset. That asset cannot be sold or traded without the permission of the charge holder.

The floating charge is different. It "floats" or "hovers" over a category of assets that changes from time to time, such as stock in trade or book debts. The company can change and alter these assets as they wish and deal with them in the ordinary course of business. The charge only "crystallises" and attaches itself to the asset in the event of the failure of the business or under some other condition laid out in the charge document. Once it crystallises, the charge becomes fixed and the company may no longer deal with the assets without the permission of its lender. The floating charge does not, in theory, affect the ability of the company to assign its book debts. However, almost every lender includes conditions within their charge documents forbidding the assignment of book debts. We can consider both fixed and floating charges to be similar in effect as far as the financier is concerned and so a "waiver" is needed (see below) to enable book debts to be purchased by the financier.

Sometimes, cashflow financiers also take charges as security for monies that their clients may owe them. This is particularly so with invoice discounters who have greater risk because no notice of assignment is given to debtors. The document containing the charge is called a "debenture". Although charges in debentures can cover a wide range of assets, the most usual are over either:
• All assets; or • Non-vesting book debts

Waivers

If the client has granted security, by a charge over its debts, to its bankers or other creditors, the financier cannot buy the debts and the invoice finance arrangements cannot work. It is essential that such secured creditor waives his rights to debts, and consents to the client entering into the factoring or invoice discounting agreement before any monies are paid to the client. This ensures that no claim can be made against the debtors by the secured creditor if the client becomes insolvent. A sample waiver appears in Appendix 1. The waiver provides that the secured lender will make no claim against the financier for debts subject to its charge but that any monies due by the financier to his client remain subject to the charge. The sample waiver ensures that the "related rights" (e.g. transferred goods) as well as the debts are likewise waived. This also applies to any trust provisions in favour of the bank. Trust provisions often occur in bank financed import transactions where pledges to the bank of shipping documents are released in return for the client signing a letter of trust in favour of the bank over the sale proceeds of the shipped goods, i.e. the debt. This could result in the financier and the bank both claiming the debt. Hence the need for a waiver.

Deeds of Priority (including consent to factoring)

Increasingly financiers take a fixed and floating charge over all the assets of a client. This is also called an "all assets debenture". It will include a charge over non-vesting book debts. There are debts intended to be assigned to the financier but which do not vest e.g because of a fault in the factoring agreement or the absence of a signature. There may be other assets such as stock or work in progress which the financier particularly wants security over. If another security holder has priority over such assets through an earlier charge then the financier may consider it essential to obtain priority over these and other assets, in order to provide funding. This is obtained by a deed of priority with the prior security holder and the client. An example is shown in Appendix 2. It is a shortened version showing only the key sections. It also includes a consent to factoring. This then does away with the need for a separate waiver.

The priorities are set out in clause 3, and allow specific priorities for items listed in the Schedule. The security holders, including the financier, agree to cooperate in appointing the same person to enforce their securities. The prior lender in this document is a bank. Increasingly banks demand clauses, permitting factored debts to be paid into the client's account at the bank without penalising the bank. You will note that if Top Financiers want to claim such monies they need to put the bank on notice before the monies are received at the bank. It is usual for the financier to negotiate standard forms of such documents with most of the major banks. This ensures that there is no delay in providing them, once the commercial terms have been agreed between all parties.

Loan Postponement

It may be that there is an unsecured loan to the client from another party . In which case the financier may make it a condition of the facility that repayment of the loan is to be postponed for the life of the agreement. In which case a Deed of Postponement will be required, under which the lender agrees not to enforce the loan or accept any repayment for so long as the financier provides facilities.

So, in this chapter, we have examined new business generation, the suitability of prospects, identifying client needs, pricing, types of risk and the role of other financial institutions. In the next chapter we will look at how we extract the information we need and subsequently examine the risks, the legal agreements and the process of taking on a client.

Structuring the Deal

Introduction

In the last chapter we examined new business generation leading to the identification of a prospective client, which we shall call a "prospect". We then examined the suitability of prospects, identifying their needs, pricing, types of risk and the role of other financial institutions. In this chapter we will look at the risks involved in cashflow financing and the information required in order to evaluate those risks before deciding whether to offer facilities.

Business and Corporate Risks

Prior to making an offer of any type of cashflow finance facility, the financier will wish to understand the business and corporate risks posed by a particular prospect. We have already seen that there are two distinct risks involved in cashflow financing:

• That the prospect company will go out of business

• That the assets being financed (e.g. invoices or stock) will not recoup sufficient value to cover the level of finance currently being provided against them.

In addition, a non-recourse financier has the risk that a debtor will fail, owing a debt that the financier had credit approved. But apart from that specialist risk, it is a fact that all financiers risk their client going out of business, so that the assets being financed are devalued or proved worthless. It is important to realise that the risk of devaluation will not in itself produce a loss to the financier until the first risk (that the client will go out of business) has taken place. So these two risks are very much intertwined.

You will almost certainly hear someone say, from time to time: "the underlying asset may be a bit risky but this company will never go bust", or, "this company may go bust but you will always collect the full value of the asset". Both of these statements must be treated with caution. Even if, on the face of it, these statements may look credible, there is no such thing as a corporate entity which is 100% guaranteed never to fail. Nor is there an invoice or item of stock that will always retain 100% of its value even if the business fails. Circumstances will change or fraud could occur, but that just serves to show that providing any sort of finance is a risky business. The key is to understand the level of risk prior to making a decision whether or not to make an offer of finance.

All prudent financiers must go through a process of gathering information on a prospect in order to evaluate the risks involved. Some of this information will be gathered by the new business manager, some of it sought from external agencies and some of it will come from a visit to the prospect which is generally called "due diligence" or the "survey".

Let us now look at the items to be examined when trying to assess the risks.

Financial analysis

Historical financial performance is just what it says – historical and does not necessarily show how a business is currently performing. Nevertheless, it is a good indicator of whether the business is capable of generating future profitable growth. It serves to add weight to the forecasts of the directors as well as highlighting potential problems.

Typically, a financier will wish to see the last three years' audited financial accounts plus any later management figures that the prospect has produced.

Most financiers use a standard analysis for accounts, usually on a computer spreadsheet. This is to produce, in a standard format, a set of financial information in order to compare like with like. A typical assessment of the published accounts and the management accounts will generate a number of ratios. As with all ratios, the financier is concerned with trends, movements and comparisons, using these to give an indication of the potential risk. Ratios however can only highlight potential problem areas and further investigation will be needed to establish exactly what is happening.

It is assumed that readers of this workbook already have a good understanding of the make-up of a balance sheet, the profit and loss account and a cashflow statement. It is also assumed that readers have a basic understanding of how to interpret the information contained in these accounts. Therefore we shall not be looking at the methodology of financial analysis but suffice to say that this aspect of risk assessment is crucial when deciding whether to offer facilities to a prospect.

Sales, profits and cashflow forecasts

Historical data will give an indication of recent financial strength but it is equally important to look into the future.

The forecast of sales over the coming, say, 12 months will affect every other forecast you are given and deserve to be challenged and tested. For an existing business, comparison with historical sales will be the obvious start and if only modest growth is expected, then perhaps not much questioning is necessary. However, if rapid growth is forecast or the business is a new start, then the directors need to justify that the market is there for their product and at the volume and price they are forecasting.

The next forecast to investigate is profit and loss. Again, comparison with historical figures will help to develop confidence in these forecasts but it becomes more difficult in a period of change or where the business is new.

Once the sales and profit forecasts have been accepted as credible, then the cashflow forecast is the final set of figures to challenge. These need to be relatively conservative because it cannot be said often enough that cash is king in any business. Lack of it is the main cause of company failure, even if the business is trading profitably.

Using a sensitivity analysis, it is possible to test what would happen if, for example, sales fell short by 10% or profits dropped by 25%. Any fall in sales or profits will automatically have a negative impact on cashflow. We saw in an earlier chapter, that some headroom is needed when forecasting the amount of finance required. Forecasts rarely go exactly as planned, therefore the access to extra cash, when needed, is vital.

Sales ledger analysis

An examination of the sales ledger is important even if the financier is considering making an offer which does not include invoice finance. If, however, invoice finance is being considered, then examination of the sales ledger is paramount before making the decision to quote. We shall investigate later the prospect's credit control procedures but first let us look at the following items to be found in the sales ledger:

Debt turn

We have already seen how to calculate the "debtor days" or "debt turn" from the financial accounts. It may also be prudent to look at the total sales ledger balances over several shorter periods to discover a trend in the debt of recent months. Any deterioration needs to be investigated. When asking those who are currently responsible for maintaining the sales ledger for explanations of issues that have been unearthed, it is at least encouraging if they are aware of the issues. If not, satisfactory control may simply not be there.

Try to compare the debt turn with those of similar industries. Most credit agencies will provide average debt turns for a variety of sectors or there may be enough data within you're the financier's own organisation. If the prospect's debt turn is longer than the norm for that industry, it could be that they offer longer terms, are dealing with slower paying debtors or simply that they do not chase their debts hard enough. It is important to find out the reasons and seek to establish what, if anything, the prospect intends to do to bring the debt turn down.

The outcome of the investigation on the debt turn may have a direct impact on the product the invoice financier is ultimately prepared to offer.

Ageing of debt

Almost all computerised sales ledger systems will "age" the debt owing. In other words it will calculate how old the invoice is and put that figure into set time bands. Typically this analysis will be as follows:

- Invoices not yet due (current)
- 1 to 29 days overdue
- 30 to 59 days overdue
- 60 to 89 days overdue
- 90 days or more overdue

This document is usually called an "Aged Debt Analysis" and is used by most businesses to highlight what needs chasing for payment and what is seriously overdue and needs urgent attention. From the financier's point of view, it is a point of reference to try to discover why certain debts are not being paid. It may well be that bad debts or potential bad debts are sitting in the sales ledger and are of no value and should be written off, thus making the current financial position of the prospect worse than they have portrayed.

It is also a clue to what may be excluded from funding in an invoice finance facility, and what needs to be taken into account when calculating the likely level of funding if an offer was made.

Quality of debtors

If an invoice finance facility is being considered, then the credit worthiness of the debtors is of paramount importance. If the offer is of a non-recourse facility, the financier will not wish to quote if the debtors are generally of poor quality. Even if the proposal is for a recourse arrangement, the financier will not be keen to fund poor quality debtors for fear that in a "collect-out", the debtors will also fail and the debts become uncollectable.

There are ways to mitigate the effect of poor quality debtors if everything else is looking positive. The most obvious is to offer less funding, either by excluding certain debtors or by reducing the overall prepayment percentage on offer. If the debtor balances are not well spread the financier may wish to impose a spread restriction, which we shall examine in the next section. Or, even if the financier does not offer a non-recourse facility, it may be that a credit insurance policy will offer cover and the financier might only fund credit insured debts. The financier, even in a recourse facility, may set finance limits on the major debtors, up to which it will provide finance. Or the financier may tighten the period over which it will provide finance on overdue debts. For example, if the financier normally wishes to "claw back" any debts that are more than, say, 90 days overdue, then it may wish to reduce this to 60 days overdue.

The mere fact that poor quality debtors exist at all, could be symptomatic of a prospect selling in desperation, or perhaps that the quality of the product or service is also poor and only poor debtors will put up with it!

Spread of debt

We saw in an earlier chapter that in an invoice finance facility, the spread of debt is most important. There are two reasons for this. The first is that the loss of a large customer can cause the demise of the client. The second is that in the event of a "collect-out", there is a danger of having all the eggs in one basket. The debtor itself could go out of business or may have a valid reason for non-payment, thus making a disproportionate amount of debt uncollectable.

Each financier will vary in their requirement for a "good spread" of debt but most will not wish to see any one debtor owing more than 50% of the total ledger. If any one debtor predominates more than this, most financiers will decline to offer. Some will go ahead but with a "spread restriction" (also referred to as a "concentration percentage") and most will have some sort of restriction on any debt representing over 25% of the ledger, some going as low as 10%.

A "spread restriction" is typically worded thus: "we shall not finance any balance representing more than (say) 25% of the total debtor balances". Using this 25%, an example might look as follows:

- Total debtor balances: £100,000
- Debtor A Ltd owes: £35,000 or 35% of the total
- The financier would only base its funding on up to 25% of the total, which in this case is £25,000
- Thus the financier would not fund the difference between the £35,000 owed by Debtor A Ltd and £25,000 and would deduct £10,000 from the total outstanding before calculating the availability at the agreed prepayment percentage

Whilst a narrow spread is never desirable, the terms of trade, credit protection, strong paper trail and good trading history can be used in support of a deal. It is possible that with insurance cover, the financier may not apply any funding spread restriction, although this is very much the exception.

Potential bad debts

We have already seen that an examination of the "Aged Debt Analysis" can provide evidence that an overdue amount is owed by a debtor that has already gone out of business. It can also be an indicator that a debtor is close to the brink of collapse. "On account" (lump sum) payments might indicate that the debtor cannot pay the whole balance in one go. It would be wise to run a check on any seriously overdue balance to see if the debtor is still trading.

Contra trading

We have also seen that an invoice financier should avoid financing a debt owed by a debtor which also appears as a creditor. When required to pay the debtor the debtor will "contra" (i.e. deduct) the amount it is owed against the amount it owes and only pay the balance to the financier.

So, an examination of the sales ledger and purchase ledger should take place in order to identify actual or potential contra accounts. Where the amount owed by the client to the debtor is always in excess of that which the client is owed by the same debtor, then it would be foolish to finance this debtor. However, if the situation was reversed and the client was consistently owed more by the debtor than it owed the same company, then some financiers might wish to finance the difference between these two amounts. So if on average £10,000 was owed by the debtor to the client but only £2,000 was consistently owed by the client to the same company, then it might make sense to fund the £8,000 difference.

There would be a risk, however, that the financier would never be entirely up-to-date with how much the client owes. In these situations, the financier will require the client to provide a monthly or even weekly list of creditors in order that it can deduct any amounts owing by the client to these contra accounts, but even that is not foolproof. The financier will not be aware of any purchases that are yet to be invoiced and posted to the purchase ledger.

Although not foolproof some financiers still consider the risk worth taking. Others might take a view that a few small potential contra accounts are worth the risk and perhaps adjust the prepayment percentage accordingly.

Industry practice and custom

Many financiers will have built up their own experience of certain industry sectors. In some cases this experience is documented and in others there will be individual staff members who specialise in certain sectors. It is good practice to compare the dynamics of a prospect's sales ledger with others in that sector. For example, it may be common practice to offer sale or return in some industries and whilst examination of a prospect in the same sector may not have highlighted any occurrence of sale or return, it alerts the financier to its potential occurrence.

Credit control procedures

We have just examined what to look for in the sales ledger in order to identify risks to the financier but that is only half the story. To understand why the sales ledger looks as it does and how the prospect company offers credit and chases overdue debt, one needs to examine the credit control procedures. The following are important points to examine:

Debtor assessment and setting limits

Perhaps the first thing to look at is how the prospect establishes the debtor's correct trading style. An incorrect style on the invoice can lead to the setting of a credit limit that relates to another business. An even worse consequence is that legal action is taken against the wrong debtor. This can lead to an award of legal costs against the financier. A key element in ensuring the correct debtor style is to obtain written orders. Some financiers insist that the prospect must in future obtain written orders, particularly for new debtors. Poor debtor styles will inevitably lead to lower levels of funding.

If the debtor is new to the prospect, does the prospect seek bank or trade references or undertake any searches through external organisations such as a credit agency or Companies House?

Having gathered information on a debtor, does the prospect make a judgement as to their credit-worthiness and if so, does it set a credit limit?

Having set a credit limit, how rigidly is it enforced and what happens if it looks like being exceeded?

How regularly are such limits reviewed?

What happens to the limit if a debtor account becomes overdue?

Invoices

As a minimum the invoices need to show the debtor's correct name, address, date, order number (if supplied), the invoice value and any payment terms. The more information on the invoice to enable the debtor to identify the order and verify its acceptance, the better.

If an invoice finance facility is being considered, the invoices need to be examined to ensure that they are of the type that can be financed. A good rule of thumb is that each invoice should evidence a legally enforceable debt in its own right. Typically, an invoice financier will not finance invoices evidencing the following:

- Cash sales
- Sale or return
- Requests for stage payments
- Sales to private individuals
- Sales of the prospect's own capital items
- Sales to associated companies of the prospect
- Requests for a deposit (or even payment in full) in respect of goods to be delivered at a later date
- Sales on extended terms (the definition of "extended" will vary from one facility to another)

Credit notes

An examination of past credit notes will give you some indication of the likely level of credit notes in the future. Initially, the percentage, by value, of credit notes to invoices should be invoiced. Depending on the prospect's industry, anything over 5% should give cause for concern and it will then be prudent to examine the causes of the credit notes. The directors of the prospect should be asked to comment on whether they are happy with this level of credit notes and what their strategy is for reducing them. For an invoice financier, it must be remembered that all credit notes reduce the value of debts purchased.

Collection procedures

An examination of any statements which are sent out is useful. Statements should clearly list all unpaid invoices, including their due dates. Ideally they should contain an "aged debt analysis" and preferably have a tear-off remittance advice.

It is generally accepted that the most effective method of chasing overdue debts is by telephone. This is partly because commitments can be gained from individuals but it is also the best way to track down any hold-up in processing the invoice for payment, especially in large organisations.

The proof of an effective collection effort will be in an acceptable debt turn and the better this is, the happier an invoice financier will be. Of course, poor collections could be why the prospect is looking to use factoring but even if the proposal is to offer factoring, the invoice financier will want to establish if its own methods will bring about an improvement in the debt turn.

Attitude to overdue debt

It is important to understand the prospect's attitude to overdue debt. Are they prepared:

- To review the debtor's credit limit?
- To withhold future deliveries?
- To take legal action and if so, how quickly?

Cash review

A review of the cash position will highlight any cashflow problems. It will also identify money going in and out of the business that hitherto had not been mentioned. The items to examine will include:

Banking facilities

Confirmation will be required of the current funding provided by the bank and this will usually be apparent from correspondence. However, examination of the bank statements will show the actual usage and, if the usage is constantly up to an overdraft limit, this is an indication that cash is very tight. A review of the bank statements will also show up any bounced cheques issued by the prospect and reveal which debtors pay by BACS. The latter will be useful in trying to prevent future direct payments to the client.

Cash book examination

Examination of the cash book, in conjunction with the bank statements, will show up any cash going out of the business that may require further investigation. Cash may be going out to an associated company and bleeding the prospect of funds. Extraordinary payments may be going to the directors or there may even be potential evidence of money laundering.

Extraordinary payments coming into the business will be less frequent but will also need to be examined. Cash book figures will highlight any other bank accounts not previously mentioned by the prospect.

Other finance

Current cash movements can be identified through examination of the books but there may be future cash commitments, such as loans or hire purchase facilities,that have not yet been made. So it pays to ask for access to all correspondence regarding finance matters.

Bank reconciliation

Every business needs to reconcile the figures in its own books with those on the statements provided by its bank. Smaller companies might do this only monthly, larger organisations more frequently but they must do it regularly or a false picture might develop as to how much cash the business has. So it is important to establish that bank reconciliations are done regularly and are up-to-date.

An examination of the bank reconciliation will show how many cheques drawn by the prospect have not yet been presented. A company with a cashflow problem may be tempted to draw cheques to pay for purchases, or VAT, or income tax and then not send them out because they realise they will not be met. If a financier examines the purchase ledger or tax records, it will appear in these circumstances that the amounts have been paid, whereas the cheques are probably just sitting in a drawer.

Contract analysis

It is important to fully understand the contractual responsibilities of a prospective client. The following areas should be examined:

Purchase invoices

Many purchases bring with them certain responsibilities. It is well worth examining the terms and conditions of the key suppliers to the prospect company. By far the most important from a financier's viewpoint, is reservation of title (ROT).

Reservation of title

Reservation of title is where the supplier retains ownership of the goods until such time as they have been paid for in full. The result is that a seller can repossess his goods and resell them if the buyer defaults in paying for them. This is a useful right to exercise upon the buyer's insolvency. An ROT clause was held to be valid in the case of Aluminium Industrie Vaassen v Romalpa Aluminium Ltd (1976) and since then ROT clauses have also been known as "Romalpa clauses" or "retention of title clauses".

The simplest clause is "Full legal title to the goods shall not pass to the customer until they have been paid for in full". However, if goods are onward sold by a buyer who has possession of the goods, the original seller usually loses his rights to repossess goods under an ROT clause. ROT can be drafted with an "all monies clause", i.e. ownership of any goods sold and paid for will not pass to the buyer until all other goods supplied by the same seller have been paid for. Such a clause might read: "Title in the goods shall not pass to the customer until all sums due from the customer to the supplier on any account have been paid".

ROT is best effected on goods with serial numbers or bar codes. Otherwise if the buyer obtains goods of the same type from a variety of different sources the seller will be unable to tell which are the ones he delivered and will lose his claim.

From a financier's viewpoint, ROT is a complex area and one which has different implications for those funding invoices and those funding stock. The important issue at this stage is to ascertain whether the prospect's suppliers have it as part of their terms and conditions.

Debtor purchase orders

It is not always possible to study the orders placed by potential debtors. However, some of these orders might include clauses which could make invoice finance difficult or impossible. Although still rare, the most frequent of these clauses is a *ban on assignment.* This is where the debtor specifically states that no part of the order, including the invoice, is to be assigned to another party.

Invoices subject to a ban on assignment should not be financed because there is no way the financier can enforce payment of the debt. In such circumstances the financier should try to seek a waiver of this clause from the debtor. Sometimes this is possible because the intention of the debtor is that performance of the contract should not be assigned, rather than the debt itself. However there are some organisations, the Ministry of Defence being a prime example, where the seeking of a waiver will prove a fruitless exercise.

Terms and conditions of sale

An examination is also needed of the prospect's own terms and conditions of sale. It may be that they too have an ROT clause for example, which can sometimes be useful. Or perhaps a long-term warranty is offered. Upon the prospect's insolvency a debtor is going to be unwilling to pay for goods subject to an unenforceable warranty. There are insurance schemes which will take over warranty claims in the event of a company, which initially gave a warranty, going out of business.

There may be occasions when the prospect is a distributor that passes on a warranty offered by the manufacturer. This can often be an advantage if the manufacturer is perceived to be financially strong and likely to remain in business even if the prospect fails.

Once again, common sense will tell if any of the prospect's terms and conditions are likely to devalue the asset which is being funded.

Other contracts

It would seem prudent to examine any other contracts, such as insurance policies, or any legal document that might have an adverse effect on the prospect's business or the asset to be financed.

Purchase ledger analysis

An examination of the purchase ledger will give an indication as to how tight the prospect is for cash. We have already seen that the purchase ledger should be examined for potential contra accounts but the following should also be undertaken:

Credit turn

The so-called "credit turn" is similar to the calculation of the debt turn except that the former shows how quickly the prospect is paying its purchase invoices. The calculation is arrived at by dividing the average purchase ledger balance into the total purchases over, say, 12 months and then expressing that as a number of days. If the prospect is buying on similar terms to that which it is selling, then the credit turn should be similar to the debt turn. If the credit turn is longer, this could mean that the prospect is tight for cash.

Aged creditor analysis

This will highlight significantly overdue creditors and will need investigation as to why the creditors have not been paid. Much will be learnt about the prospect by establishing this. The reasons could range from cashflow problems, to quality disputes (ultimately affecting onward sales) but need investigating, particularly by sight of recent correspondence.

"Crown Right of Set-Off" allows a government ministry or department, which is indebted to a creditor, to reduce its payment in settlement by the amount of any money that its creditor may owe to any other ministry or department. This can be enforced against a financier who has taken an assignment of the debt. So if the financier is the assignee of debts due from the Ministry of Defence for military equipment sold but the client had arrears of VAT owing to HM Revenue and Customs (at the time of notice of assignment) then only the balance will be payable to the financier.

Stock control review

A review of stock control procedures is useful even where the facility is just for invoice finance, and becomes more important if the value of stock held is large. However when the facility includes stock finance, such a review is essential.

We saw in Chapter 3 the importance of the stock control records kept by the client because the financier has to rely on these so heavily. The particular issues to look for in the evaluation stage include: complimentary

Stock turn

The stock turn may have been calculated from the financial accounts for the period in question but it is important to do a series of calculations to establish any trend. A deteriorating trend should be investigated. It is generally the case that from the financier's perspective the quicker the stock turn the better because fast moving stock is likely to be easier to sell in a collect-out.

Stock control

The value of stock is arrived at in two ways. The first is the quantity and the second is the value of that quantity. The quantity will be established by means of a system of counting stock in and out which is then adjusted periodically by physical stock-takes. Most stock control systems will also calculate the value of each item of stock but others may take that information from an accounting system. Time is well spent in understanding the stock control system, particularly how and by whom manual adjustments are made. It is also useful to understand how the prospect deals with returns and damaged stock.

Accounting convention

The value of the stock should be stated at the lower of cost or net realizable value. Establish the pricing method (such as First In First Out) and how long the method has been applied.

Physical stock-takes

Establish how often these are undertaken and whether they are done by independent third parties. An examination of the results of these stock-takes should then take place and a comparison made with the figure appearing on the Balance Sheet. Just as important will be a comparison with the monthly stock records as the financier must rely on these documents to calculate the availability of funding.

Policy on obsolete stock

The prospective client should be asked how they know when a particular type of stock is not moving and what action is taken to "write down" the value of such stock. If the prospect becomes a client, the financier will want to hold a reserve for stock over a certain age and it is thus important to establish how this figure is to be identified.

"Sense check" the stock

If the amount of finance in question is large, then it is likely that an external professional valuer will be asked to value the stock. However, most small deals will not justify the cost of such external expertise. So, the financier's own surveyor should at least walk around the warehouse and make a judgement as to the credibility of the stated value of stock compared with what he or she can see with their own eyes.

Evaluation of due diligence findings

Having examined the risks of cashflow financing and the aspects to be investigated, it is now time to evaluate those findings in order to make a decision on the offer of a facility. There will have been a process of "due diligence" undertaken by the financier ranging from information sent in by the prospect in the case of a small factoring deal, to a full survey and perhaps many visits to the prospect for more complex product offerings. Whatever the process, someone or a group of people, will have to evaluate the information that has been gathered.

There are some basic goals for the evaluation of this information:

• Identify the suitability of a prospect for a particular type of funding and the level to which finance can safely be made.

• Identify and evaluate the underlying strengths, weaknesses and key variables which enable the prospect's business to succeed or cause its failure.

• Determine the ability of the prospect's management to achieve its goals and required performance levels.

• Ensure that identified strengths exceed identified weaknesses by a sufficient margin in order to cope with any unforeseen circumstances.

- Evaluate the likely value of the invoices, the stock or any other assets being funded in the event of the client's failure.

- Finally, in view of the above, can the financier make a reasonable return from this prospect?

Financial evaluation

The main purpose of the financial evaluation is to decide the likelihood that the prospective company will continue to trade in the foreseeable future. In the normal course of business, the financier will never lose the funds it has provided, as long as its client remains solvent. As long as this is the case, the client can repay the funds to the financier. Even if the client gets into financial difficulties, there is usually hope that a way will be found to turn its fortunes around. So, let us not forget, that it is very much in the financier's interest that the client remains solvent. Only upon insolvency will the true value of the assets being financed become apparent.

If a financier feels that the asset being financed will retain its value, that its security over that asset is strong and the amount of finance is small, then they make take a chance with a prospect whose financial position is uncertain. This can often be the case with factoring, where the financier has a good deal of control over the asset and where the amounts of finance are, on average, smaller than invoice discounting or other forms of cashflow finance. Thus the financier looking at smaller factoring deals will tend to go through a simpler financial evaluation and will take a more liberal view as to the prospective client's financial strength.

By the same token, the greater the amount of finance on offer and the more "arm's length" the control is over the asset, then the financier will make a more extensive evaluation of the financial strength of the prospect. At this level, the financier will want to see if the introduction of their "new" money will actually benefit the prospect's future. It will want to see that the added financing charges can be absorbed, and will certainly want to see that there is sufficient "headroom" to cover any unforeseen circumstances.

The "big ticket" deals will not only go through extensive and rigorous financial evaluation but the outcome may be to impose financial covenants on the client. These may take the form of profit targets, sales targets, cash generation targets or net worth targets. Whatever the covenants, they will probably have been taken from the prospective client's own forecasts and will be written into the offer letter. The penalty for failure to meet these targets will vary from reduced funding (perhaps a dangerous and self defeating strategy) to tighter controls, or perhaps an increase in fees to cover the added risk.

In summary, the extent and rigour with which a financial evaluation will be undertaken will vary from one financier to another and from one type of facility to another. No financier will wish to take on a client whose life seems to be very limited. However some financiers will take greater risks over the financial strength of a prospect if the amount of finance is modest, the perceived security strong and the reward for that increased risk is adequate.

Business plan

Ideally the prospect will have a prepared business plan although in practice this is most unlikely with smaller companies. However, it is absolutely essential for new start companies or those being restructured.

A business plan will normally include the following:

- The aims and objectives of the business
- Details of the market place in which they intend to operate
- Details of how the business intends to operate within that market in terms of price, quality of goods or service etc. In other words how do they intend to compete with the rest of the players in that marketplace?
- Details of the senior management, their skills and background
- Details of the infrastructure of the business i.e. premises, plant and machinery, IT, administration
- Sales forecasts
- Profit forecasts
- Cashflow forecasts
- Details of funding requirements

In evaluating the business plan, it needs to be credible and robust enough to withstand a reasonable amount of unforeseen circumstances. Ultimately, the evaluation of the business plan will come down to a mixture of common sense and considerable business experience.

Management quality

This is a vital area for assessment but is almost totally dependent on subjective feedback from those who have met the prospect's management - the new business staff/surveyors.

An assessment must be made of the technical ability and attitude of the prospect's management to run the company and achieve its objectives in line with its plans. Weaknesses in terms of limited skills or missing experience must be identified and considered within the full picture.

If the prospect company has been trading successfully for many years under the same management, then that in itself indicates that the management is capable of taking the business forward. However, a stage may be reached in the growth cycle of a business, when the skills of the management no longer match those needed for running a larger organisation.

For new start companies, it is vital to check the background of the management thoroughly. This is especially important if they are not investing too much of their own money. A word of caution is necessary - fraudsters are always helpful, co-operative and believable. The evaluation of the management quality must concentrate particularly on proven track records and the level of financial commitment on behalf of those individuals.

Many financiers will check the management's personal circumstances. If the managers are house owners and have been resident in the area for some time, then they are less likely to walk away if times get difficult.

Debt evaluation

We saw earlier in this chapter, that certain types of debt are not usually financed. However, it is not as simple as that. There are some types of invoices that definitely should not be financed such as cash sales, or sale or return invoices but there are some, such as those with potential contra accounts or invoices relating to goods with an attached warranty, where the situation is less clear. This grey area contains certain categories of debt which some financiers would not finance under any circumstances and yet others might "take a view" and find a way to offer funding. Let us look at some of these categories and possible ways to minimise the risk:

Specific to the contract

There is little option but to exclude the following:

- Cash sales
- Sale or return
- Stage payment invoicing
- Contractual debt

Relating to the type of Debt

Whilst many financiers might exclude the following, there is some scope for financiers to be flexible:

- **Warranties.** Some financiers may reject any debt that relates to goods which have a warranty. Others might try to estimate the likelihood of these warranties being used as reason for non-payment by the debtors in the event of a collect-out. If the product is quite simple and unlikely to deteriorate or fail, then it might be considered unlikely that the debtors will refuse to pay in full once their warranty becomes useless. However, it has to be said that most goods that carry a warranty, do so because there is a perception that a warranty is necessary.

  There are specialist insurance companies which provide warranty cover should the original warrantor go out of business, but for a financier to arrange for such cover to mitigate its risk is a complicated affair.

- **Ban on Assignment.** As the name suggests, a debt cannot be assigned if the debtor's order was conditional upon no assignment taking place. However, that does not mean the debt is not valid or that the debtor will not pay, even in a collect-out. It does mean that the debtor will pay the client rather than the financier. If the financier has a charge over the debtor balances as well as taking an assignment through the legal agreement, then the charge should mean that payment of that debt will ultimately end up with the financier in a collect-out.

- **Inter Company Debt.** Financing invoices addressed to a company that is associated with the client is a very dangerous exercise. The whole "group" could collapse at the same time. It is also an easy way to defraud an invoice finance company by having a non-existent debt going round in circles within a group of companies.

  Having said that, some financiers may take a view that such debt is acceptable if the business relationship is at arm's length. In other words the financier may conclude that the association between the client and the debtor is such that the risk of collusion is acceptably small. It is however, uncommon for a financier to finance inter company sales.

- **Disputed Debt.** Financiers will wish to exclude any disputed debt because there is a high risk that the debt will prove to be uncollectable. However, there may be some rare cases where the client convinces the financier that ultimately a debt which is currently disputed will eventually be paid.

Relating to the debtors

Financiers may find more scope in the following:

- *Contra accounts.* We have already seen, earlier in this chapter, that some financiers will simply not finance any debtor that may also be a creditor of the same client. However, we have also seen that some financiers will take a considered risk when the client owes significantly less than it is owed by the same company.

- *Poor spread.* As we saw earlier in this chapter, invoice financiers like to see a good spread of debt. Some will have a rigid policy of insisting they will not finance any debtor owing more than a certain percentage of the total sales ledger. Others may take a more flexible approach; they will look at the credit worthiness of the debtor, the client's financial strength and perceived probity of management, and finance a debtor that consistently represents the majority of the total outstandings.

Regardless of how flexible they are, most financiers will specify a maximum percentage of the total ledger owed by a single debtor that they are prepared to finance. This is called the "spread restriction" or sometimes the "concentration limit". The effect that a spread restriction can have on the level of funding is illustrated in the following examples. In the first example, there are four debtors that in total owe £32,000 but one of them owes £15,000. The overall prepayment percentage is 85% but there is no restriction on the spread of debtors. The availability, given no other retentions, would be £27,200 as shown below:

Example 1 (no spread restriction)

	Balance	pp%	
Debtor A	£ 10,000		
Debtor B	£ 2,000		
Debtor C	£ 5,000		
Debtor D	£ 15,000		
Total ledger	£ 32,000	85%	= £27,200 Availability

However, if a 30% spread restriction is imposed, then only £9,600 of the prime debtor's balance will be funded. Therefore the remaining £5,400 will be deducted from the total ledger of £32,000 before applying the 85% prepayment percentage. This reduces the availability down to £22,610 as the following example shows:

Example 2 (a 30% spread restriction)

	Balance	pp%	Balance Allowed	Disallowed
Debtor A	£ 10,000			
Debtor B	£ 2,000			
Debtor C	£ 5,000			
Debtor D	£ 15,000		£ 9,600	£ 5,400
Total ledger	£ 32,000			
Less disallowed	**£ 5,400**			
Fundable	£ 26,600	85%	= £22,610 availability	

- **Weak debtors.** Most invoice financiers like to see debtors who are of satisfactory credit worthiness. Others may take a view that they will accept weak debtors as long as the spread is good or the client strong or the prepayment percentage lower than normal.

- **Overdue Debtors.** It would be rare for a financier to exclude a debtor just because there is overdue debt on its account, but they will certainly wish to exclude the overdue portion of that debt. Unless the facility is non-recourse and the particular balance is credit approved, the financier will require that debts over a certain age will be disallowed for funding. This retention is variously described as the "recourse period", the "aged debt retention" or the "overdue retention". It is expressed as a number of days overdue, such as 90 days. The precise number of days will depend on the normal payment terms. Thus if the terms are quite long, say 120 days from date of invoice, the "recourse period" is likely to be quite tight at, say, 30 days overdue.

The effect of holding a retention against aged debt is shown in the following example. In this case, we are following on from examples 1 and 2 where there are four debtors and the prepayment percentage is 85%, but this time, half of Debtor A's balance is overdue and a retention held against this amount.

Example 3 (in addition to the 30% spread restriction, half of Debtor A's balance is subject to an aged debt retention)

	Balance	pp%	Balance Allowed	Disallowed
Debtor A	£ 10,000		£ 5,000	£ 5,000
Debtor B	£ 2,000			
Debtor C	£ 5,000			
Debtor D	£ 15,000		£ 9,600	£ 5,400
Total ledger	£ 32,000			
Less disallowed	**£10,400**			
Fundable	£ 21,600	85%	**= £18,360 availability**	

The above is by no means an exhaustive list but it is intended to show that whilst some debt is simply not "fundable", there are ways to minimise the risks with debt which is "less than ideal". Invoice finance is a highly competitive industry and there will always be those who will take a more entrepreneurial view on which debt to finance.

Stock evaluation

This evaluation will typically cover the following areas:

- **Effectiveness of stock control system.** The financier usually has to rely on the monthly stock listing as the only day-to-day control of how much finance should be provided. Although regular audits will supplement this, it should never be forgotten how much trust is put on this single listing. Therefore the prospective client's stock control system must be reliable, robust and ideally integrated with the accounting system. Particular attention should be paid to how easy it is to manually change the stock records.

- **Categories of stock.** We saw in Chapter 3 that stock may consist of raw materials, work-in-progress and finished goods. We also learnt that the nearer the goods are to being turned into cash, the better the security they provide to the financier.

So, finished goods are generally the most acceptable to the financier because they are the nearest to being turned into cash. This cannot be said for work-in-progress and thus it is less attractive to the financier, although there may be occasions where work-in-progress is easy to convert to finished goods and a reduced amount of finance made available. Raw materials are, in theory, the furthest away from being converted to cash but if these materials are of a simple nature with a wide market, then they too may be acceptable to the financier.

There are categories that will usually be excluded and these will include:

- Materials subject to ROT
- Spare parts
- Goods in bonded warehouses
- Goods in transit
- Consignment stock

- **Type of stock.** The best type of stock from a financier's point of view is that which has a value unconnected with the value of the company that holds it, i.e. the client. Thus low margin, commodity-type goods that have a wide market will hold their value in the situation where the client goes out of business. Conversely, high margin, state-of-the-art or bespoke products, will devalue steeply upon the client's demise. The key test at this, the evaluation stage, is to ask the question: "How easy and inexpensively will disposal of these goods be in a collect-out?"

So, to summarise the stock evaluation, the key issues are:

- How much can the financier rely on the stock control listing?
- What stock should be excluded from being financed?
- Of the stock to be financed, what is its likely value, after costs, in the event of a collect-out?

The involvement of other lenders

We saw in the last chapter how important it is to involve other lenders at a very early stage. Initially, the involvement might be to see if the various financiers can provide the amount of funding required or requested, and at what price. By the end of the evaluation process, new issues may have arisen that were not previously apparent. Now is the time to talk to other lenders about the financier's likely terms and conditions. This will happen as a matter of course if the funding has been "syndicated". This is where several financiers each agree to contribute to the overall amount of finance being provided and so the risk is shared. Typically one financier will "lead" the syndication and will coordinate the overall offer. The method by which the necessary security is shared between the financiers will vary from one deal to another but syndication is a good way, where the amount of finance is large, for the risk to be kept to manageable levels for each financier. In such cases, open dialogue between financiers will occur at every stage prior to acceptance, and will continue after commencement.

If the financier is actually in competition to provide finance against the same assets, then this dialogue will of course not happen, but if various providers of funding are working together, this dialogue is important.

Whether or not there is open dialogue before an offer is made, the involvement of other finance providers will affect the financier in the following areas:

Amount of finance to be provided

Each provider will want to ensure that the sum total of all the finance being provided is adequate for the particular needs of the client. For example, if an invoice financier is to replace the client's bank for debtor finance, then the financier may wish to see the bank continuing, if needed, against any other security it may have.

Assets to be used as security

Even if one of the finance providers wishes to have a fixed and floating charge over all the prospect's assets, it may be obliged to release some of those assets to another financier. This is especially important where assets are to be purchased by the financier, as in invoice finance. However, it may be appropriate that more than one lender has a charge over the same asset, in which case a priority needs to be agreed. For example a bank may provide a loan against a property and take a "first charge" over the property. Another financier may wish to increase its security by having an interest in the same property and take a "second charge". In the event of insolvency, the first chargeholder would need to recoup its entire loan before the second chargeholder could expect to recover any of its funds.

Conflicting terms

In addition to competing for the same assets, there may be occasions when different finance providers wish to impose conflicting terms. Clearly this needs to be resolved before a deal can go ahead.

Terms and conditions of offer

Once it has been agreed that the financier wishes to offer the prospect company a facility, then the terms and conditions of that offer will be put in writing. This document, usually in the form of a letter, is called the "offer" or "quotation" and may ultimately form part of the legal agreement between the financier and the client. Such offer letters will vary from one financier to another and from one facility to another but will typically include the following:

Invoice finance terms and conditions

- *Category of debtor balances.* This will cover whether the debts to be financed are domestic or export, or a particular category of the outstanding debtor balances owing to the legal entity to whom the offer is addressed.

- *Type of facility.* This will cover the product offering, e.g. factoring or invoice discounting.

- *Whether the facility is recourse or non-recourse.* If it is the latter, there may be discretionary limits or first loss values. A discretionary limit is one which the client can set themselves provided they have adhered to criteria set by the financier. A simple example would be that the client could set a £250 limit on any debtor that appeared in the current telephone directory. A "first loss" is the amount that remains at the client's risk even when a limit has been set by the financier, and works in the same way as it does for domestic car insurance.

- *Prepayment percentage.* This will be the "initial payment" percentage that will be made available against eligible/approved debt.

- *Any funding limit.* This will be the maximum amount of finance to be made available.

- *Spread restriction.* Sometimes referred to as the "concentration percentage". This refers to the maximum percentage of the total ledger that is owed by any one debtor that will be eligible for finance.

- *Any "excluded" or "non-notifiable" debts.* This refers to any category of debt that is to be excluded from being financed. This could range from potential contra accounts to stage payment invoices. The client is not required to notify the financier of these debts.

- *Any excluded debtors.* This may include, for example, debtors banning the assignment of debt.

- *Recourse period, if applicable.* This relates to the age of debt at which funding will be withdrawn. This is typically 90 or 120 days past due date.

- *Fee.* Typically, the fee for a straightforward facility will be expressed either as a percentage of debts purchased or a set amount per month. For more complex facilities, there may also be an initial arrangement fee upon commencement or even one set some time in the future.

- *Cost of funds.* This will usually be expressed as percentage points over a stipulated bank base rate.

- *Any other fees.* These might include extra costs related to a non-recourse facility or a minimum fee based on a forecast turnover.

Stock finance terms and conditions
Specific terms and conditions in respect of stock finance are likely to include:

- *Stock to be financed.* The offer will set out the categories and type of stock that will be financed. For example it may state that only finished goods less than 90 days old will be financed.

- *Finance percentage.* This will be the amount of finance available on the "eligible" stock. Typically this will be between 50% and 65%.

- *Cost of funds.* As with invoice finance, this will usually be expressed as percentage points over a stipulated bank's base rate.

- **Fees.** There will be an administration fee, usually a fixed amount charged monthly or annually. There will usually be other charges, particularly third party costs, but may include set-up fees, audit fees and charges for non-performance of any covenants.

- **Stock to be excluded from finance.** Typically this might include work-in-progress plus any stock where the ownership might be questioned such as ROT or consignment stock.

- **Retentions or Reserves.** Slow moving stock will be reserved against after a specified date. A reserve will be made against any claims under the floating charge such as the pool for unsecured creditors. Some financiers will reserve against third party warehouse costs.

- **Audit requirements.** Regular audits by the financier are even more important for stock than for invoice finance. The financier will wish to set out the obligations of the client and the rights of the financier when it comes to the audit visit.

- **Care of stock.** The financier will require that the stock is well maintained and secure and that it is insured for the benefit of the financier.

General terms and conditions

- **The agreement.** Reference will be made to the fact that the facility will be subject to a legal agreement between the two parties. It is normal that by this stage the prospect will have been given a copy of the financier's standard agreement. Ultimately, the terms and conditions detailed in the offer letter will be transposed to the legal agreement, usually in an attached schedule.

- **Any additional security.** The agreement itself will specify how the particular assets are to be secured. In the case of invoice finance, the invoices will be purchased and with most other assets, a legal charge will be taken out over the assets in question. However, it is not uncommon for an invoice financier to take a charge over the debtors that would give them chargeholder rights over debts that might for any reason fail to become the property of the financier. Some financiers may take a fixed and floating charge over all assets, as additional security. Some may take warranties or guarantees from other corporate entities or individuals connected with the prospect and back these up with security such as a debenture.

- **Covenants.** Larger deals will invariably contain covenants. Usually these will relate to the financial performance of the client such as a sales figure, amount of profit or minimum net worth. However, they might also be non financial covenants such as a deadline to install a new stock control system. The covenants will be specific as will the action to be taken by the financier if the covenants are not met.

- **Expiry date of the offer.** To avoid an offer being accepted long after it was made, an expiry date of typically 30 to 90 days will be included, after which a fresh assessment will have to be made.

Securing the deal

The Agreement

This document must cover all the rights and obligations of both the financier and the client. In a relationship of this complexity there is no room for unwritten "understandings" or "gentlemen's agreements". In a precisely worded way the day-to-day relationship is spelt out. Because only the financier knows exactly how its facility will work, changes to the standard agreement are rarely made.

The agreement may be one single document of considerable length. Alternatively it can comprise a few pages of items that vary from client to client, such as the client's identity, the prepayment percentages, administration fees, discount rates, concentration percentages and funding limits. This will then cross-refer to a separate set of "Standard Terms and Conditions" often printed in booklet form. If the financier has any conditions which are specific to the particular client these can be added to the short agreement, or put in a schedule to a long agreement. Such conditions may include matters to be dealt with prior to the commencement of funding (e.g. recapitalisation, waivers of ROT terms or clarification of sales contracts). Other conditions may relate to matters to be taken into account to ensure funding continues (e.g. holding of government licences, credit note limitations, payment of credit insurance premiums). Conditions can also vary from industry to industry.

Each financier has its debt purchase agreements written and laid out in its own deliberately chosen style. Some use very formal language; others are typeset like a book; others use "plain English". However, all cover the same subject matter. It is suggested that you study your own company's agreement and ensure that you understand it. Such detail may be tested in an examination related to this workbook. Before doing so you may find it helpful if we explain the broad framework of a debt purchase agreement.

Overview of Master Debt Purchase Agreements

In a typical agreement you will find that:

- The parties are identified.

- Technical words and phrases are explained.

- The ownership of all present and future debts of the client is transferred to the financier (lawyers tend to call such transfer a "whole turnover assignment") or with unincorporated clients they agree to offer their debts. The offer avoids a Bills of Sale registration for partners and sole traders.

- The calculation of the purchase price is explained.

- The calculations of the discounting charge, the financier's administration and other charges are explained.

- The time for payment of the purchase price to the client is explained including prepayments and any recourse period.

- Certain guarantees are given by the client as to its present position, together with promises as to its future conduct, including the handling of disputes.

- The client gives guarantees regarding its present and future debts (often called "warranties").

- The procedure is explained for the financier to get back its prepayment of the purchase price, if the debt is not paid before the end of a set period or the debtor becomes insolvent. This is known as "recourse" and the agreement is often called a "recourse agreement".

- In a "non-recourse agreement" the prepayment is usually not claimed back except in the case of a breach of the agreement. The balance of the purchase price of an approved debt is paid upon the insolvency of the debtor. Some financiers may even pay the purchase price of an uncollected approved debt without such insolvency, provided a substantial length of time has passed, e.g. 120 days past the due date for payment.

- Certain accounting issues are explained, including the treatment of VAT on bad debts. These are worded so as to emphasize that the facility is based on the purchase of debts and is not a loan by the financier secured against the financier's debts. If such security existed then it would be treated as a secured loan requiring registration at Companies House as a charge.

- The right of the financier to contact customers of the client and other interested parties is explained.

- The financier's right of access to the client's records is emphasised.

- It is essential that the financier has the sole right to collect debts even if the client is appointed as an agent under a confidential facility.

- If the financier needs to act in the client's name then such right is given by the client's power of attorney in the agreement.

- Special provisions for partnership and sole trader clients (particularly if they take in new partners) are explained.

- How and when the agreement can be ended is clearly set out.

- The financier's rights if the agreement is ended, or if the financier has the right to end the agreement but does not do so, are clearly set out.

- The way to give formal notices (e.g. to end the agreement) is clearly spelt out.

- The consequences of termination will be unambiguous, including any additional charges for wrongful termination.

- Towards the end it specifies which of these laws applies, English, Scots or Irish.

When considering an agreement for the first time each party may concentrate on different issues. We list some of these below. Not surprisingly the client wants money for the debts and the financier wants its income.

- What does the client want to see?

- How much will be paid?

- When does it get paid?

- What will the financier's services cost?

- What does the financier consider important?

- What debts does the agreement cover?

- Is the purchase price paid on a recourse or non-recourse basis?

- Is it a confidential invoice-discounting agreement or a fully disclosed factoring agreement or some variation of either of these?

- What fees and charges will be paid by the client and when?

- What warranties and undertakings does the client give, particularly as to the validity of the debt and the non-banking of receipts?

- When can the agreement be terminated?

- What are the consequences of the client's default, even if the financier chooses not to end the relationship?

Warranties and guarantees

Any financier will be interested in the financial stability of its client. Not only will it want to be convinced of future profitability but also it will want to see that the shareholders of the business are putting up a reasonable amount of capital themselves. What is a "reasonable" amount will vary enormously but any financier will want to ensure that the shareholders (who are most often the directors in small businesses) stand to lose a fair sum if the business should fail. Otherwise there would be no incentive to keep the business going should it hit hard times.

Where there is not this "reasonable" level of investment by the shareholders, the financier might seek a guarantee or a warranty. Such a guarantee or warranty could be sought from another company (for example a "parent" of the client business) but more usually, it is sought from individuals, often the directors or major shareholders.

A guarantee is an obligation to pay or perform if someone else fails to do so. It is sometimes referred to as a "secondary obligation", e.g. secondary to the primary obligation of the client to the financier.

An indemnity is an obligation to pay or perform irrespective of whether any demand has been made by the financier on its client. So an indemnifier stands in exactly the same position as the client in relation to the financier for the obligations indemnified. He assumes a primary obligation.

There is great diversity in the way in which each financier's guarantees and indemnities are drafted but an example of both is included in Appendix 3.

Plant and machinery

We saw in Chapter 1 that some cashflow financiers will provide additional finance against plant and machinery but that typically this will be in addition to an invoice finance facility.

A professional valuer will have provided a "market value" and the financier will have considered how easy it will be to dispose of these assets in a collect-out.

Typically, a cashflow financier will offer funds in the region of 70% to 80% of the "market value" as a loan over, say, three to five years. Having established that the plant and machinery in question is unencumbered, then a fixed charge will be taken over each item, to secure the loan.

Property

Similarly, some cashflow financiers provide specific loans against property but again, usually in addition to an invoice finance facility.

As with plant and machinery, a valuation will be obtained and the same consideration given to the ease with which the property could be sold in the event of insolvency. A smaller percentage will be offered against property, usually below 70% but over a longer period of say, five to seven years. A fixed charge will be taken over the property to secure the loan.

Credit insurance

We have already seen that when a client receives a non-recourse invoice finance facility or where credit insurance is provided as part of a package, the client is protected from the risk of a bad debt if its customer fails. By protecting the client against this risk, the likelihood is further strengthened of the invoice financier recouping its money in the event that the client also goes out of business.

Let us assume that ABC Client Ltd issues an invoice for £10,000 to XYZ Debtor Ltd and that ABC Client Ltd then assigns that invoice to its invoice finance company and takes a prepayment of £8,000. Now, let us assume that ABC Client Ltd goes out of business. The invoice finance company expects to recoup that £8,000 prepayment by being paid in full by XYZ Debtor Ltd. However, what if XYZ Debtor Ltd also goes out of business? It is not uncommon for the demise of a customer to cause the failure of its supplier. The invoice financier has nowhere from which it can recoup its £8,000. But if there is protection against the debtor's failure, the invoice financier can feel more comfortable. Thus, the addition of a credit insurance policy can aid not just the client, but also its financier.

Whilst the fact that there is a credit insurance policy in existence is reassuring, it is little value unless the financier can benefit from any payout. The client has to be the insured party and as such comply with the policy requirements, but the financier can become beneficiary of any claims. The most common method of achieving this is for the financier to become "Loss Beneficiary Payee". Under this arrangement, the client informs the insurer that they have an invoice finance facility and that they wish for the financier to receive benefit of any claims paid out. Paperwork is exchanged and the insurer acknowledges the fact in writing. Under this scheme, the financier is not liable for any of the conditions of the policy but simply the recipient of any claims paid out. The financier must ensure that the policy premiums are being paid by the client and have the right to pay such premiums on the client's behalf if the client fails to pay.

The other, rarer option is for the financier to become "Joint Insured" and this gives the financier more control and access to information but makes it jointly liable for the conditions of the policy. In this case the financier is jointly liable for the premiums and it is usual that the financier will pay the insurer and recoup the amount from the client.

In both cases, it is vital that the financier ensures that all conditions of the policy are being complied with so that the insured debts remain covered.

In this chapter, we have looked at the structuring of the deal from the point where the financier gathers together the information it requires, makes an assessment and then a decision whether to quote. Once a quotation is made, we have seen what is required to pull the deal into a legal agreement. The final part of this process from finding a prospect to it becoming a client is the take-on and that is the subject of the next chapter.

Taking on the client

Introduction

So, an offer has been made and it has been accepted. We have now arrived at probably the most important event in the relationship between financier and client. usually described as the "take-on". It is important because both parties, despite their own research up to this stage, are making a significant leap of faith and, just to make things difficult, new people become involved as others start to fade from the process.

The process

Naturally the process will vary enormously from one financier to another and from one facility to another but there are some parts of the process that will be common in almost all take-ons. The process will begin with the acceptance of the offer and usually end with the initial payment from the financier to the client. The time between these two events can be anything from a few days to several weeks but usually a target date will be set for the first payment, therefore all the other steps in the process will have to be completed before then. There can be conflicting interests during this period because the financier will largely be procedure-driven, whilst the prospect will often be time-driven. A high level of communication between the two parties and even within their own organisations is absolutely vital during this process.

Building new relationships

We saw in the last chapter that in most cases the new business manager is generally responsible for the relationship with the prospect until they become a client. So in most cases the new business manager's formal relationship ceases at take-on although most will keep an informal channel open, if only for future new business generation.

It is at this stage that the client manager usually takes over the lead role, representing the financier and so will be building a new relationship with the prospect. Just to confuse matters, there will often be other members of the financier's staff who will become involved only during the take-on process. However the client manager must assume overall responsibility.

On the prospect's side, the directors will have negotiated the deal but thereafter others within their organisation may operate the facility from day-to-day. Sometimes, the people brought into the relationship at the take-on will have been unaware of the financier's impending involvement. They may be concerned for their own jobs, they may have pre-conceived negative ideas about such a facility or they may simply be afraid of change. So it is important that the financier recognises that not everyone at the prospect's company will have the same level of enthusiasm for this new facility.

Legal documentation

The agreement

This is the prime document that needs to be signed by both parties. As the agreement will almost certainly contain a power of attorney, it must, by law, be executed as a deed. In the case of a company, this means either using its company seal or the signature of two directors, or one director and the company secretary. As many companies are now formed without any requirement in the articles of association to have a company seal, the signature of two directors will increasingly become the norm for deeds. Nevertheless, there needs to be a board minute, confirming that the company is to enter into an agreement and authorising the directors to sign it. In that way, none of the directors and shareholders can claim that they were unaware of the arrangement or that the directors who signed exceeded their authority. For the same reason, where security is taken such as a charge, it is also good practice to have a shareholder's resolution approving the arrangements.

If the prospect is a partnership or sole trader then special registration provisions apply if the agreement contains a general assignment of all future debts. In the event of the partnership's or the sole trader's subsequent bankruptcy, the assignment will be void against the Official Receiver or Trustee in Bankruptcy handling the insolvent client's affairs unless the agreement is registered at the Bills of Sale Registry as if it were an absolute bill of sale (Insolvency Act 1986). In order to do this the agreement must be executed in front of the prospective client's solicitor, after the solicitor has explained the nature of the assignment to all the partners in the client or the sole trader.

The procedure is that the financier is the first to execute the agreement. It then arranges for all the partners in the prospective client or the sole trader to execute the agreement in front of a solicitor. The procedure thereafter is:

- The solicitor should fully explain the nature and effect of the assignment to all the partners or the sole trader.

- All partners or the sole trader must sign all prints of the agreement in front of the solicitor, who then witnesses their signatures.

- The client's solicitor then swears an affidavit before another solicitor as to the above events.

- The affidavit, with a copy of the agreement, then has to be filed at the Bills of Sale registry at the High Court in London within seven days of the client having signed it.

- Registrations are valid for five years and must be renewed before that period expires.

- If there is any change in the partnership, e.g. death, retirement, addition, expulsion, amalgamation etc. the above procedure must be adopted in the case of every new partner and a deed of novation will be required.

Guarantees or Indemnities

When taking personal guarantees it is essential that before signature they are either directly handed to each individual or posted to them at their home address. They should never be left with a director of the prospective client to obtain signatures from co-directors or shareholders. This is to ensure that no allegation of duress or misrepresentation can be made, e.g. "I only signed because my husband said it was unimportant". There is always a risk that spouses or elderly relatives will make such an allegation in order to avoid having to honour their guarantee. The burden is then placed on the financier to produce evidence to the contrary. This is the result of two cases (1) *Barclays Bank v O'Brien* and (2) *Royal Bank of Scotland v Etridge*.

In the O'Brien case the House of Lords set out the circumstances in which a bank is put on notice that a guarantor might set aside a guarantee on the grounds of undue influence. This is usually where a wife or elderly relative with no financial interest in the business is involved. The court held that this risk could be removed if the financier held a private meeting before signature where the proposed guarantor was told the extent of their risk and advised to take legal advice. In practice, banks and financiers have generally preferred not to have such a meeting but to have an independent solicitor separately advising the guarantor. This prevents allegations of misrepresentation or duress being raised when attempts are made to enforce the guarantee.

The House of Lords in the Etridge case set out the minimum requirements to be followed, where solicitors are used, wherever the relationship between the surety and the debtor is non-commercial. The Etridge rules would cover a wife with no active role in a company owned by her husband being asked to give a guarantee for the company's indebtedness to the financier. Apart from requiring her solicitors to advise the wife in a face-to-face meeting, the law now lays down minimum disclosure requirements that the financier must make, including the amounts and terms of the facility. In practice this means that a copy of the completed debt purchase agreement must be provided and the solicitors must confirm that they have no conflict of interest. All this is designed to ensure that the wife freely and knowingly enters into the commitment.

Taking guarantees or securities from such protected persons is unlikely to be routine. However sometimes it is unavoidable. If the husband has to give you a guarantee for his company's obligations, secured by a mortgage over the matrimonial home, it is likely that his home will be jointly owned with his wife. The mortgage cannot be obtained without the wife's signature and would be worthless without a related guarantee from her, following independent legal advice given strictly under the Etridge rules.

Corporate guarantees, whilst not subject to the same constraints as personal ones, need to be supported by a board minute referring to the facility and in effect confirming their support for the deal. Again good practice dictates a shareholder's resolution where security is taken from a corporate guarantor. Any directors common to both the prospect and the guarantor company should declare and record their interest (including as personal guarantors) at each board meeting. Ideally they should abstain from voting if there is a conflict of personal interests.

Waiver

We saw in Chapter 4 that a waiver is required if there is already a charge which includes the debtor balances because without such a waiver, the financier would be unable to purchase those debts. The existing charge is almost always held by a bank and the main banks have a standard waiver which they will issue.

Fixed and Floating Charges

It is very common for a financier to take security over all the obligations of a limited company which is either a client or guarantor. The document is usually described as a "debenture" and contains fixed and floating charges over most of a client's assets. If a financier has a charge over its client's assets this means that the charged asset can be realised for the benefit of the financier, if the client defaults in its obligations. This is subject to the rights of any other party having priority either by an earlier charge, or having been granted priority by the financier or having priority at law. Enforcement usually has to be by a licensed insolvency practitioner.

Charges are "fixed" when the client is unable to deal with the asset without the prior consent of the financier. Real estate, intellectual property such as patents and trade marks, plant and machinery are all suitable for fixed charges. Materials, unfinished goods and stock are only suitable for floating charges since it is difficult for a financier to control dealings with them. Where a financier has, or expects to have, a shortfall in its recoveries from the purchased debts of a client in financial difficulties, it can appoint either a receiver or an administrator to enforce its security. Following the passing of the Enterprise Act 2002 the choice depends upon the date of the debenture. If it is prior to 15 September 2003 and contains a floating charge, the financier will usually appoint a licensed insolvency practitioner as an administrative receiver to take over, manage and sell all the company's assets. He is the agent of the company but his prime objective is to recover the financier's money.

Where the financier has a charge dated after 15 September 2003, over substantially the whole of its client's property, then it can only appoint an administrator. This provides the company with a breathing space while it considers its option. The administrator is expected to use his best endeavours to rescue the company as a going concern. If that is not possible he must try to obtain a better result for creditors as a whole than in a winding up. Failing these objectives, the administrator must use his powers to realise property for distribution to secured or preferential creditors.

Before appointing an administrator to enforce a debenture the financier must be aware that the administrator can sell the floating charge assets and need only hand over to the financier the net proceeds after settling:

- The preferential creditors, including arrears of wages up to £800 per person, and accrued holiday pay; and

- The "prescribed part" reserved for unsecured creditors being 50% of the first £10,000 plus 20% of the remainder. The maximum amount of the prescribed part is £600,000.

- As can be seen, debentures dated prior to 15 September 2005 are inherently more favourable to the financier. This must always be borne in mind when renegotiating security over the assets of a longstanding client.

Deeds of Priority

We have previously discussed the need for Deeds of Priority where there are two or more charges over the same asset. If the financier takes a charge, then this may create the need for such a deed. Alternatively, it may be made a condition precedent that one needs to be completed prior to commencement.

Trust accounts

In the case of undisclosed invoice discounting, a trust account will need to be set up to receive debtor payments. The trust account is a bank account set up by the invoice discounter in the name of the client into which the client will pay monies received from debtors, and those debtors paying by BACS will pay into directly; confidentiality is maintained by the account being in the name of the client. Withdrawals from the account can only be made by the invoice discounter and typically funds will be "swept" from each trust account into the main account held by the invoice discounter on a daily basis.

Bank mandates

In the case of factoring or disclosed invoice discounting, a mandate needs to be signed by the client allowing the factor to bank cheques made out to the client. For example, a mandate from "A Client Ltd" will allow cheques payable to "A Client Ltd" to be paid into the bank account of the financier. The reason for this is that despite the notice of assignment, some debtors may continue to make cheques payable to the client. The mandate will avoid having to return the cheque to be made out to the financier and will reduce the temptation for the client to bank the cheque into its own bank account.

Statutory identification of directors

All financiers are obliged under laws against Money Laundering to "know your client" which includes verifying their identity and their ultimate beneficial ownership. This means that the financier must verify the identity of all applicants as soon as practicable, whether they be sole traders, UK or foreign registered companies or partnerships. Each financier should have a manual prepared by its Money Laundering Compliance Officer which will have to be followed. Having satisfactorily identified the client then some of the directors or partners will have to provide identification, unless the applicant is a public company quoted on a recognised stock exchange or a subsidiary thereof.

Proof of personal identity is usually through sight of a current passport or photo-card driving licence which is photocopied and kept on file. Individuals' addresses are verified by sight of utility or council tax bills or bank statements and many financiers also verify the address via a credit reference agency.

There may well be other legal documents to be checked and signed at this stage and many financiers now have a legal section to ensure that all the documentation is properly drawn up and stored securely in fire proof conditions.

Pre-commencement conditions

These are sometimes referred to as "conditions precedent". These are terms requiring certain events to happen before funding can start.

For example, the financier may wish to see further equity put into the prospect's business and therefore will specify an amount of new issued capital to be invested prior to commencement of funding. The financier will thus wish to see documentary proof of this and compliance with any similar condition, prior to making the first payment to the prospect.

Most financiers have a library of special conditions which they tailor to their requirements for each client and then insert into master agreements, usually by way of a schedule. Here are a few examples:

Before we start making payments:

• We are to receive the personal guarantee of XXX and YYY.

• We are to receive a letter of waiver from BBB Bank with an appropriate deed of priority, in our standard form allowing us to purchase your debts free of any third party security.

• We are to receive a loan postponement from your managing director in the sum of £ xxx.

• We are to receive a fixed and floating charge over all your assets as security for your obligations to us.

• We are to receive written confirmation from FFF Factors that upon repayment to them of all monies due in respect of your debts they will have no further interest in your debts.

• (In a disclosed invoice finance facility) all invoices must contain a "Notice of Assignment".

• Our commitment fee of £xxx will be deducted from the first prepayment".

Verification

In the case of invoice finance, it is not uncommon for the financier to seek to verify that the take-on debts are genuine. Due to time constraints, this will usually have to be done over the phone. It would not be effective to verify all debts but the financier will typically wish to see a large proportion of these take-on balances verified.

Care will be taken during the verification exercise that the phone number of the debtor has come from an independent source, rather than given to the financier by the prospective client. This will help to minimise the possibility of fraud whereby the person answering the telephone call requesting verification of a debt is in fact in collusion with the prospect. Land-line numbers are required for this exercise rather than mobile numbers, which may cause suspicion.

With disclosed invoice finance, a general notice of assignment letter is sent to all debtors. This is signed by the client and written on their letterhead. It is usually sent out by the financier by recorded delivery. In addition to assisting the debt verification process, it sets the rights of the parties and has specific connotations regarding future offset claims by debtors.

Where the financier is funding fixed assets such as plant and machinery, the financier may obtain a valuation and proof of ownership prior to take-on.

Data loading

Details of the prospect and the asset being financed will have to be entered onto the financier's database. In the case of factoring, individual debtor accounts with open item balances will have to be entered. In an increasingly large number of cases, this will be done electronically from the prospect's database onto that of the financier. However, they may have to be individually entered in which case some time will need to be allowed for this to take place.

In addition to this standing information, a client current account is set up which will reflect all the transactions between the financier and client, including invoice and credit note notifications, debtor cash, client payments, fees and all adjustments and ancillary charges.

Obligations of the parties

The obligations of each party will have been laid out in the agreement. However, it is only right that some of these obligations are highlighted during the take-on process.

The financier will wish to explain the likely reaction to a breach of the Agreement. For example, an invoice financier will want to stress that the deliberate banking by a client of a debtor payment due to the financier, is a serious breach and will warrant severe action, including termination and enforcement of guarantees. It is important to take the time to ensure the prospect fully understands how seriously such breaches will be viewed and the likely outcome. The financier will also point out the benefit of compliance, which is to maximise the level of funding available.

Procedures explained

Inevitably the financier will have some laid-down procedures that they wish the prospect to follow. Usually these will be described in some detail in a "user manual" for the prospect to keep. However, it is important that the key procedures are verbally explained by the financier not only to the directors of the prospect company but also to the staff who will have to follow these procedures. Time spent ensuring an understanding of these procedures, is time well spent and is often done face-to-face, thus allowing the Account Manager and client to meet.

Managing Expectations

The last two sections have covered the legal and procedural issues that will be faced after commencement but there will be other issues that both sides need to understand and expect.

The financier should understand any special features of the prospect's business and what the prospect hopes to achieve by this fresh injection of cash. Similarly the prospect needs to know how often the financier will be in touch with them, the sort of questions they will be asking on client visits, the rationale behind an audit, and so on.

At this stage and possibly throughout the relationship, there should be a review of the funding position in terms of what the client needs against what the financier believes they can generate. Such debates help to minimise any surprises as to the amount of funds available.

Inter-factor handovers

Sometimes, clients will change financiers for a similar facility. Perhaps they have become disenchanted with their current financier or found a facility better suited to their needs. Where the facility is invoice finance, the outgoing financier needs to be repaid and the incoming financier needs to purchase the existing debts. Members of the Asset Based Finance Association have agreed a set procedure to enable such transfers to be as easy for clients as possible and this is called the "Inter-factor handover procedure" (regardless of whether the facility is factoring or ID). All members of the Asset Based Finance Association are obliged to use this procedure and even non-members often use it.

At take-on, the incoming financier will need to make an initial payment to the outgoing financier which discharges the latter's indebtedness and allows it to release the debts for re-purchase by the incoming financier. The methodology for this is laid out in the "inter-factor handover procedure" which will be covered in more detail in the final chapter which looks at termination. At this stage however, it is worth mentioning two points relating to risk.

The first is that it is generally accepted by most members of the Asset Based Finance Association that clients taken over from other financiers have had a lower success rate than normal. Such clients have generally been more likely to fail and when they do, more likely to cause a loss to the new financier. The evidence for this is purely anecdotal but widespread enough to warrant extra care. Suffice to say that a financier is most unlikely to lose a "good" client to another financier. If the client tells the incoming financier that they have been receiving a "poor service" from their current financier, it may mean that they are not receiving as much money from the financier as they would like and there may well be a reason for that. So, it behoves the incoming financier to be even more vigilant in its assessment of the risk.

The second point is that the incoming financier needs to keep a close eye on the likely amount of the initial prepayment in the days prior to take-on. Very occasionally, the incoming financier finds it is being asked to pay the outgoing financier more than its calculations show it should do against the debts it is purchasing. A decision will then need to be taken as to whether to "overpay" in order to purchase the debts. The earlier the financier can gauge if this might occur, the better.

The initial payment

The legal documents are in order, accepted and signed, pre-funding conditions have been met, the debts verified, procedures explained and good title to the asset has been obtained. The final step in the take-on process is to make the initial payment to what will then become the client.

If all the items listed above have taken place (and there will usually be a check list to ensure that they have), then someone at the company providing the finance will authorise the initial payment to be made. This is possibly the most important single step in the whole relationship, but providing everything else is in order, it will be done at the press of a button.

The last three chapters have taken us from negotiating the deal, structuring it, and finally, in this chapter, taking on the client.

In the next chapter, we will look at the content and effect of the master agreement between the financier and its client.

The Master Agreement

Introduction

This chapter is about the content and effect of factoring and invoice discounting agreements. Before reading this, you may like to refer to Appendix 4 which covers basic contract law for financiers and Appendix 5 which is about the law of the sales of goods or services.

There is an example of a master agreement in Appendix 6 and this should be read in conjunction with this chapter. Reference in this chapter to a financier is intended to include a factor or an invoice discounter, reference to factoring is equally intended to include invoice discounting and reference to a guarantor includes an indemnifier unless specified to the contrary. These notes only apply to the law of England and Wales. Some provisions may have to change if the client is incorporated elsewhere, e.g. Scotland or the Irish Republic.

Contractual Basis

Under English law three key elements are essential for there to be a binding contract:

1. an offer
2. an acceptance
3. (a) consideration (usually a promise to pay money) or
   (b) a document signed as a deed.

Factoring, like any other commercial relationship, involves a contract between the financier and his client. In every situation, both parties need to know with precision each other's rights and obligations. Because of the complexity of the transactions and their high value, the legal basis of the entire relationship has to be set out in a master agreement signed by both sides. The master agreement may consist of one long document or be comprised of several documents. If it is in several documents it may include some or all of the following:

• Short agreement including a power of attorney
• Standard conditions
• Quotation letter (sometimes called an "offer letter")
• Supplementary modules covering situations that only apply to certain clients; e.g.
  - Computerised services
  - Export debts
  - Foreign currency
  - Partnerships
• Procedures manual
• Computer users' guide

Each document will normally show whether it is or is not intended to be a contractual document. For example, some financiers do not want the quotation letter or their procedures manual to have any legal effect. Others do.

At the end of this book there is an outline of a master factoring agreement which deals with all the major issues that you or your client would expect to be covered (except for the terms of any electronic service that may be used). Many terms which are only of minor effect have been left out.

This sample agreement is a non-recourse factoring agreement, so that protection against bad debts is offered, so long as they are within credit limits established by the financier for each *customer* (often called the "debtor" by other financiers). Since Top Financiers' agreement calls them *customers*, and defines this word, we will do likewise. We will go through this and explain the purpose of the most important sections.

In day to day practice, decisions based on the master agreement often have to be made very quickly. It is particularly important for you to have a full grasp of the content and effect of all the provisions in a factoring agreement. They tell you and your client how each of you must act in any given circumstances, together with the extent of any discretions allowed to you. The agreements explain the major aspects of your day-to-day relationship with your client.

Both factoring and invoice discounting concern the sale of debts to the financier by the original supplier of goods or services in return for the payment of a purchase price. The transfer is called an "assignment". This emphasis on the word "sale" is important and the reasons for this are explained elsewhere in this book.

Overview of Master Agreements

Before dealing with specific issues, you will find it helpful to understand the broad framework of the debt purchase arrangements set out in a master agreement. In Chapter 5 when discussing the structure of the deal we saw an outline of a typical master agreement. We also reviewed what the client considers important and what the financier considers essential. It is worth bearing such points in mind when reviewing the details in this chapter and the sample agreement shown at the end of this book.

The Schedule of Variable Items

Because the deal with each client has to be individually negotiated there are certain provisions that may change from client to client and/or product to product. To avoid having to re-type the main body of the text for each client these variables are listed in a schedule (sometimes called the "particulars") and the details inserted once the deal has been structured with the client. Often they are copied straight across from the offer or quotation letter. The Schedule helpfully cross-refers the reader to where the main provisions occur in the text. The more important details from the model agreement's Schedule include:

Paragraph of Schedule	Heading	Paragraph of Schedule	Heading
2.	Period of agreement and notice	9.	Discounting charge
3.	Debt covered by agreement	10.	Service charge
5.	Prepayment percentage	11.	Minimum service charge
6.	Concentration percentage	17.	Conditions prior to funding
7.	Prepayment review level	18.	Special conditions

Most of these terms are also defined in the agreement immediately before the signature page. We shall deal with their effect when studying the main text of the model agreement.

Party – Client

It is vital to know with precision who is the client. Its details are then inserted in the particulars (see the last page of the agreement, just above the signatures). Failure to be precise (e.g. wrongly spelling the client's name) may make the agreement unenforceable. To make identification certain most financiers insert the following:
• the jurisdiction where a company is incorporated – "place of registration"
• its registered number at the Companies Registry

Remember that in the British Isles companies can be incorporated in any of:
• England
• Scotland
• Northern Ireland
• Irish Republic
• Isle of Man
• Guernsey
• Jersey

Party – Financier

Some agreements call the financier "we" and the client "you". Others, which wish to be more formal, will refer to the "factor" or "discounter" as the case may be and to the "client". Whatever they are called it is important that the agreement extends to anyone who is substituted for the Factor if, for example, the portfolio of agreements is sold on.

Definitions

Many words in the English language are capable of several meanings. A legal agreement demands precision. In a formal document the most important words and phrases are given precise meanings in order to avoid disputes. These definitions appear in the annex of definitions towards the end of the sample agreement at the end of this book. In the rest of the agreement these words appear with initial capital letters to remind you to refer back to the definitions section for their exact meaning. We will use italics to remind you that a word (other than "debt" or "client") has a precise meaning. You should be familiar with your own company's definitions that may vary from those shown in this book.

The following are worth commenting on:

"Approved Debt"
As this is a non-recourse agreement (an agreement with bad debt protection) the financier takes the risk of non-payment of approved debts. These are debts within credit limits established by the financier for each customer.

"Associates"

It is important to know who "associates of the client" are. Debts due by such people or companies will not be funded. Experience has shown that such associates are more likely to engage in fraud and are less likely to comply with any credit terms. Such associates are defined by cross referencing to definitions in Acts of Parliament, which includes spouses, relatives and financial partners. Companies are associated if they are under the same control.

"Availability"

This shows how the amount that the client can draw down at anytime is calculated.

"Customer"

The party obliged to pay the debt; often called the "debtor" in other financiers' agreements.

"Debt"

Note that the definition includes any tax or duty payable under the sale contract. The word can include a part of a debt. It is also called a receivable in other financiers' agreements.

"Delivered"

In clause 16.1.2 the client gives a warranty that the goods have been "delivered" prior to notifying the financier of the debt. Delivery means delivery of the goods to the customer or as directed by the customer.

"Goods"

This agreement equally applies to the provision of services. To save endless repetition about "goods and services" the agreement treats any reference to "goods" as always including "services".

"Ineligible Debt"

Situations are listed which cause debts to be ineligible for prepayments and so reduce the client's availability.

"Insolvency" and "Date of Insolvency"

Under a non-recourse facility the financier has to pay the purchase price of a credit protected debt upon a customer's insolvency. It is important to know what procedures are included within this definition. Under any agreement the insolvency of the client gives the financier the right to end the Agreement forthwith.

"Purchase Price"

As this is a sale and purchase agreement then the monies paid by the financier to his client for debts are for their "purchase price". They are not loans. In a recourse agreement it is the amount collected from the customer. In a non-recourse agreement it is the amount that would be payable by the customer but for his insolvency (and sometimes also upon substantial delay in payment).

"Related Rights"

Where a debt is purchased by the financier, at the same time there are also transferred all its "related rights" (see clauses 3(1) and 3(2)). These are both tangible and intangible matters connected with the debt including:

"Securities"	e.g. charges, guarantees, indemnities securing a customer's payment
"Benefits of Insurance"	e.g. the payout from credit insurance on a bad debt.
"Accounting Records"	to assist in collections
"Evidence"	e.g. proof of delivery of goods or the order.
"Rights under the Sale Contract"	This could include the right to stop goods in transit, the right to claim interest, the right to sue and give a valid discharge for the debt, repossess the goods under a reservation of title clause or to sell goods which are returned. If the client is unable to satisfy his financial obligations to the financier, then the financier may wish to sell such goods to reduce the client's indebtedness.
"Returned Goods"	See below.
"Remittances"	See separate definition.

"Returned Goods"

You will have noted from the definition of "related rights" that, when a debt is sold to the financier, at the same time there are also transferred the "returned goods" relating to the debt. These include goods recovered from or returned by the customer. Where the financier has a shortfall upon the failure of a client he can recoup part or all of his losses by taking possession of and selling the returned goods.

Transfer of Debts (Section 3)

You need to know to which debts the agreement applies. These are set out in paragraph 3 of the Schedule. In the example given it covers only UK debts (sometimes called "domestic debts") Debts payable by customers outside the UK are often called "export debts". All debts, present and future, to which the agreement applies, are intended to come into the ownership of the financier.

Ownership of debts is obtained in two ways:

1. All debts coming into existence after the date of the agreement become the financier's automatically (see clause 3.2). Other than signing and exchanging the agreement no other action is needed to give ownership of all such debts to the financier. This type of agreement is sometimes called a "whole turnover" agreement of future debts.

2. Debts in existence at the commencement date are to be offered for sale to the financier (see clause 3.1). Those it wishes to accept (in practice usually all of those offered) will be accepted by crediting their value to one of the accounts kept by the financier, often called a "debts purchased control account", a "client account" or a "current account" depending upon the accounting system in use.

Other factoring companies' agreements may provide for acceptance by the inaction of the financier e.g. failure to serve a notice of rejection. This offer/acceptance device was designed to avoid stamp duty on the transfer value of the debts at commencement. Such stamp duty applied to agreements before December 2003 so you will still come across such offer devices.

Agreements entered into after 2003, usually include an immediate transfer of all debts existing at the commencement date.

As a back up provision, debts which do not become the property of the financier under the above provisions (sometimes called "non-vesting debts") are held in trust for the financier (see clause 14.3). If the client becomes insolvent, assets held in trust, including such "non-vesting debts", do not benefit the client (or its liquidator, receiver or other insolvency practitioner administering the client's affairs) but go to the beneficiary of the trust i.e. the financier. As an additional security over such non-vesting debts, many financiers take a specific fixed charge by way of security over them and register it at the Companies Registry. This has the added benefit of alerting any future party, such as a bank, wanting to take security over such debts, of the financier's prior involvement. This lessens the risk of another secured party having a competing interest in the debt, particularly in a confidential facility, such as invoice discounting.

Prepayments

Section 9 headed "Our Accounts" contains the most important part of the agreement which the client will want to see. How much and when will he be paid?

The "purchase price", as we have seen from its definition is the amount collected from the customer, including duties and VAT, which is credited to the client account when cleared funds are received from the remittance in settlement (see clause 9.4). As this is a non-recourse agreement monies are also credited under clause 7.2 upon the customer's insolvency.

However no client wants to wait for payment of the purchase price until the debt is collected. He wants the benefit of a prepayment facility as soon as he notifies the financier of the existence of the debt. This is provided under clause 9.2. The amount available is calculated at the percentage (set out in paragraph 5 of the Schedule), which typically will be in the range of 70% to 80%, subject to:

- a financial limit on all prepayments and other monies payable by the client. Top financiers call it "the prepayment review limit" (see clause 9.2 and paragraph 7 of the Schedule). Other financiers may call it the "limit" or the "funds in use limit";

- no prepayment being available for ineligible debts (see later) including any concentration of the debts being owed by a small number of customers; (see definitions of "availability", "concentration limit percentage", "ineligible debts" and paragraph 6 of the Schedule).

Discounting Charge (clause 10.1)

So what does it cost the client to have the benefit of a prepayment? The financier takes a discount off the purchase price. But because no-one knows when a debt will be paid to the financier the discount increases for each day's delay. This is called a "discounting charge" and is calculated at a margin over a named bank's base rate (see paragraph 9 of the Schedule). It is worked out on the debit balance on the client account and debited to that account at the end of each month (see clauses 10.1 and 10.2). You must clearly understand that this is a discount off the purchase price and not interest. Interest is only appropriate to a loan. Nothing in pure factoring or invoice discounting involves the lending of money. The financier merely makes a part payment of the purchase price earlier than the collection of the debt. For this additional advantage to the client the financier takes a discount off the purchase price via the discounting charge.

Service Charge (clause 10.3)

Apart from prepayments against the purchase price, the commercial effect of the agreement is for the financier to provide other services, of which the majority are:

• administering customers' accounts
• collection of debts
• cash reconciliations
• assisting dispute resolutions

The client has to pay a service charge for these services. Other financiers may call it an "administration charge" or a "factoring fee". This is explained in clause 10.3 and 10.4 of the agreement. Top financiers' service charge is a percentage of the total value of the debt, including VAT, before any discounts due to the customer (see paragraph 10 of the Schedule). It is payable upon notification or offer of the debt to the financier (see clause 10.3). The service charge percentage is set out in paragraph 10 of the Schedule and is also subject to a minimum periodic charge in paragraph 11 of the Schedule.

If the debt is not collected by the end of the period stated in paragraph 8 of the Schedule then a monthly refactoring fee becomes payable (see clause 10.5). Some financiers call this a an "additional factoring fee". Again, it is calculated as a percentage of the notified value of the debt. Upon the Client's Insolvency ceasing to trade or failure to repay any Repurchase price on termination the financier has enhanced risks. As recompense for these enhanced risks, the service charge and discount can be increased (see clause 18.2).

Charges to the client can be made for:

• banking charges (clause 10.6)
• services outside the scope of the agreement or for variations to the agreement (clause 10.7).

If court proceedings are needed, these will usually be in the financier's name. The financier will pass the costs to the client to pay, including any awarded against the financier (e.g. if it loses the case) (see clause 10.8.8).

Undertakings and Warranties (Sections 15 and 16)

These are matters that the financier considers of vital importance. Whilst the relationship continues the financier relies on the happening of the background matters set out in sections 15 and 16. A warranty is a guarantee by the client. An undertaking is a promise to do something.

Clause 16 contains the warranties given by the client when it notifies a debt, including that:

- the details in each notification are correct
- each debt notified relates to a bona fide sale and in accordance with the contract
- there will be no set-off
- the client is entitled to transfer the debt, which will remain free of encumbrances (such as charges)

Although there are other undertakings elsewhere in the Agreement, clause 15 attempts to bring together some of the more important which include obligations on the client:

- not to cancel a sale contract
- not to include prohibitions on assignment in a sale contract
- to ensure compliance with the Data Protection Act 1998

Breach of these undertakings may only come to light after the insolvency of the client. However, to the extent that such breach causes loss to the financier, this should be claimable from any guarantor.

Disputes with Customers (Section 8)

A financier wants "clean" debts that can easily be collected. Disputes dilute the value of the debts purchased by the financier and put at risk the funds in use paid to the client by way of prepayments. If a debt becomes disputed this is a breach of clause 16.1.8 and the client debt becomes an ineligible debt (see definition item 1). This means that the availability of funding is affected, (see definition). The financier can also resolve disputes as it sees fit (see clause 13.3), although normally the client is expected to do so on receipt of a dispute notice 9 (see clause 8.2).

Recourse/Repurchase

"Recourse" is not a word used in this agreement. Reference at section 11 is made to "Repurchase". The financier has a right to insist that the client buys an ineligible debt back. The definition of the repurchase states it has to be repurchased at the amount at which it was first notified to the financier at or the value of its prepayment. When reading some other company's factoring agreements, be careful if you see the word "recourse". It sometimes means merely the redesignation of an approved debt (approved for funding or credit protection) as an unapproved debt (i.e. with no such benefits) but without any requirement on the client to buy back the debt. Such agreements may separately refer to "repurchase arrangements" or similar terminology.

So what *ineligible debts* can be subject to Repurchase under this Agreement? They are:

1. disputed debts;
2. debts where the client is in breach of any undertaking or warranty;
3. debts not subject to bad debt protection (unapproved debts) remaining unpaid at the end of the recourse period shown in paragraph 8 of the Schedule;
4. unapproved debts in excess of the funding limit for each customer;
5. debts in excess of the concentration limit;
6. unapproved debts where legal proceedings have been threatened;
7. an unapproved debt where the customer is insolvent (which can include having assets seized)

The repurchase price in practice is usually recovered by the financier debiting it to the current account that then, for a while, will reduce the client's availability for prepayments from new debts notified.

The above explains how routine recourse operates while the financier's relationship with his client is working well. However, if the agreement is terminated following the minimum notice period in the Schedule by either party (see clause 2.1) or is instantly terminated (see clause 18.1) because of a serious event listed under that clause (called an "termination event") or could be so terminated (but is not), then clause 18.7 becomes operative. All debts have to be repurchased for the debit balance on the current account. Although the word "recourse" is not used, the effect is the same. The client has to buy the debts back (see clause 18.3.3). Ownership does not pass until the repurchase prices of all debts have been paid to the financier (see clause 11.2).

If the financier does not terminate the agreement following a termination event then any newly created debts still come into the ownership of the financier. This adds to the value of the ledger to be collected from which the financier can recoup any prepayments previously paid against debts. In addition Top Financiers can increase the discount and service charges, if the client is insolvent or ceases to trade.

Customer Credit Balances (Clause 9.6.1)

Sometimes a credit balance will appear on a customer's ledger. The reasons for this can be numerous, e.g.

• double payment for one invoice
• payment for an invoice that has not been notified to the financier
• a credit note issued which is larger than the invoices notified to the financier.

If a client becomes insolvent, liquidators have been known to make financial claims on the financier for those credits. This places the financier in a difficult position. Some credits may be a liability of the financier to repay to the customer, some may not. The legal position on many claims is complex and untested. In order to resolve the legal position a great deal of the financier's time may be involved. To avoid such disputes, the client agrees that the financier does not have to pay such credits to the client (see clause 9.6.1). This provision should be binding on a liquidator or insolvency practitioner appointed in relation to the client.

Collection of Debts (Section 13)

One of the most important rights that a financier needs is to be able to collect debts in his own name. This right comes automatically by general law as a result of giving notice of assignment to the customer. It is reinforced by clauses 13.2 and 13.3. These give the financier total discretion as to how and when to issue, defend or compromise any legal proceedings relating to a debt. If the financier wants to sue in the client's name, he can do so under the power of attorney (see clause 20). Where the facility is fully disclosed then the client's name in practice is rarely needed except where the customer denies that the debt was ever assigned to the financier. The client is responsible for all legal costs involved (see clause 10.7.8).

Client's Accounts (Clause 17.2)

The financier will want to know about its client's financial position. The client is obliged to send in periodic financial statements and annual audited accounts (see clause 17.2).

Power of Attorney (Section 20)

A power of attorney is the right given to the financier to use the client's name and sign documents on the client's behalf. This power is given irrevocably as security for the performance of the client's obligations under the agreement or to customers. This means that the insolvency of the client does not render it unenforceable. Other purposes are for perfecting the financier's ownership of debts or related rights e.g. by drawing up formal documentation and signing it for the client. The financier and its officers can also in turn appoint or remove substitute attorneys. This can be useful if an overseas lawyer requires to be appointed with a power of attorney to issue collection proceedings. Apart from the financier being appointed as the client's attorney each of the financier's directors, its Company Secretary, its General Manager and its officers are also appointed to act as attorneys. "Officer" is a very wide term and in practice is any manager or senior executive.

Partnership and sole trader clients

Most of the agreement applies equally to clients that are companies, sole traders or partnerships. However, certain extra administrative provisions have to be made for partnerships and sole traders. Examples include:

1. the financier's ability to settle with one partner without affecting its claims against the remaining partners;

2. a demand by one partner (e.g. for a prepayment) can be treated as being binding on all the partners even if not signed by them all.

These would be the subject of a specific partnership module. Space does not permit a copy to be included in this book.

Commencement and Termination (Clauses 2.1 and 18)

Each side will want to know when the relationship starts and how and when it can be finished. The start is usually straight forward. With most financiers it is either the commencement or start date specified in the Schedule or, in the example used in this book, the date of the agreement.

Ending an agreement is by:

- a period of notice from one party to the other (often of three or six months); or
- instantly by the financier if something seriously detrimental occurs (often called an "event of default"). This is a phrase often used in commercial agreements, although some factoring agreements (including the example in this book) call them "Termination Events". They are set out in clause 18.1.

Termination with a Period of Notice (Clause 2(1))

You should note the strict requirements imposed on the parties under this agreement in giving notice; i.e.

- a minimum of 6 months written notice (see paragraph 2 of the Schedule); and
- only to expire after the minimum period of 12 months shown in the Schedule.

If the client wants to go earlier, this potentially could give rise to a claim by the financier for compensation, which is usually settled by payment of a negotiated early termination fee. In the first year, the financier has to recover his start up costs through his income stream. Such compensation could be substantial. Because the negotiations for such compensation can be complex it is important to indicate the method of calculation (see clause 2.3). Remember that whatever method is set out in the agreement it must reflect the parties' genuine pre-estimate of the financier's losses. Anything more would constitute a penalty clause and be unenforceable.

Termination Event (Clause 18.1)

The rights of instant termination by the financier in clause 18.1 break down into:

- those associated with insolvency e.g. 18.1.8, 18.1.9, 18.1.10.
- those associated with adverse financial circumstances, e.g. 18.1.3, 18.1.4
- those which could adversely affect the basis on which the financier entered into the relationship, e.g. 18.1.5, 18.1.6, 18.1.7, 18.1.11, 18.1.12
- Breach by the client or any associate in its contractual agreements with the financier e.g. 18.1.1 and 18.1.2.

The most common grounds for the financier terminating an agreement are:

- insolvency
- breach of the agreement by either:
  (a) notifying non existent debts (a breach of the warranties in clauses 16.1.2 or 16.1.3)
  (b) banking monies received into the client's own bank account and failing to tell the financier (a breach of the undertaking at clause 14.2)
- retirement from the business of a key guarantor who wants to withdraw his guarantee (or his insolvency or death) (see clause 18.1.10).

As we explain below, it is rarely wise to terminate an agreement.

Effect of Termination

You will have noted that a serious termination event without an actual termination by the financier, puts the financier in a very powerful position because of clause 18.3. The financier continues to obtain ownership of all debts newly created thereafter, but can if it wishes accelerate the recovery of its funds in use by:

- reducing the prepayment percentage(see clause 18.3.1)
- demanding back all prepayments made against debts at that time unrecovered (see clause 18.3.2) by adjusting the prepayment review level. Other financiers may call this the maximum funds in use figure.

The financier still has to collect the debts and hand over the proceeds (once the above recoveries have been made). Usually the mere threat to invoke this clause is sufficient for the client to mend his ways e.g. if he has been diverting collection remittances away from the financier.

You must be absolutely certain of the financier's rights upon termination or his further rights following a Termination Event. They can vary from financier to financier. If you claim to exercise a non-existent right the client will have a claim for substantial damages and guarantors may be released. Clauses 18.2, 18.3 and 18.4 set out Top Financiers' rights in the situations stated including:

- The client must repay the debit balance on the client account;
- the financier can increase the service charge; and
- the financier can increase the discounting charge.

Top Financiers very wisely have taken care not to breach the Unfair Contract Terms Act 1974, which they would do if they could instigate serious consequences for the most minute breach of the agreement. Unfortunately for the reputation of the asset based lending industry there are still some financiers who retain the rights to enforce massive penalties for minor infringements of the agreement. Clause 18.3 very wisely states that only certain termination events will be considered as "prejudicing" the financier's position. These include:

- failure to honour payment obligations
- breach of any warranty or undertaking in the clauses so headed
- failure to provide accounts
- failure to hand over collections from customers.

If the financier's position is so terminated then, under clause 18.3.1, it can without ending the agreement:

- reduce prepayments to zero
- make all existing debts ineligible debts, without funding
- demand repayment of the funds in use.

Under the last sentence of clause 18.3, the client then has 30 days within which it can immediately end the agreement, effectively without penalty. However it must then repurchase all the debts.

The effect of clause 18.5 is that the financier has a continuing obligation to collect debts until the repurchase price is paid and all debts become revested in the client. In turn, the financier is entitled to rely on the client's indemnities as to legal costs of litigation for unapproved debts.

To avoid lengthy arguments as to the amounts needed to be paid by a client in any legal proceedings against it, clause 9.8 states that a certificate by a director or the Company Secretary of the financier will be conclusive evidence of the amount due. The Courts will uphold this unless there is an obvious error e.g. the figures in the certificate do not balance. A similar clause appears in guarantees and saves considerable time in enforcing them through the courts.

Applicable Law (Clause 20)

It is important to know which law applies to the agreement. In this case, it is English law. For ease of administration, the client accepts that English courts can hear any proceedings brought in respect of it.

Exclusion of Other Terms (Clause 21.1)

To avoid any suggestion by a client that he entered into the factoring agreement because of some statement by a new business executive or some misunderstood letter or advertisement it is essential to state that only the matters set out in this written document affect the relationship. This means that Top Financiers do not intend to rely on any "letter of offer". Nor can the client claim that any advertising terms are incorporated.

Special Conditions and Pre-funding Conditions (Paragraphs 17 and 18 of the Schedule)

It may be that the deal has special requirements e.g. as the client's recapitalisation or new shareholders. In which case, these requirements would be inserted in the Schedule, usually as preconditions to any monies becoming payable to the client. An explanation with examples appears in an earlier chapter. Ongoing special terms would be inserted under paragraph 18 of the Schedule.

Execution of Agreement

You will note from the last page of the sample agreement that the document is described as being executed as a deed. This is because it contains a power of attorney, which by law must be executed as a deed. In the case of a company this means either using its company seal or by having it signed by two directors or one director and its Company Secretary (as in the case of the client). Since many companies are now formed without any requirement in their Articles of Association to have a company seal then the signature of two directors will increasingly become normal for such agreements. Where a financier has many agreements to sign it is easier to appoint senior executives with power of attorney to sign the document as a deed, thus saving the time of busy directors. This is what Top Financiers have done.

Non-Recourse Agreement

This is a non-recourse agreement (i.e. with bad debt protection) which means that the financier takes the credit risk of non-payment by a customer of an approved debt, which is a debt within a credit limit established by the financier. Usually debts at take-on cannot be approved debts. These provisions do not appear in a recourse agreement. On the agreed date after the due date (typically 90 or 120 days after such date) funding for an invoice is withdrawn and the financier has no more financial interest in it. The financier takes no credit risk and the debt can be reassigned back to the client.

Reassignment and Value Added Tax

If the debt proves to be uncollectible the VAT is recoverable from HM Taxes and Customs. The VAT Rules do not allow the assignee of a debt (such as a financier) to claim VAT Bad Debt Relief. Only the client as the supplier of the goods and services can claim. Section 7.2 of the agreement enables the debt to be reassigned to the client. The client will normally wish to reclaim VAT bad debt relief through its periodic return. The client also has to hold in trust for the financier any dividend received from the estate or any recoveries of an insolvent customer (less VAT).

Receipts (Clause 13.4)

Where some debts are credit approved and some are not, the financier can take any remittance from a customer where there is no remittance advice and use it to clear approved debts before unapproved debts. Under a non-recourse agreement this then transfers part of the credit risk to the client for debts outside a credit limit. Likewise the same procedures apply to lump sum payments on account.

Invoice Discounting

The principle differences between confidential invoice discounting and factoring is that in invoice discounting:

- no notice of assignment is given to customers;
- the client, as the undisclosed agent of the financier is authorised to collect debts;
- but the financier can step in at any time, give notice of assignment and collect debts.

The client is obliged to send monthly aged debt reports. However the financier will not keep a sales ledger or allocate remittances against specific invoices. Other than these matters, all the clauses in the sample agreement at the end of this book will appear.

Supplementary Documents

In chapter 5 there is an explanation of issues surrounding guarantees and indemnities. Other supplementary documents that you will come across include:

- waivers
- deeds of priority

Waiver

If the client has already granted security, by a charge over its debts, to its bankers or other creditors, the financier cannot buy the debts and the factoring arrangements cannot work. It is essential that such secured creditor waives his rights to debts, and consents to the client entering into the factoring or invoice discounting agreement before any monies are paid to the client. This ensures that the secured creditor can make no claim against the customers if the client becomes insolvent. A sample waiver appears at the end of this book. The waiver provides that the secured lender will make no claim against the financier for debts subject to its charge but that any monies due by the financier to his client remain subject to the charge. The sample waiver ensures that the "related rights" (e.g. transferred goods) as well as the debts are likewise waived. This also applies to any trust provisions in favour of the bank. Trust provisions often occur in bank financed import transactions where pledges to the bank of shipping documents are released in return for the client signing a letter of trust in favour of the bank over the sale proceeds of the shipped goods i.e. the debt. This could result in the financier and the bank both claiming the debt. Hence the need for a waiver.

Deed of Priority (including consent to factoring)

Increasingly financiers take a fixed and floating charge over all the assets of a client. This is also called an "all assets debenture". It will include a charge over non-vesting book debts. There are debts intended to be assigned to the financier but which do not vest e.g because of a fault in the factoring agreement or the absence of a signature. There may be other assets such as stock or work in progress which the financier particularly wants security over. If another security holder has priority over such assets through an earlier charge then the financier may consider it essential to obtain priority over these and other assets, in order to provide funding. This is obtained by a deed of priority with the prior security holder and the client. An example is shown at the end of this book. It is a shortened version showing only the key sections. It also includes a consent to factoring. This then does away with the need for a separate waiver.

The priorities are set out in clause 3, and allow specific priorities for items listed in the Schedule. The security holders, including the financier, agree to cooperate in appointing the same person to enforce their securities. The prior lender in this document is a bank. Increasingly banks demand clauses, permitting factored debts to be paid into the client's account at the bank without penalising the bank. You will note that if Top Financiers want to claim such monies they need to put the bank on notice before the monies are received at the bank. It is usual for the financier to negotiate standard forms of such documents with most of the major banks. This ensures that there is no delay in providing them, once the commercial terms have been agreed between all parties.

This chapter has been about the content and effect of the master agreement between the financier and its client. In the next chapter, we will look at managing the risk. We will first examine the potential risks before describing ways in which any deteriorating trends and contractual non-conformance can be identified and then managed.

Change

Introduction

In Chapter 6, we looked at the procedures for taking-on a client. Following this commitment, circumstances will inevitably change, and will affect how the financier will manage the facility.

In this chapter, we will look at how the financier responds to change. These changes to the client may be brought about by external market forces or internal management decisions. They may be changes for the better or changes for the worse but one thing is certain – change is inevitable.

Later in this chapter, we will look at mechanisms for identifying change and then, finally, how to respond to the positive change. In the next chapter, we will discuss negative changes in the context of managing the risk. But first, in this chapter, we will look at the many stages where change can occur.

Where change can occur

Sales ledger profile

For an invoice financier, the first and most obvious place where they will see a change is in the profile of the sales ledger. This will manifest itself almost immediately in the case of factoring, and will soon become evident with invoice discounting. Such changes will include the following:

Spread

Gaining new customers is the lifeblood of many businesses and a change in the mix of its debtor base is almost inevitable. However, the financier will watch for the emergence of a major debtor which will lead to a poor spread of debt. This is serious for an invoice financier but is also of general concern to any provider of finance, if the client is acquiring too many of its eggs in one basket. It increases the risk that if the debtor's business fails, so too can the client and even if the debtor simply stops buying from the client, the hole that this will create can have a serious effect on profitability.

What may have seemed a well spread ledger, with no one debtor more than around ten per cent of the total outstanding, can change very quickly. Most financiers will have an automated system for calculating and flagging the largest debtor balances. If, as is usual, there is a "spread restriction", then the system will automatically reclassify any balance over that limit as ineligible for prepayments.

Ageing

A change in the ageing will occur if the debt turn deteriorates or quickens. It will also look different if the debtor mix changes or any particular debtor changes its payment pattern. Whatever has caused the ageing to look different, it should be investigated, especially if the debt turn has slowed. Conversely, if the debt turn is "too good to be true", then this could indicate the existence of money laundering.

Debtor quality

The financier will have assessed the quality of debtors prior to take-on. It will almost certainly have an on-going method of monitoring that quality. This will be easier if the facility is factoring because each debtor balance will need to be set up and thus there is an opportunity to assign credit ratings and perhaps finance limits for each debtor. It is more difficult for invoice discounting although most financiers will monitor the debtor quality of, say, the top ten debtor balances.

The significance of a change in debtor quality, particularly if it is a deterioration, is that this may reflect a change in the type of product or service being offered. Generally speaking, poor quality debtors tend to buy poor quality products and this may be indicative of a fundamental change within the client's business. A change in debtor quality also increases the risk that there could be more bad debts and that has serious ramifications for an invoice financier. Even well known names, such as MG Rover, occasionally fail and so it is important to ensure that there is a tight credit policy and that shipments are withheld if a debtor account becomes overdue. But surprises do happen, which reminds us again of the importance of ensuring a good spread of debt.

Dilution

Dilution is the word used to describe anything that reduces the value of an invoice other than cash. Thus credit notes, reassignments (charge-backs) and write-offs will each contribute to dilution. If the dilution rises, then so too will the expectation that less of the debtor balances will be collectable if the client goes out of business. Thus a significant rise in dilution is likely to be met with a reduction in the prepayment percentage.

Again, early warning of dilution is much easier with factoring. As the financier is in direct contact with the debtors, it will quickly notice a rise in debtor disputes. Some of these may be spurious in an effort to delay payment but some will be genuine reasons why an invoice is being disputed and these may lead to future credit notes, reassignments or, worst of all, an indication that the invoices are fictitious.

Domestic/Export balance

The financier will be interested if more of the invoices are in respect of export debt, because they are more difficult to collect if the client ceases to trade, and therefore involve more risk. There is also the added risk that collecting debts in certain countries is difficult, even in the best of times.

The facility may be for domestic sales only and so any export invoices will, once discovered, be ineligible for prepayments. Or it could be that the extent of exports is growing to unexpected levels. Whatever the change, there are risk and pricing implications for the financier.

Stock profile

Obsolescence

The danger of obsolete stock to a financier is that it will be difficult to sell in the event of the client's demise and even if eventually sold, will only fetch a fraction of the price attributed to it when it was originally financed. Thus all stock facilities will define an obsolence date as part of the finance agreement. This will usually be expressed as a period of time after the category of stock was created. For example, if finished stock of, say, fashion garments is being financed, such stock may become ineligible for finance after a period of 90 days.

In addition to adding to the financier's risk, an increase in obsolescence may also indicate a worrying trend in the client's business which ultimately will lead to stock write-offs and possible losses.

The financier will have to rely on the client's stock listings to determine the extent of any obsolescence but will also wish to confirm these values by periodic stock revaluations.

Stock revaluation

A stock revaluation can be both a cause and an effect of a change in the client's circumstances with a stock financier.

Let us first look at revaluation as an event which caused the change. We have previously noted that stock finance is perceived to be riskier than invoice finance and that one reason for this is the relative arms' length control that the financier has over the asset. Looked at simply, there will have been a stock valuation at some point, followed by periodic (usually monthly) listings provided by the client showing the movement in stock since the last return. Any mistake or deliberate manipulation of the listings may not show up until an audit or another valuation is made.

Needless to say, if the eligible stock is shown to be much lower than thought following a revaluation, then the financier may find itself seriously exposed. In these circumstances, a plan needs to be put in place to gradually reduce the level of finance until it is back in line with the agreed criteria. Even then, the financier will wish to investigate the reason for the discrepancy and may then seek to impose tighter controls or perhaps a reduction in funding until trust in the figures can be regained.

Now let us look at revaluation as being the effect of changed circumstances. This will be when the stock financier has some concerns about the facility. It may be that the client's financial position has deteriorated or that other assets are being financed and they have changed for the worse. It may also be that the financier has reason to doubt the stock figures being produced by the client. Under these circumstances, the financier may decide that a stock revaluation is required. We shall look at the mechanics of these in the next chapter.

Product

Some clients might slowly change the way they do business to suit their market, and in all innocence not think to inform the financier. It may not be a clear change of product but just a change in their modus operandi. The change in a client distributing "off the shelf" software to one selling software it has written itself, will be of interest to an invoice financier. The change in a client previously selling plain plastic bags but now selling these with a trendy slogan on them, will be of interest to a financier funding the stock. The type and nature of the product is a key part of the decision to take the client on so any significant change will prompt a reappraisal. Some changes to the modus operandi will improve the risk profile because they add to the client's profitability.

So changes in product can be positive or negative from the financier's point of view. However, deteriorating product quality is always bad news. Let us look at the impact this can have on both an invoice finance facility and one funding stock.

Impact on an invoice finance facility

For an invoice financier there are two issues to consider concerning deteriorating product quality. The first is the relationship between product quality and the asset being financed. For example, if the client manufactured furniture and the standard of workmanship declined even though the selling price remained the same, the debtors would start rejecting the poor quality furniture. Such merchandise disputes would dilute the value of the asset, be it invoices or stock, which is being financed. Thus deteriorating product quality means deteriorating asset quality and for the financier, that is bad news.

The second issue is that deteriorating product quality means that there is a problem within the client's organisation. The problem can usually be traced back to poor management, whatever the obvious cause, and this does not bode well for the future of the client's business. Under these circumstances, the financier is faced with a deteriorating asset being made by a client whose financial future is in doubt, run by management which has proved itself poor in at least this aspect of its control of the business. Clearly an immediate review of the situation is required and some swift action necessary.

Impact on a stock finance facility

We have just discussed the fact that deteriorating product quality means deteriorating asset quality. For the stock financier, this is more serious than for those funding invoices. At least with the latter facility, it will quickly become apparent that all is not well with the product either through debtor disputes or an increase in credit notes. The stock financier, however, could be funding poor quality goods for months before this issue comes to light. A stock revaluation or an audit should uncover the decline in quality but probably far too late. This is why a tight policy on ensuring that old or obsolete stock becomes ineligible for finance is so important.

Management and corporate profile

Change in management

Change in personnel. It perhaps goes without saying that questions should be asked if directors suddenly leave the client company and the same goes for new directors, especially a new managing director or finance director. In the case of the latter two, a swiftly arranged visit should be undertaken to meet the new directors. An important part of the decision to take on the client was the capability and probity of the management. So if the management changes to a significant extent, then a reappraisal should take place.

Businesses which are owned and run by families can be a problem when the management is passed down to the next generation which may not be as capable as its predecessors. The new managers may not posses the skills or indeed the motivation to manage a business. Many business text books talk about "rags to riches and back to rags in three generations". Of course there are many highly successful family-run businesses, but the financier needs to be satisfied that new management from the same family possess the skills required to run the client's business.

The swift exit of directors or any key staff should be investigated in case it uncovers a serious problem within the client which can affect its future.

High staff turnover within the client's organisation can be a symptom of poor morale, the causes of which should be discreetly investigated. It can be that the staff do not approve of some of the business activities of the management or perhaps they can see the "writing on the wall" and think the business is heading for trouble.

How the financier finds out about such changes is important. If the client informed the financier that will enhance the level of trust in the relationship but the converse may apply if the financier finds out from other sources. Departing personnel is not always bad news of course and it may be that the departure is a welcome one as far as the financier is concerned.

Lack of change in personnel. There can be situations where the client personnel does not change but their business does and leaves them behind. An example of this can be where the directors enjoyed a "lifestyle" business from which they gained the satisfaction of knowing everything that went on and had total control. Following substantial business growth, however, they might not possess the skills to keep up or they may simply lose interest because the business no longer satisfies their original needs. It may be useful to bring in a qualified financial director when a business gets to a certain size.

It is a truism that "businesses must change or die" and if the management does not change then inevitably the business will eventually die.

Management buy-outs. In "Management buy-outs", (MBOs) the existing management takes over ownership of a business. The good news is that it has presumably run the business successfully and should be able to continue. In addition, it now has a financial stake in the business and the risks and rewards entailed and thereby an added incentive to run the business successfully. A disadvantage may be that they miss the expertise (and perhaps financial muscle) of the previous owners of the business.

In management buy-ins (MBIs) a group of managers is brought in to take control of a business. They may not know the business in question but they will usually have considerable corporate experience. They are likely to go into a business that has not been trading very successfully and make the radical decisions that its previous managers were unable to make. The financier should seek references and examples of previous businesses that these managers have run.

Change in legal status

Client companies will occasionally change their legal status and the financier needs to look at the ramifications of this. Such a change may be from sole trader or partnership to limited company; the reason for this needs to be understood and the financier will want to re-evaluate the financial commitment of the owners of the business. Clearly a sole trader is personally liable for any business debts and yet the same person may invest just a small amount into the issued capital of a limited company. In such a case, the financier may wish to obtain a personal guarantee.

Moving up the scale, a limited company may seek flotation on the stock market and this is usually very positive news to the financier from a risk perspective. However, it may mean that with more access to fresh capital, the client may decide that it no longer needs the services of the financier. Paying attention to the needs of the client will be especially important in the run up to a proposed flotation.

Financial performance

All the items listed above can affect the ultimate performance of the client if they have not been resolved in time. Strong, proactive management will be able to come up with swift effective action to counteract most of these problems but weak, complacent management will almost certainly end up fire fighting the effects of the problem. From the financier's perspective, it is thus more beneficial to discuss with the client as soon as any of these difficulties occur rather than wait until the negative effects become apparent. Nevertheless, the financier may not always be aware of these difficulties and the first they may know of a problem is when the financial performance starts to deteriorate. Deteriorating financial performance will manifest itself in one or more of the following ways:

Increased sales

Usually where sales have increased, it is good news, but if badly managed it can bring stress to the business. If sales are in excess of forecasts, then it could be that the client is overtrading and this may lead to extra pressure on cashflow, notwithstanding the existing cashflow finance. For example, the client may need to purchase large stocks of raw materials that may be outside its stock finance facility until they are turned into finished goods.

Increased sales can also put other pressures on the business and the client may find itself struggling to keep up. At its very worst, increased sales may consist of some "fresh air invoicing".

Falling sales

If sales are actually falling, then this is a serious issue. Less serious is that they are growing but not in line with forecasts. Either way, the client needs to explain the reason and its strategy for reversing the trend. The financier will become aware of falling (or below forecast) sales by examination of its monthly statistics. Most computer systems will be designed to flag up declining sales.

Falling gross margin

The financier will become aware of falling gross or net margins by comparing the latest set of management accounts with previous sets. Gross margins which are falling will indicate either that purchase prices have risen or that selling prices have fallen or at least not kept pace with the rise in the cost of purchases. Once again, the client will be questioned on this and their strategy must appear credible.

Falling net margins

If gross margins are being maintained yet net margins are falling, then overheads are too high. These overheads can be anything from rising staff costs to an increase in bad debts or perhaps a rise in the cost of borrowing. Again, credible remedial action should be taken to reverse the situation.

Changing asset values

Liquidity will suffer if there is an increase in fixed assets which has been paid for from working capital. The total value of the assets remains the same but the liquidity deteriorates. For a company with significant cash reserves, this is no problem but for a business that is already stretched, then fixed assets must not be financed out of working capital but by longer term funding.

Even changes in current assets, such as an increase in stock, need to be investigated and could be indicative of an obsolete product line.

Extraordinary items

By definition, these items are not in the ordinary course of business and must be investigated. They may be the result of a reorganisation or revaluation or they may simply be a prudent exercise in taking a one-off hit for a project rather than trying to spread the cost over some years.

Cashflow problems

Falling sales or margins will have a negative effect on cashflow if left unchecked. However, if cash is tight, there can be other reasons. Too much capital expenditure or the "big project" will soak up cash. Too much cash being taken out of the business in directors' remuneration or being siphoned off into another company will quickly drain the client of cash. The onset of a cashflow problem will manifest itself to the financier if the client constantly takes maximum "availability" or makes regular requests for overpayments. Lack of cash is the most obvious indicator of a problem and later in the chapter we will look at how to spot it quickly. Suffice to say at this stage that the sole reason for most business failures is lack of cash. Many things can cause cash to dry up but it is always this lack of cash that will cause a company's insolvency.

Auditor's comments

The auditor's report should always be checked to see if they have any particular comments to make. They may pass comment, for example, on the way the stock has been valued or that they have had to rely heavily on some assurances from the directors.

There are two other financial changes that sometimes occur and need special attention:

The "big project"

The "big project" can mean anything from developing a new product to investment in state-of-the-art machinery or a bespoke computer system. The problem with "big projects" is that they become all consuming. They may take the management's eyes off their prime function of managing the business. Or the "big project" can simply consume too much of the client's cash. Large projects, particularly ones which have not been tried before by the managers of the client, have a tendency to go over budget and consume significantly more cash and/or time than was initially budgeted for. The financier thus ends up funding capital expenditure out of current assets and the client will very quickly end up with a serious cashflow problem.

The question is does the client have a plan in terms of desired outcome and how to fund the project? It can also present an opportunity to the financier in that it could assist in financing the project either directly or indirectly.

An acquisition

Many clients will go through a stage of considering making an acquisition considering a bid to be acquired. This needs particular skill and the financier needs to assess whether this expertise exists within the client's organization.

Increasing regulation, such as the "Transfer of Undertakings (Protection of Employment) Regulations (TUPE)", makes acquisitions more complex and can increase potential long term liabilities. The TUPE Regulations preserve employees' terms and conditions when a business or undertaking, or part of one, is transferred to a new employer. Any provision of any agreement (whether a contract of employment or not) is void so far as it would exclude or limit the rights granted under the Regulations. Employees employed by the previous employer when the undertaking changes hands automatically become employees of the new employer on the same terms and conditions. It is as if their contracts of employment had originally been made with the new employer. Thus employees' continuity of employment is preserved, as are their contracts of employment (except for certain occupational pension rights).

Making an acquisition can have some of the negative effects of the "big project" and in particular may take the directors' eyes off the ball. Assuming the financier is aware of the proposed acquisition at an early stage, it will ask to see the plan that puts the business case for the acquisition. Even if that plan is not written down, it is important to listen to why the directors see this acquisition as the right way forward.

The plan will be examined by the financier in the same way as any business plan, and challenged if it does not appear to be credible. Even if a successful acquisition is made, there still may be unforeseen problems particularly if two different business cultures are being merged or over-zealous job losses have to take place to make it work.

The process of being considered for acquisition is even more debilitating for a company. If a quick purchase is made with job security made clear from the start, then the financier need not be too concerned or may even see the benefits of faster, profitable growth. However, many long-drawn-out acquisitions will sap staff morale of the company being taken over and the business will be in limbo, unable to execute vital actions in a difficult environment. This will be compounded if the acquirer is seen as a "white knight" who will resolve all the current cash headaches of the client. "It can also present an opportunity to the financier, who could assist in financing the project either directly or indirectly".

Market

Increased competition

There will inevitably be changes in the client's market place. Such changes may be as a result of the economic cycle, but can just as well be a result of the dynamics in the client's industry. It should be part of sound client management practice to keep up-to-date with what is happening in the industries in which a financier's clients operate. A comparison with the client's actual experience and the trends within its own market can be useful. If the market is growing but the client is not, then the problem clearly is within the client itself. By the same token, if margins are falling in the wider market, then the client, when questioned, needs to have a solution that goes against the market trend.

The cause of a change in the market could be the sudden influx of cheap imports or a new product. For example, mobile phones which take photographs have dented the sales of cameras.

New legal encumbrances

New legislation which affects the client's product can be both an opportunity and a threat. Years ago, the introduction of the compulsory wearing of crash helmets on motor bikes was a great opportunity to manufacturers of helmets. More recently, the increased legal obligations of operating as an electrical contractor have put some smaller players out of business. The list of examples is long. Suffice to say that awareness by the financier of new and impending legislation in relation to the sale of goods and services is most useful.

Product requirement

Compulsory changes to products can occur for reasons other than legislation. Mobile phone manufacturers and networks are constantly under pressure to make their products less attractive to thieves. Food manufacturers are being asked to produce foodstuffs of more nutritional value and with greater clarity of ingredients. These two industries are operating in highly competitive markets and these consumer-led initiatives require investment and increased operating costs in an environment where prices are difficult to increase.

Economy

Inevitably the economy will move through various cycles. A client taken on in a favourable economy might not fare so well if there is a downturn. Prior to offering facilities the client will be evaluated to determine how robust it is to withstand the vagaries of economic cycles. Even if the client is thought to be fairly robust, a review should take place if a change in the economy is likely to affect the client.

Changes in the financier's criteria

Occasionally, the financier's own criteria will change. This may be due to a change in the economy but can equally result from internal reassessments of "acceptable risks" because of higher than expected bad debts, weak profitability or even a change of ownership. Whilst not strictly an external market change, this is nevertheless outside the client's control. However unfortunate for the client, such a change in criteria will have to be sensitively communicated and appropriate action taken.

Finance from other sources

Additional or replacement finance from other sources may also represent a significant change. It could affect the security, terms or longevity of the funding already provided by the financier or it may significantly change the gearing and financial profile of the client.

Underlying security

Guarantors

We have seen that financiers will sometimes take guarantees as additional security. They will have assessed the worth of the guarantor prior to quotation but of course the worth of the guarantor will change throughout the course of the relationship. Keeping track of the worth of a personal guarantor is not easy and so the financier, through its account manager, should try to stay close to the individual. Usually the guarantor is one of the directors or shareholders of the client company, so it is relatively easy to track any changes in personal circumstances. Clearly individuals can go bankrupt, making the value of a guarantee worthless.

Should a personal guarantor leave the client, they may think that this automatically releases them from the guarantee and should be reminded that this is not the case. However, should a personal guarantor request that they are released from the guarantee, this is a change that needs to be assessed. Either the client's financial circumstances have changed for the better and a guarantee is no longer necessary or additional security is required if the guarantee is to be released.

Similarly, the worth of corporate guarantors can change and if they fail then once again the value of their guarantee becomes worthless. However, it is easier to track the worth of a corporate guarantee through the provision of audited accounts. It may prove more difficult if the guarantor is based overseas.

Charges and Liens

Financiers will always take a legal charge over stock or any fixed asset they are financing and often invoice financiers will take a charge as additional security. We have discussed the different types of charges in chapter 6. Liens confer the legal right to hold or take an asset(s) belonging to a creditor until they (or if they fail to) discharge a financial obligation. Clearly any changes to a legal charge or lien, will affect the security belonging to the financier. As they are legal documents, there is little that can change without the financier's consent, other than a subsequent dispute regarding priority if there are other charges in place. Providing a charge has been taken and registered in accordance with the legal requirements and before any previous charge over the same assets, then a dispute over priority should not arise. However, a financier should seek immediate legal advice should there be any doubt over the validity of a charge.

Mechanisms to identify change

Economic and market information

The economy is constantly changing, sometimes in subtle ways and sometimes more dramatically. Any significant change in the economy will affect a client in some form. Periods of growth, low inflation and strong consumer demand will present opportunities for clients. Economic downturns with negative growth, rising unemployment or a reduction in consumer spending will present threats. Financiers will wish to keep abreast of such changes to the economy and be aware of the impact on its clients.

Financiers will also wish to understand and keep abreast of issues within the market place of each of their clients. Some financiers set up units within their organisation that will specialise in certain industries – e.g. clothing, provision of temporary manpower or computer technology. They will subscribe to trade magazines on these sectors, train their staff to understand the issues that make these industries tick and perhaps attend relevant seminars and exhibitions.

Client relationship

All financiers wish to maximise their profits over the long term. We have already seen that it is a costly business taking on a new client and therefore the longer the client is retained by the financier, the more profitable it will be. So, client retention increases profits and, of course, minimising bad debts has the same effect.

Usually, the day-to-day responsibility of maximising client retention and minimising bad debts is vested in the account manager who thus performs the role of "diplomat" and "policeman". The precise roles of account managers will of course vary from one financier to another but will generally be:

- To oversee and protect the financier's investment.
- To provide the client with information, help and assistance, and be the person to whom the client will make requests and complaints
- To be the most knowledgeable within the financier's organisation about that individual client account.
- To be the main negotiator for the financier over all matters relating to the agreement between the two parties.

The account manager's involvement in risk management will vary from one financier to another as will their authority to raise or lower the client's fees. However, nearly all account managers will be judged on their ability to keep contented clients which are profitable to the financier and avoid any losses should a client cease to trade. This is a big responsibility but one that will be shared with other areas of the financier's organisation and of course, its management.

The account manager is thus in a unique position to spot changes relating to the client. They will do this in the following ways:

The client visit

Most account managers visit each of their clients on a regular basis at intervals set by the financier. Almost all clients are visited within a few weeks of take-on in order to iron out any niggles but also to check that the facility is running as expected at the time a quotation was made.

Thereafter, clients will be visited at predetermined intervals with maybe an occasional visit in between, either at the client's request or because the financier has an urgent issue that needs addressing. Most financiers expect their account managers to write a report following the visit to cover some fundamental points, typically:

- Comment on the financial performance of the client
- Comment on the client's trading outlook and forecasts
- Is the client happy with the financier's service levels?
- How profitable is the client to the financier?
- Comment on the asset quality (i.e. invoices or stock)
- Comment on conformance to the legal agreement
- Comment on client's management
- Comment on any changes since the last visit
- A summary of the overall relationship
- A list of actions points

An inexperienced account manager might view the visit as an exercise in telling but a good account manager will spend much more time listening to what the client is saying about their business. By so doing, the account manager will not only have a far better relationship with the client but will possess the knowledge to spot potential problems before they occur, and take the necessary action.

Day to day contact

Account managers will talk to their clients on the phone quite often. Apart from dealing with specific issues, there is an opportunity to pose questions such as: "When I visited, you said your turnover was going to increase in the Spring and yet I notice that in fact sales are falling?" etc.

Payment authorisation

Many financiers require the account mManager to authorise or at least be aware of payments to clients. This is not always possible when the aAccount manager is out visiting other clients and many financiers have a system of automatic payments within certain criteria. But most account managers will be aware of payments which breach these criteria or are unusual or "overpayments".

Client reviews

We will look at this issue in more depth later in this chapter but suffice to say that most financiers will have a regular formal review of each client and that the account manager will be present at this review.

So, there are plenty of opportunities for the account manager to become aware of changes in the client's circumstances or in the relationship with the financier. It is worth mentioning here that a conflict can occur if the account manager is left alone managing the risk and the relationship without any checks and balances within the financier's organisation. Thus if the account manager, in all good faith, gets too close to the client, there needs to be another independent person within the organisation who can flag up worrying trends. It is therefore usual for the audit function to be completely separate from the account management function and for each side to have an input into the monitoring process. Risk management structures vary from one financier to another. However most know from experience that checks and balances are essential when setting out the responsibilities of those closest to the client.

Audits

Why audit a client?

Many financiers do not routinely audit their clients because the amount of cash at risk is relatively small and because, for certain facilities, the financier feels that it has sufficient control over the asset it is funding. Indeed most factoring facilities, unless the amount of funding is large, are not normally audited, although most factors will send out "audit letters" to debtors asking them to validate stated sales ledger balances. Apart from "standard" factoring deals, almost every other facility does carry an audit including:

- The larger factoring facilities.
- All confidential invoice discounting facilities.
- All stock finance facilities.

So why do these types of facilities attract an audit? Because the reason is that the amount of finance is high and/or the asset is not being managed on a day-to-day basis by the financier. As a result of this, the financier needs to check periodically that the client is doing everything that it is contractually bound to do.

Perhaps at this stage, we can examine what is meant by "periodically". Most audits will occur at predefined times, typically every three or four months (but sometimes every month and occasionally just twice a year). These set times will have been decided by the financier and may often be set out in the agreement between the two parties. However, there will be times when an audit takes place as a result of an adverse event or because the financier has some concerns. These "event-driven" audits can happen at any time.

What is the purpose of the audit? There are four aims:

- To establish that the client still exists
- To establish the current financial and trading position
- To confirm that the assets being financed are in good order and the documentation being sent to the financier is accurate
- To look for evidence that the client is not conforming to the requirements of the agreement

Most audits are undertaken by one person over the space of just one day. Clearly it would prove impossible to comprehensively achieve all three objectives under these circumstances. If a comprehensive audit is required, then more people and more time will be allocated, however that will only be necessary for very large deals or where there are serious concerns. For more routine cases, the financier will set out some priorities, based on the particular circumstances. If the financier (perhaps through the risk manager and the account manager) is more concerned with the asset being funded than the financial position, they will direct the auditor to spend more time looking at the underlying asset.

Preparation for the audit visit

The auditor, having booked the date with the client, will wish to receive input from the account manager and other operational staff to establish the current position and any operational issues that need to be addressed.

The auditor will need to read the previous audit report, the client visit report, any client review notes, the latest audited and management accounts and the up-to-date statistics on the asset being funded. In the case of invoice finance, the auditor will wish to look at trends in invoicing, levels of disputes or credit notes, the debt turn, the ineligible debt and any other documentation regarding debtor balances. In the case of stock finance, the auditor will wish to see the latest stock listings, a list of potential ROT. suppliers and a copy of the purchase ledger aged analysis.

Most auditors will have laptops with templated forms to complete with spreadsheets and risk analyses which may, prior to the audit, flag additional potential problem areas to be investigated.

At this stage it is worth commenting upon the much debated issue of whether the same person should continue to conduct the audit on the same set of clients. The advantages are that the auditor gets to understand the client's systems, will spot any deterioration from a previous visit and of course it is more cost effective to have clients visited by the same auditor who is usually based in the same locality as the client. The disadvantage is that the auditor may become complacent by having looked at the same information in the same format over and over again and may fail to spot a "creeping trend". In practice most financiers have some form of rotation policy.

Let us now look at the areas that will be examined during the audit visit:

Establish the current financial position

The auditor will almost certainly already have looked at the most recent management accounts and so will seek to verify the figures with the accounting records of the client. A more recent picture of the modus operandi will be gained by examining:

• Sales ledger
• Purchase ledger
• Bank statements
• Nominal ledger
• Cash book
• Dependant upon the circumstances, the auditor might examine any relevant correspondence, in particular with the client's bank or any other lender.

Basically the audit will attempt to achieve the same level of understanding of the financial position that the initial survey did prior to quotation. If the client is in financial difficulties, the level of that understanding will necessarily be that much deeper and more detail will need to be collected and taken back to the financier's office for review.

Asset verification
In the case of invoice finance, these will include:

• **Invoices or day book listing** The auditor will normally adopt a standard financial accounting audit technique and select, at random, a sample of invoices. The amount and number tested will depend upon the procedures laid down by the financier but will normally concentrate on some of the larger debtors where the majority of the financier's funds are, as well as some of the smaller debtors to give a good overview.

The listings sent by the client to the financier will be checked with the sales day-book records. This is to enable the financier to confirm that the invoices and/or day-book listings that it has financed are the same as those raised by the client. It does not prove the invoices are necessarily genuine but at least they appear in the client's own books.

• **Credit notes** As well as checking invoices, the situation concerning credit notes must also be investigated. The auditor should ensure that credit notes are correctly and quickly raised and that copies have been passed to the financier. Also certain general checks on credit notes will be carried out, such as comparing percentage of credits against total turnover and checking validity of credits issued, i.e. not just credit and re-invoicing to gain longer funding periods.

In addition to reviewing selected invoices/credits the auditor will use a sample of these to conduct a trace audit in which the process will be followed through the client's systems from the order being placed, goods supplied, invoices raised and payment received from the debtor.

A useful check on the ledger is to compare the value shown on the VAT return against the value of debts assigned to the financier. Any difference in figures will require an explanation and must be investigated. If a client is raising fraudulent invoices it will be unusual that they will pay the VAT element to the tax man.

• **Aged debt analysis** Having conducted these checks the auditor will move on to a debtor review with the objective of establishing that all concentrations are known about, cash has been allocated correctly and credit notes applied as needed. Non-funded/excluded accounts will be checked and the general pattern of debt aging will be reviewed to ensure it remains similar over an extended time period.

There are many tests/checks that an auditor may carry out under this heading including:

• Identifying the top five or ten current highest concentration accounts and confirming debtor credit worthiness;
• For these accounts examining their purchase orders/contracts for ban on assignment clauses, agency and distribution agreements, contractual supply terms over extended periods with potential liquidated damages claims;
• Comparing the current month balance on the aged analysis against the current month day-book totals to ensure all debts are being assigned and processed;
• Comparing the last three aged debt reports to check that debts are moving from the current column to the one month column etc. - this is useful to see if the client is re-ageing invoices;
• Reviewing all new debtor accounts including credit limits and searches;
• Reviewing all debts over 90 days old, obtaining reasons for late payment and update information on legal actions being taken against debtors;

- Checking the assigned ledger to ensure that items excluded from the invoice finance agreement have not been notified e.g. inter-company accounts, contra accounts, capital sales or other excluded sales;
- If the client has export accounts, checking to ensure that all paperwork procedures are correctly followed.

- **All cash receipts** Here the auditor is trying to satisfy himself that the client is passing debtor receipts onto the financier and that all cash is being correctly allocated and reconciled.

The normal review will include checking the client's bank statements and cash books and tracing where each cash item has gone. The aim, of course, is to ensure that all applicable cash receipts have been paid into the trust account. Any item that has been paid into the client's own bank account must be challenged, even though it may transpire that they relate to items that are outside the discounting facility. An examination of the bank statements will also uncover dishonoured cheques, in or out. This examination is probably the most important aspect of an invoice finance audit.

- **Examine purchase orders.** By examining the debtor's purchase orders, the financier will be able to spot any terms or conditions that make the resulting invoice difficult to finance. For example, the debtor may require to be invoiced in stages, or state that they will hold a retention pending testing of the product. This would fail to make the invoices "legally enforceable in their own right" and thus difficult to finance.

In the case of stock finance, the auditor will also:

- Compare the stock listing sent to the financier with the stock records.
- Check that the purchase records and the sales records reconcile with the stock control records.
- Ensure that stock over a certain age has been notified correctly to the financier and that the agreed method of defining obsolete stock is being adhered to.
- Take a physical stock-take of part or all stock, if practicable.
- Ask key staff to confirm the recording process and then look for any alterations to the agreed process.

- **Talk to key staff.** The benefits of the auditor talking to key members of the client's staff cannot be underestimated. At best, such conversations will confirm the information already passed to the financier via the account manager. At worst, some members of the client's staff may tell a different story to the one being told by the directors. This may simply be as a result of poor internal communication within the client company but it could reveal a cover-up of something that the client does not wish the financier to know.

Of a less sinister nature, more junior staff may sometimes offer information in all innocence of which the directors of the client may be unaware. For example, in an invoice discounting facility where the client is chasing the overdue debt, the person doing the chasing may have noticed that the major debtor is not returning their phone calls. It may not be a problem but it would be prudent for the financier to follow this up.

Statistics and trends

The financier will store a range of statistical information relating to the client. They will retain some sort of financial spreadsheet reflecting changes to the financial performance of the client, but perhaps more importantly they will keep statistics regarding the assets they are financing.

Factoring companies will have the most information because they actually run the sales ledger and keep individual debtor accounts. Thus factoring companies, in addition to the information kept by invoice discounters, will be able to spot trends in debtor disputes, debtor quality and will have the most up-to-date information relating to all aspects of the sales ledger. Those offering export facilities will have additional information relating to the different markets, currencies and often, details of collection activity from associated factoring companies abroad.

Invoice discounters will have monthly figures showing the level of invoices, credit notes, write-offs, bad debts, debtor spread and many other statistics relating to the sales ledger.

Stock financiers will have less information than those offering invoice finance but at the very minimum will have all the details supplied by the client in their stock listings, usually supplied at least monthly. In addition, they will have trends from their regular stock audits.

So, there is a wealth of information from which the financier can spot changes. The process by which these statistics are studied and then acted upon, will vary from one financier to another. At the very least, these statistics will be presented, perhaps as an exception report, to the client review. All are useful when looking at, say, deciding whether or not to "overpay" a client or when there is some concern that all is not quite right with the underlying asset being financed.

Internal reporting

In addition to the reports on trends and statistics that we have just looked at, there can be a variety of exception reports that are very useful, particularly to an invoice financier. Such reports might typically highlight the following:

- The notification of a particularly high value invoice or batch of invoices
- The notification of a particularly high value single or batch of credit notes
- The slowing down of debtor cash
- The deterioration of the debt turn
- An increase in the level of debtor disputes (factoring only)
- A debtor balance exceeding the "spread restriction"

There are some organisations which provide specialist software that will monitor all these items and more. This software will then assign scores to these items and flag these clients using a "traffic light" system. In this way, the account manger or risk manager is not just reacting to one big change but to a series of smaller changes which, when added together, are worth investigating.

Client Reviews

The two main advantages of a system in which a client's facility is formally reviewed on a regular basis are:

• The review is proactive rather than awaiting an event to trigger a review which would inevitably be reactive.

• It allows all the interested parties, within the financier's organisation, time to study all the relevant information upon which to make a judgement about the progress of the facility.

These "interested parties" will typically include the account manager, a person responsible for risk management, operational staff, perhaps a representative from the finance department and almost certainly someone in a senior management position. Who attends a client review will of course vary from one financier to another but the greater the amount of finance involved, the greater will be the number and seniority of the people attending.

The regularity will also vary from one financier to another and most financiers will have a set of criteria which will lead to larger, perhaps riskier clients being reviewed more regularly than smaller, stronger ones. Many financiers have a rating system for their clients which may well be used as the trigger for how often each client is reviewed.

The aims of each review will vary but will typically include:

• A review of the client's current trading and financial performance.
• A review of the performance of the assets being funded (e.g. invoices or stock)
• An assessment of the risk aspects attached to the facility.
• A review of any operational issues.
• A review of the relationship between client and financier.
• A look at the costs of running the facility and a review of the pricing.

Let us now look at the type of data which is likely to be studied during a client review. The types of information looked at during a review of a client which has both invoice finance and stock finance facilities will typically include:

• Minutes or action points from the last review
• The latest client visit report
• The latest audit report
• Spreadsheets of the latest financial accounts
• Sales ledger statistics on invoices assigned, credit notes, items "charged back", debt turn, cash turn, etc
• Credit information on the major debtors
• Recent bad debt losses
• A recent stock listing and reconciliation with the previous listing
• A report on any recent stocktake
• A costing based on recent throughput

All of the above will of course be supplemented by verbal reports from the various operating areas.

Outcomes from a client review

The review itself will no doubt involve much discussion and perhaps even some disagreements. However, the most important aspect of a review is that if it uncovers a problem or a situation that is continuing to get worse, then some action must be taken.

To ensure this, it is vital that minutes of the review are taken, action points listed with the name of the person responsible for taking that action and, if appropriate, a deadline.

A deteriorating risk profile is rarely something that will just go away and resolve itself; it needs action. Thus for all the preparation and analysis that goes into a client review, it is pointless uncovering a potential risk without then taking appropriate action to restore the situation.

External sources

Identifying change from external sources can also be valuable. There are a variety of sources the financier can tap into in order to identify changes, or potential changes, to its client base. Whilst by no means exhaustive, these can include:

The client's bankers

If the financier belongs to the same group as the client's bank, then dialogue will be easy and ought to happen as a matter of course. Even banks which have no association with the financier have a vested interest in gleaning as much information as possible on their mutual client. So a voluntary dialogue is highly desirable. In addition, there may be certain obligations for the financier and bank to disclose information. An example of this is the waiver (of the debtors from its charge), in which the bank is often required to notify the financier if any suspected debtor cash is paid into the client's bank account.

Other financiers

Clearly where there is a syndicated package of finance, provided by a group of financiers with an agreement between themselves, there is an obligation to notify each other of changes. In these circumstances, there will be a lead member of the syndicate who will co-ordinate such information. Apart from syndicates, clients will sometimes receive funds from a number of specialist financiers; perhaps invoice finance through one and a loan against some fixed assets through another. There may be no obligation for the financiers to exchange information about the client but subject to any constraints (such as the Data Protection Act), the sharing of certain data could prove very useful.

Companies House

All limited companies in England and Wales must register with Companies House. They must submit a set of annual accounts, even if they are non-trading, and an annual return. This latter document includes the accounting date, the names of the directors and secretary, the registered office, the shareholders and share capital. Any changes to this information have to be notified to Companies House shortly after the change occurs. In addition, all mortgages and charges must be registered within 21 days. Certain special resolutions also need to be notified. For full details of what must be sent to Companies House, go to its website on www.companieshouse.gov.uk.

Under normal circumstances, one would hope that the client would notify the financier of any of the changes that it is obliged to notify to Companies House, but there may be occasions when the client chooses not to do so. To circumvent that, many financiers subscribe to one of the many agencies which pass on changes notified to Companies House on a given company. They send a list of all their clients to the agency who will then notify them, usually within 24 hours, of any changes registered at Companies House. The main reason that financiers use this service is to be made aware of any new charge registered against their clients. It is surprising just how many clients forget to tell their financier this information!

Credit reference agency reports

These agencies are more likely to be used in checking out debtors but may be used occasionally to obtain information on a client. These agency reports will normally give details on payment performance, and any county court judgments that have been registered, but will largely list data already known to the financier.

Trade circles

We discussed earlier in this chapter the usefulness of financiers subscribing to trade magazines and attending seminars and exhibitions if they have many clients in a particular industry that would make this research worthwhile.

Press cuttings service

A few agencies offer a press cuttings service whereby it will provide its customer with any press cuttings on a given subject or name. It is rare that clients of cashflow financiers regularly appear in the press but some financiers offering big ticket deals may find this kind of service useful.

Responding to positive change

The final section in this chapter looks at responding to positive change. The next chapter will look at negative changes insofar as they will affect how the risk is managed.

Review limits

When cashflow finance started in the UK it was rare to set a limit to the amount of funds available. It was thought that the facility would automatically be capped by the asset being financed. In the case of invoice finance, the facility will grow (and be constrained) by the value of outstanding debtor balances. However, as the use of invoice discounting grew, it was thought too risky to offer facilities without a limit. Experience had shown the value of setting a limit which triggered a review of the facility.

Nowadays, limits are almost always set for invoice discounting and stock facilities, and are generally set for factoring facilities as well. In most cases these limits are known to the client but in other cases the limit is known only to the financier and exists as a trigger to review the facility.

When reviewing the changes that have occurred in their relationship with a client, the financier may often find that, on balance, most of those changes are positive. Thus, if the client is forecasting growth, the financier may wish to raise the review limit and still maintain an acceptable risk.

Switching to another product

As the client's business grows, so too will its needs. For example, it may be that a small business will opt for factoring not only because it provides finance but also a credit management service. This service is something that a small business may not have the expertise to undertake itself and so it makes sense to "buy it in". However, as the business grows, it may feel that it can undertake the credit management in-house and would prefer confidentiality and so invoice discounting may be more appropriate.

This same client perhaps started selling just within its own country but now wants to export and may add export factoring to the invoice discounting facility it has for its domestic sales. As the business becomes more sophisticated, then so too will its finance needs and so other assets will be used to raise more cash.

It behoves the financier to keep abreast of the client's changing needs and even pre-empt them. The financier, after all, will prefer to offer a different product to a good client than lose its business to a competitor.

Lifting constraints

Even where a product change is not appropriate, there will be other options open to the financier to proactively lift some constraints. Some examples of these are:

- Allowing electronic transfer of invoice notifications
- Allowing automatic payment authorisation within agreed criteria
- The financier requiring less hard copies of invoices or other documentation. provided they are retained for inspection by the client
- Allowing CHAPS payments (same day telegraphic transfers) if they have not previously been allowed
- Relaxing the "spread restriction"
- Increasing the prepayment facility

Pricing

When the balance of change has largely been positive, then it will not just be the financier that recognises this fact, the client will be equally aware. Thus the client may be looking for its "reward". They may feel that having had some constraints lifted or a review limit increased, they have been adequately rewarded. But they may not. They may be looking for a reduction in their financing costs.

The pricing policy will vary enormously from one financier to another but what they all have in common is strong motivation to retain clients for as long as possible, providing that the risk is acceptable and the reward sufficient. Thus, when there have been positive changes since the price was set and constraints have been lifted, the choice is either retain the same fee structure and risk losing the client or proactively reduce the fees.

There is, of course, no right or wrong to this dilemma and each financier will have to make up its own mind taking into account all the circumstances at the time. Suffice to say that retaining a client which is highly profitable to the financier has to be matched by first class service and strong relationships.

Outgrowing the need for cashflow finance

So, the financier has increased the review limit, removed some constraints, reduced the price and yet the client wishes to move on, not to another similar offering but something more suited to their needs. The financier will of course talk to the client, exploring ways in which it can retain the business. But sometimes the client, for all the right positive reasons, will wish to move on.

The range of products offered by cashflow financiers is wide enough to appeal to most small to medium enterprises, but not all of them, and rarely to the very large corporations. A client that has grown successfully by using cashflow finance and then parted company easily and amicably, will be a source of excellent PR to the industry as a whole.

Throughout this chapter, we have discussed the issue of change. The circumstances that were apparent when the client was taken on will inevitably change, some for the better, some for the worse. We have looked at the areas which could change and we have discussed mechanisms for identifying change. Finally in this chapter, we looked at responding to positive changes.

The next chapter will look at some negative changes which can affect the risk, the contractual tools to protect the funds, poor trading indicators, fraud and how financiers manage these changes in risk.

Managing Risk

Introduction

Understanding risk is about understanding change. As we saw in the last chapter, as soon as a client is accepted, the circumstances under which the financier took on the business will begin to change. Identifying those changes is important but the most important thing of all is taking prompt action if the changes are for the worse. The reaction to these changes in the risk profile will not necessarily lead to an exit route but may present opportunities. The key is that the financier is: a) picking up the signs early, and b) responding accordingly.

In this chapter we will look at identifying increased risks such as negative trading indicators and fraud. We will then look at responding to these negative changes. But first, we will look at how the financier is able to protect its funds through use of the contractual provisions.

Contractual provisions for protecting the funds

Most commercial transactions rely on a large dose of trust between the parties. This is particularly so with invoice finance. The financier is buying an asset for a very large upfront payment with little opportunity to inspect what it is purchasing. It is unlike buying a motor car where the shiny new vehicle is paraded for inspection and testing before any money changes hands.

So, how does the financier protect its investment in prepayments made against uncollected debts? The protection measures break down into the financier's rights against:

- The client
- The debt
- The associated rights
- The guarantors
- Non-contracting third parties

In the last resort, a financier wants protection against an insolvent client unable to pay back monies overdrawn from the financier. Such requirement to pay back may happen because:

- The notified debts are non-existent (fraud)
- The debtor is insolvent or fails to pay
- The debts are disputed

The financier's rights will largely be found in the documentation and to a lesser extent in the general law. The most important documentation for the protection of funding will be:

- The invoice finance agreement
- Guarantees and indemnities
- Mortgages and charges (particularly with stock finance but also for any additional security for invoice finance)

All three of these documents may provide protection from third party claimants who might otherwise dilute the financier's security. There is also the intangible value that these documents provide. For example, a guarantor may not have sufficient fiscal worth but the threat of direct action may encourage them to assist the financier in getting back the money owed.

The invoice finance agreement

In an earlier chapter we examined the invoice finance agreement in detail. However, it is necessary to revisit this major document when helping to protect the funds in use.

Rights against the client

A financier often sets out preconditions before funding commences. Such conditions can cover any additional matters that the financier considers necessary for its protection, e.g. the assignment of the client's credit insurance policies or an increase in the paid-up capital. Such special conditions can also cover matters to be continued during the relationship.

Agreements will be written in such a way that if there is a breach of the special conditions or any other term of the agreement during the relationship then the financier can, in its absolute discretion, withhold all prepayments and demand repayment of any prepayment previously made together with all present and future liabilities. Monies due by the client are set off against collections and the debit balance is immediately payable by the client to the financier.

Upon breach of the Agreement funding will cease and the financier can claim recovery of its exposure. If the right to terminate the agreement is not the financier's chosen path, any further debts created belong to the financier but with no obligation to increase the funding through further prepayments.

Apart from a breach of the agreement, the financier can likewise protect itself if any other event of default occurs, such as insolvency-related events or changes in third party positions.

Once the financier becomes aware of an event of default, how does it protect its funding? The most usual demand by the financier is for repayment of the funds in use (?? Heather)) account balance. Under these circumstances the financier retains the unpaid debts as security for such payment.

If there is a breach of a client's warranty about a debt (e.g. because the goods have not been delivered) then the debt becomes an unapproved debt for funding purposes and credit protection, if applicable. The prepayment must be repaid. The reality of this situation is that the amount is clawed back through set-off if there is sufficient availability, although this is a fine balancing act where client continuation is the financier's desired outcome.

Notwithstanding these legal rights against the client, it is important to remember that dialogue is part of the whole process.

Rights in respect of debts

In most agreements all future debts vest in the financier immediately upon their creation. This is often called a "whole turnover" arrangement. This gives excellent protection to the financier because all the debts of the client, whether or not notified to the financier, are the property of the financier. This is useful in failed client situations when the client may have sold goods without telling the financier about the debts. They are automatically the property of the financier, even if it is unaware of them.

However, the financier will wish to ensure that it is being notified of all debts being created. This it will do by reconciling the client's stated turnover in its accounting statements, to the value of debts notified, and any difference investigated. Due care needs to be taken that debts that have been specifically excluded from the facility are deducted from the stated turnover figures, when making such a comparison.

The strongest right of the financier in respect of a debt is to be able to sue for its collection. As the assignee of the debt, a financier can give notice of assignment, sue for and/or give a valid discharge for a debt. This includes the right to resolve any dispute.

With disclosed facilities, such as factoring, the debtor is told of the financier's purchase of debts by a "notice of assignment". This is affixed to invoices when sent to the debtor. This notice is also repeated on statements.

This notice of assignment is important for three reasons:

• To prevent the debtor paying the client and gaining a good discharge of the debt.
• To avoid set-offs arising (see below).
• To avoid the obtaining of priority by subsequent charge holders.

The financier will often experience the situation where the debtor has ignored the notice of assignment and continued to pay the client direct. A payment to the client, ignoring a notice of assignment, will not discharge the debt. The debtor can be made to pay again. However it is important that the financier makes a particular point of advising the debtor of the correct procedures for discharging debts to avoid the time and expense of suing the debtor.

Provided that the financier can prove that notice of assignment was given of the specific debt prior to the payment to the client, the financier is entitled to demand payment again. This is important where the client fraudulently demands payment from the debtor and then goes into liquidation or the client and the debtor conspire to avoid paying the financier.

This situation can cause ongoing problems for financiers because debtors that have had to pay twice may place a ban on future assignments of debt. It is good practice for a financier to put the client's bank on notice that debtor receipts are the property of the financier, not the client.

Sometimes the debtor will claim that the client also owes money to the debtor. Then the debtor exercises its claim by reducing the amount that it will pay to the financier to discharge the assigned debt. This is called a "set-off" or a "contra- account".

The financier must then decide which claims to allow. Helpfully the law has developed rules covering these situations:

- **Rule 1** Contra arising from client's sale contract.

If the contra claim comes from the sale contract giving rise to the assigned debt, or is closely connected with it, then valid claims must always be allowed, up to the value of the assigned debt. Anything in excess is the client's responsibility and claimed directly by the debtor from the client.

Example: Goods as per the sale contract, where time of delivery was "of the essence", delivered by the client to the debtor but delivered late. Debtor suffers damages from such late delivery (e.g. loses onward sale). Debtor's claim for damages for late delivery can be set-off against the financier up to the value of the debt. Any claim in excess must be made against the client. The date of notice of assignment is irrelevant.

- **Rule 2** Any other contra claim by the debtor must be allowed if it has accrued due and is also payable before receipt of notice of assignment.

Example: Client sells goods to the debtor worth £200. Notice of assignment given on the invoice on 31 January with a credit period expiring on 28 February.

By way of contra account the client had also purchased a variety of goods from the debtor prior to 31 January with three different credit periods expiring (i) before notice of assignment, (ii) before client's credit expiry, and (iii) after client's credit expiry. The result by reference to the following credit expiries is:

(i) 15 January	£100	allow full set off
(ii) 15 February	£100	allow full set-off
(iii) 15 March	£100	deny any set-off

(i) and (ii) are allowed because their credit periods expire prior to the client's credit period of 28 February. (iii) is not allowed because its credit period expires after the client's credit period, even though the goods were delivered before notice of assignment.

So the giving of notice of assignment can be valuable in reducing the number of contra-accounts diluting the value of assigned debts. As such notice is not given in confidential invoice discounting there is a greater risk of dilution of the assigned debts.

Associated rights

We have noted that the financier not only buys the debt but its "associated rights", which are defined in the agreement. Some agreements call these "related rights". Disputes with debtors increase in frequency upon the insolvency of the client. Financiers find it valuable to be able to take possession of the client's ledgers, computerised data, proofs of delivery and contractual documentation as soon as such insolvency looms. These will assist in resolving disputes. These documents are usually within the definition of "associated rights" purchased and owned by the financier. This clause will also entitle the financier to take possession of the goods, which can sometimes have some salvage value.

Rights against non-contracting parties

Under confidential invoice discounting arrangements, the client will receive payments from debtors discharging debts. In factoring situations debtors sometimes continue to make payments to the client. The financier must trust the client immediately to pay over such funds to the financier. The client must not bank them into its own bank account. In most invoice finance agreements, the client specifically undertakes to deal with debtor payments by handing them unbanked to the financier. In addition the client will normally undertake "to hold such remittance in trust for the financier and separate from the client's own monies". Clients in financial difficulties have been known to bank debtor payments into the client's bank account in order to reduce an overdraft (and thereby reducing the directors' own liabilities under personal guarantees given to the bank). The financier is then left with a shortfall upon the client's failure. If the defaulting director has also given a guarantee to the financier, demand can be made for the shortfall. If he has not given a guarantee he can still personally be sued for the tort (a civil wrongdoing) of conversion of funds belonging to the financier plus interest. The limited liability of an incorporated client will be no protection to the defaulting director.

Guarantors and indemnifiers

Guarantees and indemnities are used to protect the financier against loss under a recourse agreement when the value of debts held does not realise the full value of prepayments made against them and the client becomes insolvent. We have already seen in the chapter concerning the "take-on" that it is vital to follow the set procedures when taking guarantees.

A guarantee and indemnity may be held by a non-recourse financier to protect it against breaches of the client's warranties about debts or for funds paid against debts which are not credit approved.

Guarantees and indemnities can:

- Cover everything that the client is obliged to do;
- Be limited to cover certain aspects, e.g. any or all of:
  - The client's warranties
  - Wrongful banking of remittances
  - Fraud
- Be of unlimited financial value or limited to a specified figure, plus interest and costs;
- Be irrevocable or revocable by a period of written notice.

The financier may have taken security for the guarantee, e.g. by an all assets debenture from a corporate guarantor. Failure to comply with a demand under the guarantee will allow the financier to appoint an administrator to the guarantor in order to recover amounts due. Personal guarantors can also be asked to provide security, such as a mortgage or charge over a home.

In the absence of security the financier will normally issue proceedings against the guarantor for the amount due by the client.

Charges

In a stock finance facility, the financier will take a floating charge over the stock. Where the stock is easily identified and sales can only take place with the financier's consent, a fixed charge can be taken, although this is rare.

Apart from the rights under an invoice finance agreement, some financiers will take security over the other assets of a client through an all assets debenture. If the client is unable to repay the funds in use following proper demand then the financier may appoint an administrator, (or if the debenture is dated before 15 September 2003 an administrative receiver is appointed). The administrator will realise the client's assets and make distribution to the creditors (including the financier) in accordance with insolvency law and priorities and this will be discussed in the final chapter in the section about basic insolvency procedures.

The types of charges and their differences have already been discussed in some detail in the previous chapter regarding "take-ons".

Negative trading indicators

One of the keys to spotting an increase in risk, for whatever reason, is noticing a change in the client's behaviour. This can manifest itself in many ways. Increased demands for more cash may become more desperate and for relatively small sums. Visits by the financier will be cancelled at short notice or telephone calls or letters will go unanswered. Problems with the client's IT system will be blamed for late production of reports or credit notes. Any of these situations can alert the financier to the fact that there may be an increase in risk.

Increasing demand for additional funding

Traditional bank overdrafts have a limit set on the basis of historical financial information. If there is an increasing demand for additional funding, it could be that the borrower is growing quickly and needs the finance to fund that growth. In contrast, the beauty of invoice finance is that the amount of cash available grows in direct proportion to the growth in sales. Whilst most financiers set a limit to that availability, when that limit is reviewed it can quickly be seen whether or not the cause of the requested increase is a result of increased sales.

Thus an increasing demand for additional funding through an invoice finance facility should be commensurate with growth in sales. If that is not the case, then there could be a problem because the cash provided by the financier has not been used to finance growth.

The financier of course is alerted to the demand for more cash very quickly. The client will start taking the maximum cash available and then perhaps make requests for relatively small and relatively frequent "over-payments". The client may also demand fast processing of invoice notifications and become over concerned with small changes to the ineligible debt.

So where has the cash been going? The financier needs to ask the question and here are some of the possible answers:

Building up stock

This will be easy to identify if there is an additional stock facility. If stocks are rising faster than sales then the financier needs to question why. If the business is seasonal, then the stock build-up should match the pattern set last season but if it does not, further investigation is required. If stock is being built up for a particularly large order, then the financier might wish to see a copy of that order and to verify it. If stock is being built up in order to satisfy customer demand more quickly, then the financier may wish to compare the client's stock levels with that for similar businesses. Whatever the reason, it needs to be credible and needs to be monitored in future to check its authenticity.

Paying creditors more quickly

A laudable aim but it needs to have been done for a reason. Perhaps the creditors are withholding deliveries because of previous slow payments and supplying on a cash only basis. Again, the reason needs to be challenged and it needs to be credible.

Debtors are paying more slowly

This aspect is covered as a separate cause for concern in itself, later in the chapter.

Capital expenditure

Cashflow finance should not be used to fund capital expenditure because if cash comes out of current assets to fund long-term expenditure, it leaves a cashflow shortfall to pay for current liabilities. Capital expenditure should be financed by appropriate long-term finance.

A temporary increase in overheads

The financier needs to challenge the reasons and any answers given should be credible and easily verifiable.

Diversion of funds out of business

It could be that cash is being taken out of the business for reasons that were previously unknown to the financier. Examples of such diversions range from extra cash being paid to directors, to funding a pet project of the directors or to propping up loss-making associated companies. Wherever the destination of these funds, chances are they are not directly related to normal expenditure within the client's business and should be investigated thoroughly.

The cash is funding losses

Other than the above six reasons, there can be no other answer to where the cash is going. The client must be losing money and the additional funds are being used to fund these losses. If the financier comes to the conclusion that the client is making losses and yet the latest management accounts show they are making profits, then that begs more questions:

- Is the financier wrong in concluding that the client is making losses and if so what is the true reason for lack of cash?

- Are the losses so recent and so sudden that they have yet to be reflected in the management accounts?

- Are the assumptions being used to prepare the management accounts erroneous?

- Are the management accounts being manipulated to give the financier the impression that the client is trading profitably?

Whatever the answers to these questions, the financier must investigate the reason for this additional demand for cash until it is satisfied that it has the correct reason and that appropriate action is being taken to bring the situation back into line.

It is worth remembering that there is only one reason why most businesses fail and that is lack of cash.

Deteriorating sales ledger performance

This section looks at ways in which the profile of a sales ledger can deteriorate. In exceptional cases, some of these patterns may be as a result of fraud but we are principally looking at a change in profile caused by genuine trading reasons as we shall be discussing "fraud" later in this chapter.

Let us look at some of those changes in profile, their likely causes and what the financier might do to counteract the increased risk.

Deteriorating debt turn
There can be a variety of causes of a slowing debt turn including:

- A change in the economy
- A change in the debtor profile
- A particular debtor paying slowly
- An actual or potential bad debt
- Product quality problems
- Administrative or credit control problems
- Slowness in issuing credit notes
- Fraud

If the facility is factoring then the financier will have all the information to hand in order to establish the exact cause. If it is an invoice discounting facility, the financier will still have most of the information to hand but may need to seek more data from the client. Having established the cause, the next step is to ask the client what action they intend to take to reverse the decline in the debt turn. Finally, the financier will need to decide whether or not to take any action. The nature of that action will vary from one financier to another and from one facility to another. However if the situation is deemed serious, then the financier may reduce the prepayment percentage until the debt turn is brought back into line. Some invoice discounters may set some targets and the most useful one, is to set a target for debtor cash, perhaps weekly or monthly. This will concentrate efforts on bringing in cash which, it cannot be stressed enough in relation to invoice finance, is all important to both financier and client. It is important to the financier in terms of the recovery of the finance being made available against that debt, and is important to the client in terms of the finance charges being paid to the financier for every day the debt remains outstanding.

Change in debtor profile

Although this can cause the debt turn to slow, it may not and, if this happens, the financier can find:

- Credit-worthy debtors have been replaced by poor quality customers. If the facility is non-recourse, then the financier may already be aware of this change and could well be holding additional retentions from the client's availability. Even a recourse facility may have finance limits on the major debtors and the same reduction in availability will occur. However, if the change is in the smaller balances, then the change will be less obvious but also less serious.

- Increasingly poor spread. It could be that one debtor has become so dominant within the sales ledger that the spread has deteriorated. If there is already a "spread restriction" in place, this will cap the prepayments on this prime debtor. However, there comes a point (80% of the ledger? 90% of the ledger?) when whatever the spread restriction, having such a prime debtor is just too great a risk.

Change in product or service

Whilst not strictly a change in the sales ledger profile, it is certainly an important change and will ultimately affect the collectability of the debt. The business of some clients may change, slowly perhaps, from selling goods or services which are "stand alone" to being made up of a series of inter-related parts. An example would be a client that used to sell "stand alone PCs" but then started providing complete bespoke IT systems. The client may not realise the impact this has on the financier and thus may not think to even mention it.

We have seen in previous chapters that each invoice should be a legally enforceable debt in its own right. Clearly, if a bespoke IT system is invoiced in stages, the invoices will fail that test. To illustrate this, let us assume that the debtor ordered a bespoke IT system and agreed to be invoiced in stages, the first of which was an initial payment on acceptance of the order. Let us then assume that the client invoiced this first amount of, say, £10,000 and obtained finance on that invoice from the financier. The client then fails. The debtor has an invoice for £10,000 which whilst part of the contract, did entail receiving a finished product at the end of it. The debtor will refuse to pay the £10,000 and the courts will say that they are entitled to do so because the client failed to complete the contract. The action to be taken by the financier in such a case can vary between deciding that financing such a debt is an acceptable risk to terminating the facility.

Deteriorating stock profile

Later in this chapter, we will look at the likely indicators of fraud when receiving a manipulated stock listing from a client. This section will look at the stock itself rather than the documentation sent in by the client.

A deteriorating stock profile will include one or more of the following features:

Change in type of stock being financed

If the type of stock being produced changes to one that is less saleable in a collect-out, this is clearly bad news for the financier. The key to effective stock financing is to correctly estimate the value of the stock being financed if the client goes out of business. If that stock changes to one that has less value in these circumstances, then there should be an immediate review as to what level of finance to provide against this "new" type of stock.

Changes in the proportion of stock within the production cycle

If, say, finished stock previously accounted for 50% of all stock, yet now it accounts for only 10%, then something significant has happened to cause this change. There could be a production problem, there could be a large batch of faulty raw materials or it may just be that demand is outstripping supply. Equally if the mix had changed in the other direction, then the cause should also be investigated.

To the financier, such a change could signal two things. There could be a fundamental problem within the client's business, such as a production problem, or if the mix has changed, then so too will the level of finance unless it has been capped.

Deteriorating stock turn

If the stock being financed is moving more slowly or if the whole stock is taking a longer time to shift, any deterioration is a serious matter and must be addressed with the client quickly. If the stock is simply not turning into sales quickly enough, then the financier must consider how much more difficult it will be to sell this stock if the client goes out of business.

Deteriorating financial performance

In this section, we will look at the effects of a deteriorating or unrealistic financial position. Remember that a financier will not lose money unless the client becomes insolvent and a client is unlikely to defraud a financier until it is in financial difficulties. Accordingly it is vital that these difficulties are spotted as early as possible.

Before looking at the figures themselves, let us first look at potential problems with the information itself:

- Delays in producing audited accounts. There can be any number of reasons why the production of audited accounts is delayed and the financier must judge each case on its merits. Well-run companies will produce audited accounts in good time. However, the most serious delay is when the auditors take a long time to sign off the accounts. It could be that the auditors have come across a problem that is unknown to the financier and one that, in the worst case scenario, can be terminal for the client.

- The audited figures are much worse than the corresponding management figures. There will always be differences between management and audited accounts but the more accurate the management figures are, then the better the financial controls are within the client's business. Wildly differing figures either mean poor financial controls or an attempt to mislead a financier. Both matters are serious but the latter issue, if proved, will invariably lead to the end of the relationship between client and financier. The same will be the case if the management figures prove to be incorrect during an audit by the financier.

- Delays in producing management accounts. There may occasionally be genuine reasons for such a delay, such as sickness in the accounts department. However, it is more likely that the figures paint a poor picture and the client wants to put off the day when they will be seen by the financier. Many financiers impose a penalty if management accounts are not received by a certain date. It is a time for swift action on the part of the financier.

Now let us turn our attention to the figures themselves. Predicting corporate failure is a huge subject and merits a book all to itself. It is a mixture of understanding the figures, the dynamics of the business itself and a large amount of common sense. As far as this workbook is concerned, we shall briefly focus on where to look and what to look for.

Leaving aside any deterioration of the asset being financed, the financier has access to a few types of financial information. It has the client's audited financial accounts, and hopefully management figures. In some cases it will have its own audit report. Sometimes the financier will have external information, perhaps from the client's bank. In all cases, the financier will know how much cash is being drawn down by the client from the financier itself. Adverse information will usually include one or more of the following:

- A decline in profitability. Unless reversed, loss-making will ultimately lead to failure. So the issue for the financier is how quickly the client can return to profitability. Because loss-making saps cash, this will usually be accompanied by an increase in the amount of funds being drawn down by the client; the extent of this will show how acute the problem is. The options open to the financier will vary enormously depending on the circumstances but they may be faced with a dilemma. Do they restrict cash in an effort to reduce the amount of money they can potentially lose, or do they continue funding the same or even more cash to give the client a bit more time to turn the business around?

- A decline in liquidity. If a decline in liquidity is shown in the accounts, it will probably show up in the increased funding being taken by the client. The options open to the financier will be similar to those if the client had declining profitability.

- Increased funding being taken for no apparent reason. If the client's liquidity hitherto appeared to be unchanged and there were no other apparent reasons for taking an increased amount of funds from the financier, the reason must be established and quickly. A sudden demand for extra cash is a definite warning sign and the financier may be faced with the dilemma of whether to provide more cash, the same amount, or try to reduce it.

Fraud

We have seen before in this workbook that a major risk to the financier of the client's insolvency is that the asset the financier has been funding proves to be worth less than the amount of finance still outstanding. In most cases where a financier loses money, it is because the asset simply is not worth as much as it was because the client had gone out of business. However, in a small minority of cases, the asset is worth less because of fraud. In other words, there may not have been an asset to finance in the first place. Or if there was, it had been deliberately devalued (or reduced to nothing) by the client.

Thus fraud adds yet another dimension to managing the risk. The financier must:

• Monitor the risk that the client may get into financial difficulties which may lead to insolvency.

• Monitor the risk that the assets being financed will be worth less than the total finance outstanding to the financier if, or as a result of, the client going out of business.

• Monitor the risk that the assets being financed will be worth less than the finance outstanding due to fraudulent activity by the client.

Of course a client could defraud a financier by failing to fulfil its contractual obligations simply to continue to have access to funds it otherwise legitimately generates. However, we shall focus on the type of activity which fraudulently generates more cash than would otherwise be available.

Very occasionally, although some say increasingly, criminals deliberately set out to defraud a financier right from the start. They are often very clever, know how invoice finance works, and ensure they do not attract the spotlight, sitting carefully under the radar. It needs considerable attention and experience to spot them. However, more often than not, most frauds against cashflow financiers are perpetrated by owners or directors of businesses that find themselves in financial difficulties and are then tempted to fraudulently obtain additional funds just to keep their business afloat. Their mindset is almost certainly that the financial difficulty is temporary and that they will be able to "repay" the financier quickly and before the financier finds out what has happened. Either way, it is fraud. However it helps in managing the risk to understand that even the "nicest" of clients might be tempted to defraud the financier when the client is in financial difficulties.

Invoice finance fraud

There have been many frauds against invoice finance companies over the years and almost as many different stories to tell of how the client defrauded the financier. However, most frauds are a variation on four themes. They involve:

• The client raising a fictitious invoice. Put simply, the client sends the invoice financier a fictitious invoice for, say, £10,000 and receives a prepayment of, say, £8,000 against it. Upon the insolvency of the client, the financier goes to the debtor to request payment, only to find out that the invoice is fictitious and thus loses £8,000. This, the most common type of fraud, is usually referred to as "fresh air invoicing". A slight variation on this theme is where the client raises an invoice before having delivered the goods or service. This is known as "pre-invoicing". It is just as much in contravention of the invoice finance agreement as a fictitious invoice and has the same effect on the financier if the goods still have not been delivered prior to the client's insolvency. The same applies to goods that have been ordered on the basis that they are called off when needed but the client invoices them all even though they have yet to be delivered.

If fictitious invoices are being raised, the financier might see:

- An unusually large invoice notified. The financier will almost certainly have a system which flags "large" invoices which fall outside set criteria. This will be followed by a procedure that attempts to verify that invoice, even if the facility is undisclosed. It is important that unusually large invoices, or a series of smaller ones, are picked up on the day they are notified and before a fresh prepayment is made.

- The value of debts assigned rising unaccountably. This will not usually be spotted immediately, but only after a series of assignments which in total are higher than normal. The financier may still wish to verify some of the larger values although this will be after prepayments have been made.

- Debtor cash not coming in fast enough. Many financiers will have their own system or they may purchase a third party system which predicts debtor cash on a daily basis based upon the predicted debt turn from the date of assignment. These systems are very good at highlighting a fast deterioration in the debt turn.

- Large invoices being credited out. The systems we have just looked at which measure predicted debtor cash will also reveal where invoices are being credited out rather than being paid – another sign of fictitious invoicing.

- Increases in debtor disputes. Where the facility is for factoring, the level of disputes will rise as debtors query the amount they are being asked to pay. Most factoring companies will claw back any debtor disputes from a client's availability, classing them as "disallowed" or "ineligible" debts. This is only prudent whilst the financier waits to hear what the client has to say about the debtor dispute. Even an increase in debtors wanting copy invoices should trigger some suspicion.

- The audit reveals fictitious invoices. Ultimately, although perhaps a long time after a fraud, an audit should pick up fictitious invoices.

- The client banking debtor cash. This starts by the client raising a genuine invoice of, say, £10,000 and receiving a prepayment of, say, £8,000. Then the debtor accidentally pays or is enticed to pay the client direct. The client banks and then hangs on to the cash. Upon the client's insolvency, the financier will find that the debtor has paid. Again the financier could lose £8,000. The could has been underlined because in a disclosed facility like factoring, the financier may take action against the debtor if it believes it can prove that the debtor paid despite having received a valid notice of assignment. Very few financiers wish to take this route for fear of the damage it may cause the invoice finance industry by making debtors pay twice. A variation of banked cash is where the debtor pays a deposit which is banked by the client who then invoices the full order value.

If cash is being banked by the client, the financier might see:

- Predicted debtor cash falling. The system we looked at in the previous section will quickly pick up a fall in the level of predicted debtor cash. What is required in these circumstances is a verification exercise on some of the larger debtor balances.

- A rise in credit notes. In an attempt to rectify the situation caused by their banking of debtor cash, the client may, as soon as they can afford it, raise credit notes to cancel the invoices that have in fact already been paid.

- An increase in debtor disputes. Again, debtors will ultimately start claiming (rightly) that they have already paid.

- Cash banked being revealed by an audit. Ultimately an audit will look for evidence of alternative bank accounts and look at cash banked by the client which should reveal cash belonging to the financier.

- The client withholding credit notes. The client may have raised a genuine invoice and received a prepayment against it but if, for normal trading reasons (e.g. the goods are returned), a credit note is due, then it withholds it from the financier. The client may send the credit note to the debtor but just not send it to the financier. Once again, upon the client's insolvency, there is no debt payable from which the financier can recoup its finance.

If the client is withholding credit notes, the financier might see:

- Predicted debtor cash falling. A system which can predict when to expect debtor cash will pick up that invoices are not being paid and one of the causes of non-payment can be that the client is withholding credit notes.

- Increase in factoring disputes. As debtors are being chased for cash, they will notify the financier that they are awaiting a credit note, which is then classified as a dispute. A variation on this theme is that the client has raised the credit note and sent it to the debtor but not the financier. Under these circumstances, the debtor will also dispute the debt and will in the end send the credit note to the financier as proof.

- The audit should ultimately pick up credit notes which have been sent to the debtor but not the financier. It will probably not flush out a delay in issuing the credit note.

- The client manipulating data it sends the financier. A variety of documents can be forged in a situation where a client wants to fraudulently obtain more cash than is due. Fake credit insurance limits or credit information can be sent to the financier in order to make a debtor seem credit worthy enough to be financed. This will not show up in the ledger of course but financiers should always seek to obtain independent credit information on debtors. Fake proof of delivery documents can also be used to wrongly gain the financier's confidence in the validity of the debt.

The document that is sometimes manipulated to gain more funds from an invoice discounter is the aged debt analysis. The client, wishing to avoid a debt becoming ineligible because of its age, will "re-age" a debt in order to stop it falling into the column where it will have become ineligible. If that is happening, the financier might expect to see a rising debt turn and/or coupled with a falling value of "aged ineligibles". The key to spotting this type of manipulation is a thorough reconciliation between the latest aged debt analysis and the previous one.

There can be a variety of ways in which these four methods of fraud are enacted but all are mainly variations on these themes. When the facility is factoring, a "fresh air invoice" or an invoice that has been paid or credited out, will soon come to light. However, clients that are defrauding the financier will go to great lengths to ensure that the fraud remains hidden for as long as possible. This can entail collusion with a debtor, who may just go along with being chased for a debt it knows it does not owe. Alternatively the client may repetitively go through the process of raising a fictitious invoice, crediting it out and raising another fictitious one.

With invoice discounting, particularly when it is undisclosed, the scope for fraud is wider as it is much easier to hide fictitious invoicing for a longer period and easier to retain debtor cash. Thus regular and thorough audits are most important, as are ways in which the financier can verify debtor balances. Most invoice discounters will have a method, agreed with the client, whereby the financier can actually telephone or write to debtors, asking them to verify how much they owe. Sometimes, the financier will have authority to telephone the debtors in the name of the client and in other cases the financier will have an arrangement whereby a third party audit firm is used to verify balances. Whatever method is used, it is vital that a financier is able to verify balances quickly, if thought necessary. As we shall see in a later chapter, financiers operating an undisclosed invoice discounting facility will have the right, under the agreement, to disclose their involvement should the need arise.

It can be seen that a vital indicator of a possible fraud is that debtor cash is drying up. Traditionally, invoice financiers will examine the debt turn each month and act upon a deterioration. The disadvantage of this is that it can take several months before the financier is alerted to a problem. More subtly, a deteriorating debt turn will hide the fact that fictitious invoices are being credited out. A more useful calculation is that of the "cash turn". Whereas the debt turn divides the total debtor balance into the turnover and expresses that in a number of days, the "cash turn" takes the debtor balance and divides it into the cash received and then expresses that in a number of days. It thus takes the debt turn and excludes all types of credit (i.e. credit notes, re-assignments, adjustments etc.) other than cash. Most sophisticated systems will measure the cash turn over any period. Too short a period may just miss large, "lumpy" payments and yet too long a period will be alerting the financier too late. Some third party systems will use the cash turn, a credit note percentage and a series of adverse trends in cash and disputes to produce a risk score. Such devices are useful in flagging potential problem areas but should be used in conjunction with more traditional indicators.

Stock finance fraud

A client that defrauds a stock financier will usually do so in one of the following methods:

• The stock listing sent to the financier will exaggerate the value of stock. This can be done by over-valuing the amount of stock purchases or by undervaluing the amount of stock turned into sales. This latter method can be checked by reconciling it with the corresponding sales ledger balances (relatively easily done if invoice finance is also being provided). The former can be checked by reconciling it with the purchase ledger balances, but neither checks are foolproof without a more detailed examination of the accounting records of the client which can only be achieved at an audit inspection.

- The stock listing will exaggerate the value of stock eligible for funding. This can manifest itself in a number of ways. The total stock figure may be correct but there will undoubtedly be some stock which is ineligible for funding. This can be a category of stock, such as "work in progress" or it can be stock over a certain age. It is almost certain that the client will be able to manipulate these figures themselves and they are difficult to check without an audit. However, comparisons with previous stock listings and the inclusion of a verifiable "stock movement report", should uncover a blatant fraud but there is no doubt that this is an area fraught with potential weaknesses for the financier.

- The values being placed on the stock, from the start of the facility, are too high. Reliance will be placed on third party professional stock valuers where possible, particularly where the amount of finance being provided is large. Where stock valuers have not been used, the financier must ensure that the annual stock take has been undertaken by someone independent of the client and carries the approval of the client's auditors.

  As can be seen from the above (the reliance by the financier on reports that are produced by the client but are unverifiable by a third party such as a debtor) there is more opportunity for a client intent on fraud if they have a stock finance facility. This is one of the reasons that funding stock is a riskier proposition than funding invoices.

So, we have seen ways in which a client can defraud a financier and we have noted that most frauds occur only when a client is in financial difficulties and that some, although by no means all, financial difficulties result in insolvency. A client is less likely to commit a fraud if it is in a financially strong position with more cash than it needs. Thus effective risk management is about exception reporting and focusing on known indicators or potential problems.

Responding to negative changes

Having looked at types of negative change, including fraud, we will now look at ways in which the financier can respond to these changes.

Review limits

We briefly looked at the subject of review limits in the last chapter in the context of how they can be used to respond to positive change. Let us now look at these limits in the context that they serve as a trigger to the financier for the purpose of managing the risk. These limits will have been set when the client was taken on and will be reviewed either when the amount of "funds in use" are about to be exceeded or as part of a regular client review.

In setting a review limit for a certain period, the following will usually be taken into account:

- The current limit and how recently it was changed.
- The anticipated value of the assets being financed over the forthcoming period.
- The anticipated cash requirements over the forthcoming period.
- How well the asset is "performing" (e.g. dilution rates and debt turn if the case of invoice finance or stock turn and level of obsolete stock in the case of stock finance).
- The recent financial performance of the client.

If all or most of these items are positive and the amount of funds required is likely to exceed the current limit, then it may well be appropriate to raise the limit. However, even if the finance required is likely to exceed the limit, there will be times when the financier chooses not to increase the limit or indeed to reduce it.

If the facility is invoice finance and the limit is not to be increased or will be reduced, then the emphasis will be on faster cash generation from the debtors. If the service is factoring, then the financier will agree faster collection procedures with the client. If it is invoice discounting, then the client will be targeted with improving the debt turn so that the impact of the static or reduced limit, will have less or no impact. Clearly this is not a permanent resolution because if sales invoicing is rising, then there will still come a point, despite improved credit control, where the limit starts to bite. Nevertheless, it is a short term solution and one used by financiers if they want to manage the limit down.

A similar technique can be used for stock finance in that the client can be set targets to reduce the level of stock to counteract a limit which has become a constraint. A more likely solution though is to cap the stock finance facility and allow a bit more flexibility on the invoice finance side because it is easier for the financier to control, and considered less risky.

As a risk management tool, capping the limit is generally more effective than reducing the prepayment percentage, particularly if there is a perceived risk that the assets may devalue significantly in a collect out. After all, 70% of a worthless asset is no safer than 80% of the same asset.

Changes to the review and visit functions

Client reviews
In normal circumstances, client reviews will take place at set times, according to the financier's policy on reviews. However, if there is a serious risk issue or a number of minor ones, then an immediate and thorough review ought to take place. The review may even unearth some smaller but significant indicators that all is not well. The important point is that the review will give the financier the whole picture and an opportunity to set a formal action plan.

Account manager
The role of the account manager is key when responding to negative change. An experienced Account Manger will know that however good their relationship is with the client, there will be times when tough action is required. A client will not be happy if restrictions are imposed on its funding and so good communication

is vital as the financier needs to get across its points clearly in a polite but firm way. Inexperienced account managers will need help in this difficult phase and in some cases their role may be taken over by more senior staff within the financier's organisation.

Audit

In the same way as increased risk should trigger an "extraordinary" client review, the same applies to audits. Whatever the risk issue, an audit will establish its extent. If the issue concerns suspected fraud, then a thorough audit of the "collectability" of the asset needs to take place. Not only that but if fraud has occurred, there is almost certainly a cashflow problem and the audit needs to ascertain the extent of that as well.

Stock financiers will have a particular interest in verifying the stock listings and attempting actual stock verification.

Verification and increased collection activity

If there is any suspicion that the asset being financed may not be worth what the financier thought when it parted with the funds, then urgent attempts should be made to verify the value of the asset.

In the case of factoring, increased collection activity needs to take place to verify the invoices. With invoice discounting, the financier may put pressure on the client to tighten its own collection activity. One way to ensure this is for the financier to set cash targets and to impose penalties if these are not achieved. Invoice discounters will also wish to seek verification of the invoices through whatever means they can. We have outlined these methods in a previous chapter, but where there is increased risk some urgency is required and so telephone verification is more appropriate.

Increased financier vigilance

Specialist risk teams

Some financiers, as soon as there is a significant increase in risk, pass the day-to-day running of a client onto a specialist risk team. Such "intensive care units" have the advantage of being staffed with risk orientated and skilled individuals who are used to dealing with high risk situations. They will also have regular access to external help such as legal advice and contact within insolvency practitioners who might specialise in corporate recoveries or "turnarounds".

Increased authorisation

When negative change occurs, the financier's prime responsibility is to protect the funds it has extended to the particular client. So on top of tightening up procedures with the client, it may also look to tighten up procedures internally. The key method of doing that is to require additional, or more senior authorisation of payments to clients. The financier may also require that more senior personnel must chair the client reviews and perhaps take over the decision making.

Prepayment percentage

The agreed prepayment percentage allowed against debtor balances in an invoice finance facility is variously referred to as the "Initial Percentage" or "Prepayment Percentage".

This prepayment percentage is agreed at the commencement of an invoice finance facility. The financier, having made an assessment as to the likely "collectability" of the debtor balances, will arrive at a percentage with which it feels comfortable. Thus, with an 80% prepayment percentage, the financier is making a judgement that it is likely to collect 80% or more of the outstanding debtor balances.

It thus stands to reason that if circumstances change, once the facility has been running for a while, then the prepayment percentage should be reconsidered. The following will usually influence that fresh assessment:

- **The dilution has changed.** Dilution is the word used to describe anything that reduces the value of an invoice other than cash. Thus credit notes, reassignments (charge-backs) and write-offs will each contribute to dilution. If the dilution rises, then so too will the expectation that less of the debtor balances will be collectable if the client goes out of business. Thus a significant rise in dilution is likely to be met with a reduction in the prepayment percentage.

- **The client's product or service has changed.** The acid test is to judge how much of the debt will be collectable upon the client's insolvency. If the nature of the client's business has changed, this is likely to have an effect on the collectability of the invoices. We have seen in earlier chapters that good quality, simple products, without any warranty are likely to make good collectable invoices. So significant changes in any of these areas may lead to a reduction in the prepayment percentage.

- **Other causes for concern.** If there are other causes for concern, such as a deteriorating financial position or a suspicion of fraud, then a reduction in the prepayment percentage is probably not the right method to reduce the risk. A reduction in the prepayment percentage is not appropriate in cases where the financier suspects fraud because a smaller percentage of nothing, is still nothing. What is more appropriate is a reduction in the review limit with emphasis on generating faster cash receipts from debtors.

There may, however, occasionally be good reason to temporarily increase the prepayment percentage with no increase in the review limit, particularly if the facility is invoice discounting. If the prepayment percentage is increased but the finance limit capped, then it will encourage even more effort into generating cash from debtors. Thus the client gains by receiving more cash against new invoices but has to work harder to collect cash from debtors as quickly as possible. Clearly the financier still needs to be vigilant to ensure that the new debt it is purchasing is valid.

Debtor spread restriction

Debtor concentration happens, in an invoice finance facility, when one prime debtor owes a significant proportion of the total sales ledger balance. An invoice financier will wish to see a fair spread of debt within the sales ledger for the following reasons:

- A prime debtor can result in one large uncollectable debt in an insolvency. Let us look at an extreme example of, say, the client having just one debtor. If that one debtor has a valid reason for non-payment of the debt should the client go out of business, then the financier has lost its one and only chance of recovering the amount of finance it provided the client. It is for this reason that, unless there are exceptional circumstances, financiers will not offer funding against a one debtor sales ledger. The example does, however, highlight the problem and so it can be seen that the greater the spread of the debt across many debtors, the smaller the risk to the financier.

- A prime debtor can result in a large bad debt. The same principle applies here except that the risk is not that the debtor will fail to pay but that there will be no debtor left to pay. In addition, a significantly large bad debt, unless insured, could lead to the collapse of the client as well.

- The client is too reliant on one prime debtor. In addition to the bad debt risk, a large debtor can simply stop trading with the client, leaving a vacuum that might be difficult to fill. If the client is a manufacturer, or has large overheads, then it will need to replace lost volume quickly and that may not be easy. The client could start making losses which might even lead to its demise.

Thus it can be seen that if the level of debtor concentration changes for the worse, some action needs to be taken.

Most invoice financiers have what is called a "spread restriction" or "concentration percentage". This is a maximum percentage owed by one single debtor of the total sales ledger that will be allowed for funding purposes. An example is as follows:

Key statistics

Total sales ledger:	£500,000
Prime debtor:	£250,000 (i.e. 50% of the total)
Prepayment percentage:	80%
Spread restriction:	35%

Calculation of availability

Prime debtor:	£250,000
35% of sales ledger:	£175,000
Disallowed for funding:	£ 75,000
Sales ledger:	£500,000
Less amount disallowed:	£ 75,000
Net amount allowed for prepayment:	£425,000
80% of net amount:	£340,000

Inevitably, the mix of debtors will change during the course of the relationship between the client and an invoice financier. If that change means that the spread of debt is deteriorating, this aspect will be reviewed. If there is already a spread restriction in place and the increase in the concentration of the prime debtor is only modest, then often no further action is necessary. However, there will be times where the spread restriction needs to be amended or perhaps two differing restrictions put in place. This latter event may be as a result of the prime debtor being highly credit-worthy and therefore warranting a higher or more liberal spread restriction, but for a tighter restriction to remain in place for other debtors.

As we have seen, there may come a time when whatever the spread restriction, the proportion owed by the prime debtor is so high that it is considered too risky by the financier. Unless a very creative solution can be found, the usual outcome is for the relationship to be terminated.

Stock revaluations

As discussed in the last chapter, stock financiers will often seek revaluations if there is a significant change in the perceived value of the stock they are funding.

We have seen that there is an increase in the usage of stock appraisers in the UK. Their usage is widespread in the USA where stock finance is a more sophisticated and mature product. In the UK, stock appraisers are increasingly being asked to undertake stock valuations at regular intervals. The larger, more sophisticated deals might have quarterly valuations or, in a distressed situation, the financier may insist on the movement of all stock being under independent control. Such cases are rare but will entail a person, or group of people, answerable to the financier but on the client's premises, controlling the movement and recording of the stock.

More likely will be the financier requesting a fresh valuation as part of a review of the facility. The financier's right to require such a valuation and at whose cost (usually the client's) will have been set out in the legal agreement between the two parties.

The result of the revaluation will form a key part of the review of the facility. Needless to say, the closer the revaluation is to the figures produced by the client, the happier the financier will be and the facility may remain unchanged. However, if the actual stock is much less than the "book" figure, then a plan needs to be put in place to reduce the level of finance to an acceptable level.

Increased security

Product change

Whilst a move to another product at the request of the client is usually a result of positive change, a switch of product requested by the financier is often a result of negative change.

At best, the financier may suggest that the client changes to another product simply because the current one is not appropriate for its needs. However, more frequently, the financier will insist on a change of product because it feels too much at risk with the current facility. If that happens with a stock facility, there is usually no option to switch to another facility because the client almost certainly has an invoice finance arrangement. In such cases, the likely outcome is for the financier to seek to exit the stock facility if it has become too risky. So we are talking about product changes within the invoice finance group of products.

The reasons that the financier might feel at too much risk and the possible solutions, will include:

Client has deliberately banked some debtor cash

Occasionally, clients deliberately bank cash from debtors which rightfully belong to the financier. If that occurs in an undisclosed invoice finance facility and the financier believes it can happen again, then the option is open to switch the facility to one that is disclosed. Legal agreements for undisclosed invoice discounting always contain the right for the financier to disclose the facility. In the event of client failure, the financier will need the ability to disclose in order to pursue the debtors for payment. However, the right to disclose is open to the financier at any time and is used when the financier believes there is a risk that debtor cash will be banked by the client. In a distressed situation, the financier will insist upon disclosure and will enforce it immediately but under those circumstances, the relationship between client and financier has usually broken down.

There are occasions when the situation is less serious and the financier will insist on an orderly change to a disclosed facility. In these cases, the relationship can usually be maintained and perhaps after a period of improvements in the client's financial position and contractual compliance, the client may return to an undisclosed facility.

If the banking of debtor cash happens in a factoring facility and the financier believes it could happen again, then the financier is likely to write to all debtors reminding them that the debts have been assigned and that payment can only be legally discharged by paying the financier. As factoring is already disclosed and collection activity controlled by the financier, the option to change the product is not open to the financier. In these situations, the only option might be to terminate the agreement.

The client's credit control is poor

One of the prerequisites of an invoice discounting facility is that the client must have sufficiently strong credit management. During the lifetime of the invoice discounting arrangement, the client's credit management may weaken with no improvement in sight. Under these circumstances, the financier may request that the client change to a factoring arrangement, and will undertake the credit management itself. Clearly before this happens, both sides need to agree that the reason for the deterioration in the sales ledger is a result of lack of credit control. If the reason relates to a change in the debtor mix or level of disputed debt, these problems need to be investigated first and an alternative solution might be more appropriate.

In extreme cases, there could be some other enforced product changes in order that the financier can reduce its exposure but these techniques will be discussed in the final chapter.

Tightening of terms and conditions

Some examples of tightening the terms and conditions other than those already mentioned, are:

- Reducing the recourse period (the age of an overdue invoice when it no longer becomes eligible for prepayments).
- No longer making prepayments against "doubtful" debts such as potential contras, those where the original purchase was subject to ROT, or where there is a ban on assignment.
- Not making CHAPS (same day telegraphic transfer) payments to clients.
- Not making any payments on new invoices until the high value ones have been verified.
- Imposing penalties if management or audited accounts are not sent to the financier within the agreed timescale.

Taking additional tangible security

Some examples of additional security are:

- Taking additional personal or corporate guarantees.
- Taking a first charge over assets not already taken as security by the financier.
- Taking a second or subsequent charge over assets already charged to other lenders.
- Offering invoice finance to an associated company if the financier feels this will have a beneficial effect on the overall risk profile.

Additional supporting documentation

Some examples of additional supporting documentation are:

- A full day-book listing instead of an abbreviated list of invoices as the means of notification.
- Copy invoices with each notification schedule.
- Proof of delivery (or signed time sheets) with each invoice.
- Copy orders from the debtors with large invoices.

Pricing

Within the price charged by any financier to its clients will be an element that reflects the perceived risk.

In the case of a non-recourse invoice finance facility, there is an additional risk; i.e. "approved" debtor bad debts. In the case of the non-recourse facility, the amount charged to the client will be expressed as a percentage of the debts purchased. This will usually be an element within the main fee but can sometimes be a separate percentage fee specifically covering the non-recourse debtor risk. Clearly if the level of "approved" debtor bad debts is consistently above that expected prior to take-on, then the financier may wish to increase that element of its fee. It may also reduce it if the bad debts have been lower than expected!

All financiers carry the risk that the client will fail and that the assets being funded will not generate sufficient cash to cover the finance provided to the client. In other words, the financier suffers a shortfall. The cost of that risk is usually reflected in the rate being charged for the finance. Thus if the financier perceives that the risk has significantly increased, it may wish to increase the price of the funds being provided.

Also, during a period when the risk has risen significantly due to the client breaching the legal agreement, the financier will usually wish to pass on all its additional costs involved in bringing the situation back into line. These costs might include increased audits, verification, legal charges and corporate recovery fees.

Involvement of other financiers

Where negative changes have occurred, it may be appropriate for the financier to involve other financiers.

If a syndicate is involved there will almost certainly be an obligation to share details of any negative changes seen by any of the financiers involved. Where there is no syndication but the financier is aware of other types of funding, there is the option to share any concerns the financier may have but there is a risk that it might precipitate action from others that is not in the financier's best interest.

There could be parts of a funding package that the financier is quite comfortable with, and parts that it would prefer not to have. For example, the financier might be content with funding the invoices but feels less comfortable funding the stock or the fixed assets. It may be that a specialist stock financier, or the client's bank, could take over the funding of those whilst the financier keeps control of the invoice finance.

The final option is that the financier wishes to terminate the relationship altogether and the best exit is to arrange an orderly transfer to another financier who will, in effect, pay off the original financier's financial commitment. In the highly competitive cashflow finance market, there will often be another hungrier financier willing to take a greater risk.

In this chapter we have discussed the contractual provisions open to the financier in protecting its funds, some negative trading indicators, fraud and the responses to negative changes. We have primarily considered managing the risk but concluded with the option of exiting from the relationship, and this is the topic of the next and final chapter.

Determining and Managing an Exit Strategy

Introduction

In this, the final chapter, we look at what happens if or when the relationship between the financier and its client ends. In many cases the client leaves for positive reasons, particularly when it has achieved early growth through the use of cashflow finance and is now, perhaps, self-financing. We have already discussed in previous chapters the fact that clients may wish to switch to an alternative financier that provides a product more suited to its needs, or perhaps return to bank funding. Most terminations are amicable affairs and go smoothly. However, there are some situations where either the relationship has broken down or the client's financial situation has seriously deteriorated, when the termination needs to be managed very carefully. Although such cases are in the minority, this chapter will focus on what the financier needs to do in these circumstances. After all, the financier's prime consideration is to recover the funds it has provided to the client.

It should be noted that phrases such as "terminating the account" or "terminating the relationship" are generic, non-legal phrases to describe the end of the business link between the financier and its client. However, "terminating the agreement" is a specific legal action that needs to be carried out strictly in accordance with the terms of the agreement and confers certain rights and obligations as a result. We shall see later in this chapter that where the client has committed an "event of default", the financier has powerful rights without the need to actually terminate the agreement. The financier can stop any further prepayments and demand the immediate repayment of funds, yet continues to obtain ownership of all debts newly created thereafter. Under these circumstances, the financier will rarely actually terminate the agreement.

Identifying circumstances requiring action

We will start by looking at some events leading to termination, which require the financier to take action.

Client ceases to trade or threatens to cease trading

The most obvious reason for the ending of the relationship is that the client ceases to trade or threatens to cease trading.

It is generally the case that the larger the facility, the closer the financier will be to the financial performance of the client, because better financial information is generally required. Thus financiers with the bigger ticket deals will sooner be aware of their clients' impending insolvency than those financiers with small factoring clients. Nevertheless, all financiers should be watching for the key warning signs of impending insolvency and these will include:

• Increasing demand for additional funding
• Deteriorating financial performance

- Deteriorating sales ledger and/or stock profile
- Uncovering a significant fraud by the client

We discussed in the chapter "Managing Risk", that lack of cash is a major cause of insolvency, so the financier will be looking out for symptoms. The client will be making more frequent calls to obtain maximum availability and could become aggressive if the funds available are not as much as the client needs or wants. Most financiers will subscribe to a service that informs them of any adverse information in the public domain which concerns their clients. The type of information would include winding-up petitions, county court judgments and any formal notice of insolvency.

In most agreements, either the threat of or actual insolvency will constitute an "event of default" entitling the financier to terminate the agreement, even if it chooses not to do so. As we shall see later in this chapter, this puts the invoice financier in a powerful position because it not only continues to obtain ownership of all debts newly created thereafter but can, if it wishes, demand immediate repayment of some or all of the funds provided.

The ways in which financiers will manage the threat of ceasing to trade or actual or apparent insolvency will be described later in this chapter.

If a client threatens to or does cease to trade, the financier is forced into a reactive termination of the agreement. However, aside from insolvency, there may be situations where the financier will consider proactive termination of the agreement. We shall now look at those circumstances, all of which require some action by the financier.

Serious breach

We have seen earlier in this workbook that the client's obligations are numerous and there will almost certainly be times when the client unintentionally breaches a relatively minor clause in that Agreement. Such minor breaches are usually dealt with in discussion between the client and financier and, if serious enough, perhaps a sanction such as an additional fee or a written warning will be deemed appropriate. However, there are some breaches that will be considered so serious that the financier will decide there is no alternative but to terminate the relationship. This is obviously a considerable step and not taken lightly, therefore even if there has been a serious breach, the financier will wish to take into account all relevant issues affecting the relationship.

Breaches considered to be cause for termination will vary from financier to financier but will usually be for one of the following reasons, most of which relate to some kind of fraudulent activity:

The client raises fictitious invoices
We saw in the chapter about "Managing Risk" how this kind of fraud results in an invoice financier financing non-existent debts. It is rare that, upon discovering this kind of activity, a financier will wish to continue the relationship with its client.

The client banks debtor cash

An invoice financier will continue to finance a debt that is non-existent because it has now been paid. Often, there will be some ambiguity as to whether the payment was deliberately banked by the client or was "an oversight". An example of the latter might be a BACS payment being made by a debtor to a client that has an undisclosed facility. It is possible (albeit an indication of poor administration) that the payment could go unnoticed by the client for some time. Thus the occurrence of banked cash does not always result in the financier terminating the facility unless it judges the act to be deliberate.

The client deliberately withholds credit notes

The effect of this is, again, that an invoice financier finds itself with all or part of a debt which is now uncollectable. The financier will have to decide if the delay was deliberate and make an assessment of the seriousness of the situation before deciding to terminate.

The client manipulates data sent to the financier

This can range from a doctored aged debt analysis sent to an invoice financier, to a false stock listing sent to a stock financier. It can also relate to deliberately misleading or false management accounts or any other piece of information designed to give the financier a rosier view of the client's position than is actually the case. Stock finance relies very heavily on the stock listings sent by the client to the financier and if the credibility of these is compromised, then it is almost certain that the financier will seek to terminate the relationship. The same applies to a doctored aged debt analysis supplied by a client that has an invoice discounting facility. Finally, rather than manipulated data, there can be deliberate refusal to provide information.

Accumulated non-conformance

There will be times when the client is given the benefit of the doubt when a serious breach has occurred and the relationship is allowed to continue, albeit with increased vigilance by the financier. However, if there are further breaches, then it is likely that the financier will decide that the client's probity is compromised and the relationship should be terminated.

Similarly, there may be some less serious breaches of the Agreement which on their own do not warrant termination but if they persist, then the financier may decide that enough is enough. Examples of these are:

- Continuously late submission of management accounts
- Failure to provide audited accounts within the agreed timescale
- Delays in passing on debtor cash received
- Delays in resolving debtor disputes
- Continuous breaches of warranties and undertakings
- Continued late delivery of invoice discounting monthly returns, such as the aged debt analysis and the associated reconciliations
- Late delivery of stock listings

The above list is not exhaustive but it serves to illustrate that continuous failure to comply with the Agreement will increase the perceived risk and will inevitably lead to stringent penalties or actual termination.

Insufficient reward for effort and risk

There are circumstances when a financier will decide that the risk associated with the provision of facilities to a client does not justify the reward. These can include:

- The client's projected business activity, upon which the pricing was based, failing to materialize.

- The workload of the financier far exceeding what was expected.

- A deterioration in the client's financial performance which increases the likelihood of business failure.

- A change in the client's business activity which seriously reduces the perceived quality of the assets being financed.

- In the case of invoice finance, there is a decline in the ledger profile, such as loss of spread, extended terms, poor quality debtors or a shift towards riskier export debtors.

Under these circumstances, the financier may:

- Increase its fees or charges; or
- Reduce the risk by, for example, reducing the prepayment percentage or finance limit; or
- Terminate the facility.

If a financier is able to turn the situation around so that sufficient reward can be achieved, then termination may be avoided. However, if the risk cannot be reduced or the income increased, then the financier may have to terminate the facility.

Changes to third party situations

A related party's activity or operation may have a significant adverse affect upon the success of the client or the security of the assets being financed. These are circumstances or actions beyond the financier's control that may cause it to terminate the facility in order to protect the funds it has provided. Examples of these can include:

- The client is part of a group of companies whose financial fortunes have deteriorated. The financier finds that the funds it provides the client are being used to support loss-making activities elsewhere in the group, despite the financial stability or success of the client.

- A guarantor to the Agreement between the client and the financier has become weakened to the point where the guarantee becomes worthless. Alternatively, a guarantor may wish to withdraw its guarantee.

- Action by another financier, such as a bank, leaves the client without sufficient finance to meet its future obligations.

- A credit insurance policy may lapse or be withdrawn.

Assessing the situation

Importance of timing

The financier's primary aim, when faced with an exit strategy, is to recover its funds in use. When faced with a client that is already insolvent, the financier has no control over the timing of its action. It will wish to commence a collect-out as soon as possible. However, if the client is continuing to trade, then the financier may be able to take control of the timing of the exit.

Why is timing important? By choosing the timing of an exit, the financier may be able to maximise its chances of recovering its funds and/or it may be able to assist the client to trade out of its problems. But the financier needs to be aware that the client will always prefer to delay any precipitative action. Ever hopeful that all will turn out well, the client will either seek to prove that it can trade out of its difficulty or that a "saviour" is about to come marching over the hill. These "saviours" can be another lender or a new investor or company which will take over the business. The latter two, often referred to as "White Knights", may well be interested in the client's business but may prefer to pick up the assets from an insolvency. So the financier needs to be convinced that any saviours are genuine and, to that end, needs to obtain proof of intent and perhaps meet with them in order to be satisfied that its patience will be rewarded. Under these circumstances, a delay in the timing of an exit may prove worthwhile.

Timing is also important if the client is about to enter a trading period which will help to maximise the recovery of the financier's funds. For example, if the client is about to enter its prime selling season and will be converting a lot of stock into invoices, then a financier funding both assets will probably feel more comfortable seeing more of its funds in debtor balances than stock. Or the financier may simply cap its total funds in use whilst taking on more invoices that may give it more security against the same amount of finance.

Every situation will be different but timing can play a key part in the financier's desire to protect its funds and perhaps help the client to trade through a difficult patch.

Negotiation

In the event that a financier has decided to exit from the agreement with its client, the situation is clearly very serious. There are risks that the client could fail (assuming it has not already done so) or that the financier could lose a considerable amount of money.

Thus there is considerable scope for negotiation between the two parties and perhaps others as well.

The objectives of the financier and the client will be different but there should be some common ground. If the financier finds itself "over-exposed" (unlikely to collect its investment from the assets it has financed) then it will wish to correct that situation before it is too late. The financier can either reduce the amount of money it has financed or raise the value of assets without necessarily parting with any more cash. In this latter case, the financier needs the client to continue to trade so that it can generate fresh assets. The client, on the other hand, will nearly always want to stay in business and thus both parties share the same objective. It is often better, from the financier's point of view, to have a client which is still in business and still willing to help the financier resolve any problems with the assets.

With an invoice finance facility, there may have been some invoices for goods yet to be delivered or in need of repair and this can only be achieved by having a client that is still trading. Similarly, some stock may have been financed in the belief that it was finished goods when in fact it was work in progress. A client still trading may be able to convert this into finished goods ready for sale.

Even when fraud has taken place, the financier may be better off negotiating with a client, albeit with a high degree of scepticism.

There may be other providers of finance involved, such as a bank, that wish to take a different approach, so it is essentialthat the financier and bank open a dialogue in order that they can achieve each other's objectives. Similarly, the client may have a prospective investor waiting in the wings that may need some reassurance, or a guarantor who is anxious to help the client stay in business. The list goes on but it is important that the financier at least attempts to negotiate with other parties before taking precipitate action. However, the dilemma is that the financier may have to part with more cash just to keep the client afloat, with the risk that it is "throwing good money after bad".

Role of audit in exit strategy

Whatever the reason for the financier considering an exit from the relationship, it needs to be sure of the facts before implementing its decision. The financier may think the assets it has financed have a certain value. It may think that it understands the client's financial position. However, an audit will give it a better understanding. Of course, an unsatisfactory audit may have been the original trigger that led the financier to want to extricate itself from the relationship.

Whilst not conclusive, an audit should give the financier a clearer idea about the following issues:

The client's current trading and profitability

The client's current cashflow needs
- Invoices:
  - Have they all been notified to the financier?
  - Have goods or services been provided in respect of them?
  - Are they the same ones that have been notified to the financier?
  - Have any invoices been paid direct and banked by the client?
- Credit notes:
  - Have they all been notified to the financier?
  - Have they all been raised yet?
- Stock:
  - Is the amount of stock being financed correct?
  - Is the value of that stock correct?
  - Is the stock physically on the premises?
  - What is the value of fresh invoices or relevant stock to be created in the immediate future?

- Is there any correspondence to back up what the client is saying?
- Is there any correspondence from other providers of finance?

It can be seen that an audit can give the financier a better picture of the situation before it implements its strategy. It may also prove useful, when a large amount of finance is involved, to keep an auditor on site whilst the strategy is actually implemented. If fraud has occurred or has been suspected, then representatives of the financier may wish to oversee the delivery of goods, the raising of invoices, the movement of stock or the banking of cash. This is obviously an expensive option and one that is only short-term because by this stage the relationship has probably broken down. Nevertheless, with "big ticket" deals in particular, it is common practice if the financier is still providing funds yet trust has broken down.

Client enters into a formal insolvency procedure

[Refer to Appendix 7]

It is possible for a company to enter into a formal insolvency procedure on its own accord or it could be initiated by its financier. The rights and powers of the financier when its client enters into a formal insolvency procedure will largely depend on the type of insolvency procedure and the nature of the security held by the financier.

Where the financier only provides invoice finance it is possible that the financier might not have a charge or it may only have a charge on book debts and therefore has no power to appoint an administrator or administrative receiver. In the circumstances where stock, plant or other asset finance is provided it is likely that the financier will have a registered fixed and/or floating charge over the assets of its client which entitles the financier to appoint either an administrator or administrative receiver. If the financier's fixed and floating post dates 15 September 2003 then under the Enterprise Act 2002 the financier may only appoint an administrator.

We will now look at each form of insolvency procedure.

Company Voluntary Arrangement

On receipt of a proposal for a composition in satisfaction of the client's debts, the financier should review the proposal which will outline why a voluntary arrangement is desirable, give details of the assets and liabilities of the client, the proposed duration of the arrangement and details of the proposed distribution. The proposal will also outline how the claims and rights of the secured creditors will be dealt with during the course of the arrangement.

In most cases the arrangement will provide for the continued trading of the business with a view to the client paying an agreed level of contributions to the Supervisor of the arrangement over a specified period for distribution to creditors. The financier may therefore be approached by the client at an early stage with a view to procuring new facilities to finance any working capital requirements during the course of the arrangement. Financiers should be cautious about providing new facilities to a client proposing a voluntary arrangement unless it can be satisfied that there will be significant improvements in the client's business operations which allow it to trade profitably going forward. They should assess why the business failed and why future trading will be different by considering any changes (e.g. new money, new product, new people).

Where the financier provides invoice financing the continued trading of the business will assist in preserving the value of the existing book debts and allow for any contractual work to be completed which will enhance book debt collections. The financier should consider whether it should allow the client to continue collecting book debts or whether to enforce its right to "collect out". Any shortfall on book debt collections will rank as an unsecured claim in the arrangement although the proposal could allow for the shortfall to be carried forward.

Where the financier holds a fixed and/or floating charge then the financier needs to assess whether the proposal provides for a better recovery than would be expected if the client was to enter into either an administration or liquidation procedure.

Unless the company is eligible for a small companies moratorium which restricts the rights of the financier to enforce any security over the company's property without the leave of the Court, the financier should assess whether a better return could be derived from another form of insolvency procedure and enforce its security prior to the holding of the meeting of creditors provided for in the proposal. This may include the appointment of either an administrator or administrative receiver (depending on the date of the charge).

If the financier does not elect to enforce its security then it is entitled to vote only in respect of the balance (if any) of his debt after deducting the estimated value of his security (as estimated by the financier) i.e. the estimated unsecured portion of his debt.

Administration

We know that an administrator may be appointed by:

- the company (or its directors);

- the holder of a qualifying floating charge (essentially a holder of all-embracing security) including the financier; or

- the court on the petition of the company, its directors or a creditor.

and must satisfy at least one of the objectives referred to in the Appendix.

In the case of a company appointment, the company or its directors must give at least 5 business days' notice to the holder of a qualifying charge, during which time the financier can elect to make its own appointment. The financier could be one of or the only floating charge holder.

In the case of an appointment by the holder of a qualifying charge, the charge holder must give at least 2 business days' notice to a prior ranking charge holder (either the charge was created first or pursuant to a Deed of Priority), during which time the prior ranking charge holder can elect to make its own appointment.

Administrators have wide ranging powers to manage the affairs, business and property of the company and to sell assets which are subject to a floating charge (e.g. stock, plant & machinery, etc). They may only sell assets subject to a fixed charge (e.g. property, goodwill) if it is likely to promote the purpose of their appointment and a court order is obtained. Accordingly, financiers with an invoice finance facility can elect to either collect out or allow the Administrator to collect book debts and should seek to agree an appropriate arrangement with the Administrator as soon as possible.

The Administrator's power to continue to trade the business will also help to preserve the book debts particularly if a purchaser for the business can be found in a relatively short period of time. However, it is likely that the Administrator may require funding in the short term whilst a purchaser is sought and will look to the financier to provide such funding particularly when the financier has initiated the appointment. The benefit to the financiers of providing funding to the administrator may likely result in:

• enhanced floating charge realisations from the sale of the business as a going concern; and/or

• enhanced realisations from preservation of the book debts; and/or

• enhanced realisations from the ability of the administrator to convert stock into debt.

It should be noted that if the qualifying floating charge was created on or after 15 September 2003 then the Insolvency Act provides for the carving out of a "prescribed part" as a sliding scale percentage of floating charge assets (limited to a maximum sum of £600,000) for payment to the unsecured creditors (after full payment of preferential claims) before the balance of realisations are paid to the floating charge holder.

Administrative Receivership

An administrative receiver may only be appointed by the holder of a qualifying floating charge created prior to 15 September 2003. This does not prevent the holder of any other charge from also appointing its own receiver.

An administrative receiver has similar powers to those of an administrator (limited to the assets charged under which he was appointed) but has a primary duty of care to the floating charge holder and limited responsibility to unsecured creditors whereas an administrator has a general duty to the general body of creditors as an officer of the court.

Accordingly, the same commercial considerations apply to that of the administration appointment including funding, collect out and book debt preservation. On deciding on which type of appointment would be preferable (where the option exists) financiers should consider the differences shown in the table in the Appendix and apply them to the existing client circumstances (e.g. tax considerations, administration protection provisions, reputational risk).

Liquidation

A liquidation is a terminal process and will result in the closure of the business and dissolution of the company. This does not preclude the invoice finance provider from collecting out its debt albeit debtor realisations are likely to be significantly lower than they would be in the event of a going concern sale of the business.

However, there may be instances where the financier could fund the liquidator in order to complete work in progress for conversion into book debts in order to enhance realisations.

Matching exit strategies to the circumstances

It should be stressed that not all the events listed under the previous sections will necessarily result in the financier exiting the relationship. Leopards may not change their spots but individuals may leave the client company or are no longer involved in the relationship with the financier. Similarly, the financier may find a creative way forward in order to retain the client on a profitable basis with an acceptable risk.

Nevertheless, some situations will result in termination and in this section we will look at matching exit strategies to the prevailing circumstances.

Legal provision for protecting the funding

In the last resort, a financier will want protection against the funding it has provided to a client that has breached the legal agreement. The financier's rights are largely found in the documentation (the agreement, any guarantees or any charges) and to a lesser extent, in the general law.

It was mentioned earlier in this chapter that an "event of default" without actual termination by the financier puts the financier in a very powerful position. Legal agreements will vary from one financier to another but it is usual that the financier will continue to obtain ownership of all debts newly created thereafter but can if it wishes exercise total recourse by:

• Withholding prepayments due
• Demanding back all prepayments made against debts still outstanding at that time
• Withdraw the credit protection element under a non-recourse facility

The financier still has to collect the debts and hand over the proceeds (once the above prepayments have been repaid). Usually the mere threat to invoke some of the financier's rights is sufficient for the client to mend its ways if, for example, it has been diverting debtor payments away from the financier.

Collect-out

Upon insolvency or where the relationship has been terminated and the financier still has to recover its funds in use, the financier will make a decision to "collect-out". This is the process whereby the proceeds from assets which have been financed are collected to recover the funds in use.

In most cases a collect-out will be as a result of insolvency but there will be other situations where no other financier or bank is taking over the financing of the assets in question, and the financier has to liquidate those assets. For example, the account may have been terminated by the client who cannot afford, or refuses to repay, the financier's funds in use.

In some circumstances a new company is formed to carry on the same business previously carried out by an insolvent client, and the financier may take some comfort from that. Such re-starts are called "phoenixes" and are discussed in more depth later in this section.

As soon as the financier has decided to collect-out, then it will wish to take a series of actions which will include:

Stop all payments to the client

Most payments to clients are by electronic transfer and as these leave the sender's bank on day one, there will probably not be much scope for trying to stop any payments already in the pipeline. Nevertheless, the financier must check this and put a stop to such payments. The next task is to ensure that any automatic system for making client payments is cancelled.

Check the validity of the asset

The sudden demise of a client will also trigger suspicion in the mind of the financier that all may not be well with the assets it has financed. All sorts of desperate actions are taken in the last few days and weeks of a client heading towards insolvency and these could include the banking of debtor cash, fresh air invoicing or fictitious stock listings. In the case of factoring, the financier will wish to quickly telephone most of the major debtors in order to agree the balance owing. In the case of invoice discounting, the financier will either disclose the arrangement immediately, if the facility is undisclosed or use its usual method of telephone verification. This disclosure, in the case of confidential invoice discounting, is paramount to the success or failure of the financier recouping its funds. Hitherto, the financier has parted with cash based on a large element of trust that there is indeed a valid debt in existence. Whether the arrangement is disclosed or not, the financier will immediately write to all debtors putting them on notice or reminding them that the debts have been assigned to the financier and that the debtors can only discharge the debt by paying the financier. In the case of stock finance, an urgent visit will be made by the financier to the client's premises to physically inspect the stock.

Obtain ownership of any remaining assets

Under most invoice finance agreements the financier will obtain ownership of any future debts that may still be invoiced. However, the financier will wish to ensure that all sales have been invoiced by the client before the appointment of an insolvency practitioner. Any invoices raised thereafter will belong to a different legal entity. In the case of stock finance, the financier will wish to ensure that as much stock as possible falls under its legal charge. The best way of achieving this is by securing all the stock that can be found and bringing it under the control of the financier. Any subsequent claims by other parties that some or all of the stock belongs to them can be dealt with through the legal process.

Meet with the client's directors and/or the insolvency practitioner

First and foremost such a meeting will be about fact finding. There may be events about which the financier has no prior knowledge that will come to light once the client has ceased to trade. These events, including possible fraud, will assist the financier in determining its strategy for the "collect-out". It will be important to have a dialogue with any insolvency practitioner, especially if the latter is looking for finance for any new legal entity. The types of potential new entities following insolvency will be discussed in greater detail later in this chapter. It is important that prior to meeting with an insolvency practitioner, the financier has tried its best to establish the likely recovery figure. This often influences the approach adopted by the financier.

Working with the insolvency practitioner can assist the financier in many ways. For example, if there has been pre-invoicing it is sometimes possible to get goods released or work completed and this may increase the recovery prospects. Also, the financier may be able to generate some extra income by agreeing to carry on collecting for the Insolvency Practitioner after the financier has got its money back.

It is quite often the case that a "phoenix" company is being considered. So called after "a phoenix rising from the ashes", such phoenixes will usually carry on in the same business having purchased certain assets and crucially having none of the old liabilities. The phoenix company may even have the same directors as the previous entity. The financier will need to consider whether they wish to finance the phoenix if they are invited to do so. Part of that consideration will be whether the financier thinks that by doing so it will be able to increase the recovery from its former client.

Recovery of paperwork

Where a debt is purchased by a financier, all the rights associated with the debts are also transferred. These are both tangible and intangible matters connected with the debt and include instruments, securities and benefits of any insurance. More specifically, in the case of a collect-out, the financier has the rights to the evidence that a debt has been created. This evidence, such as copy orders, proofs of delivery etc., will need to be collected from the client by the financier.

The rights transferred to the financier also include the rights under the contract of sale. This could include the right to stop goods in transit, the right to sue for the debt or to repossess any goods which are returned.

Giving notice of assignment

The financier will write to all interested parties, including the client's directors and any guarantors, giving notice that the agreement has been terminated by default and demanding immediate repayment of the funds provided. These parties can also be put on notice without termination having occurred, to ensure continued accumulation of discount charge.

Put into action a plan to recover the funds

Most financiers will have a set procedure if a client ceases to trade. It may be that the account is handled by a separate section although in many cases the account manager retains responsibility for the recovery plan. In any event, there will be a set of procedures to "collect-out" the amounts owed by the debtors or put in place the sale of stock held by a legal charge.

Collection activity

If the facility is invoice discounting, all collection activity will be brought under the control of the financier. Some financiers have a specialist section which carries out the collection activity for collect-outs. Others may even use external firms to undertake this task. Either way, the collections need to be robust and sensitive to the fact that debtors will probably be looking for a way of avoiding payment, as they will no doubt feel aggrieved that their source of supply has been stopped. Naturally, spurious claims for non-payment need to be tackled vigorously, perhaps with legal action. However, there will be occasions when the financier may have to reach a compromise with the debtor and accept a lower amount rather than risk getting nothing.

Debtor litigation

An invoice financier may need to take legal action against overdue debtors of a terminated client to recover its funds in use. Specialist lawyers can play a significant part in the recovery process. If the client is insolvent there is every incentive for debtors to raise spurious defences or set-offs to avoid payment. There is little motivation for a debtor to pay when they are no longer reliant upon the client for the future provision of goods or services. In addition, customers resent disruptions to their supplies. This can be mitigated through the continuing co-operation of the client's directors and employees even though the client may have ceased to trade. The threat of enforcing their personal guarantees can act as a powerful incentive.

It is vital that the financier can provide information related to the sales ledger, such as copy invoices, delivery notes, purchase orders, copy correspondence, remittance advices, and collection letters. Collection through the courts can fail if the financier cannot prove that goods or services were actually delivered.

Litigation can be expensive, especially if the case is complex. The financier will need to make a decision as to whether to start a potentially costly piece of litigation in light of the outstanding funds in use.

Sale of stock

Where the facility has provided finance against stock, then the process must commence to turn the remaining stock into cash. The urgent need is to secure the stock as soon as the client ceases to trade. Stock might be moved to a separate location or may be duly labelled to confirm ownership by the financier. This is because there may be attempts by other lenders or suppliers to lay claim to the stock and in the case of the latter, it is not unknown for lorries to turn up as soon as there is any hint of insolvency and take the stock back. Some of these claims may of course prove to be valid, either through a successful ROT claim or another legal charge that has priority over that held by the financier. However these are issues to be decided through the courts. The immediate priority is for the financier to have control over the movement of stock until ownership is proven.

Having established ownership, the financier will now wish to set about liquidating the stock and that is usually achieved with the help of specialist firms who will assist in obtaining the best possible return. Some stock valuers will help in this regard or at least put the financier in touch with a business specializing in liquidating the particular type of stock. Timing is an issue with seasonal goods as it is clearly better to wait until the prime buying season in order to obtain the best price.

Securing the stock, storing it, transporting it and using external firms to help sell it, will of course all cost money. These costs will have to be taken into account when deciding on the price to sell the stock. The financier will have to make some important decisions at this stage. It may be that there was also an invoice finance facility or perhaps finance against other assets; then the financier will need to take a holistic approach in looking at the likely recoveries from each particular asset. If there is likely to be a surplus of funds from the debtors, for example, then this can be taken into account when deciding on the price to accept for the stock.

Indemnity and guarantee action

Directors of a company often give the financier personal guarantees and indemnities in support of the facility. Should a financier be unable to recover its funds from the recovery of the assets then legal action taken against the guarantors and indemnifiers may be instigated as a means of recovering the shortfall. However a guarantee only has value if the guarantor has sufficient assets. If the directors of a failed client have personal financial difficulties, then the financier will have an actionable guarantee of no value. If the financier issues proceedings it may well obtain a bankruptcy order against a director although clearly this will not result in recovering the financier's loss.

Guarantees can be useful as a lever to convince a guarantor to assist with the collection/recovery process. The directors' input can often be useful in resolving queries and disputes that would otherwise be used by debtors to avoid payment. The value of this lever cannot be underestimated. After all, a guarantor, faced with possibly having to sell their house to raise enough cash to pay the financier, has a huge incentive to help maximise the recovery from the sale of the assets.

Corporate guarantees, when taken, may have had a substantial worth but if the guarantor was part of the same group as the failed client, then it too may have failed. Nevertheless, if the corporate guarantor is still in business, then pursuit of the guarantee may mitigate or even clear the financier's shortfall.

Inter-factor transfer

Under an inter-factor transfer the outgoing invoice financier is repaid its funds in use by another financier who will be offering a fresh invoice finance facility. The debts are then transferred back to the client in order that they can be dealt with under the incoming factor's legal documentation. Thus the incoming financier only acquires title if it buys out the outgoing financier. Although these procedures are usually called an "inter-factor" transfer they can also be applied between a factor and an invoice discounter and vice-versa or between invoice discounters.

Members of the Asset Based Finance Association operate under a set of guidelines for transfers between members. These guidelines allow the incoming financier to repay the outgoing financier from the initial prepayment. The outgoing financier agrees to release interest in all the debts on the day of transfer on the basis that the incoming financier underwrites any claims made against the outgoing financier. So, if a cheque that has been paid to the old financier is returned unpaid after the date of transfer, then the new financier will repay the old financier. Such transfers can occur for a variety of reasons including:

• The client outgrows its existing facility and no longer fits the preferred client profile of its current financier.

• The client requires a change of facility, for example from factoring to invoice discounting which the outgoing factor is either unwilling or unable to provide or the terms are unacceptable.

• The client no longer fits into the financier's risk profile.

- The client is unhappy with the service provided by the outgoing financier.

- It is the client's perception that the incoming financier is offering a significant reduction in overall price..

- The client wants an additional service which its existing financier cannot provide such as stock or trade finance or finance against export debtors.

- There has been a complete breakdown in the relationship.

Transfers between financiers are becoming more common as the financing market matures and businesses become more aware of the range and diversity of services being offered by competitive asset based financiers. However, it behoves the incoming financier to be very cautious in its assessment of the risk because the client may be seeking alternative facilities for reasons that it might not be prepared to discuss in detail. It may be that the client has committed a serious breach of the agreement with its existing financier and is suffering penalties as a result. It may be that the client's business no longer provides an acceptable risk to the existing financier and yet the client will obviously not mention this when talking to the new financier.

Return to bank finance

Sometimes a client will wish to cease using a cashflow financier and return to (or perhaps use for the first time) a facility offered by their bank, usually an overdraft. The reasons for this will vary but for more mature businesses, it is possible that its bank may be able to offer a single source of funds using many assets as security which is perhaps not something that is offered by its current financier.

Almost certainly the bank will wish to take the outstanding debtors as security for its new facility. As with inter-factor transfers, the outgoing financier will agree to release its interest in the existing debts and will be repaid its funds from the first payment by the bank. Unlike inter-factor transfers however, the outgoing financier is not protected against unpaid cheques and may wish to hold a retention against this eventuality until all debtor cheques have been met.

In the case of stock finance or in any case where the financier has a charge over some of the assets, the financier will have to acknowledge that the charge will be extinguished upon receipt of payment in full discharge of the funds it has provided the client.

No further funding requirements

Having funded their early growth through cashflow finance, the client may reach a stage where they simply become self-funding either through a capital injection or through accumulated profits.

Business closure/run down

Not all relationships between financiers and their clients end in formal termination. Perhaps there is a partnership split, or the founding directors split or perhaps the loss of a major order leads to a decision to close the business down. There are occasions when the client's business simply dries up, no new invoices are created, no more finance taken and the existing debts are collected in to repay the "funds in use".

Often, in such cases, the client is a new start business or perhaps a new division of an existing client that has its own separate legal agreement. Typically, these situations are more common with factoring clients that tend to be smaller and often of more recent inception. If turnover is well below expectations, then the financier will be aware of this and discuss the situation with the client. There will undoubtedly be a pricing issue. Either the financier has insisted on a minimum income, in which case the client will find the cost is now too high to be justified or the price was based on much greater volume and the financier is running the facility at a loss.

Whether the collect-out of the existing facility is "managed" or just left to take its natural course, no further finance will be provided and the facility brought to a close when the financier has recouped its "funds in use" and the debts are collected or re-assigned.

As we have seen, clients occasionally cease trading or their financial position becomes untenable from the point of view of the financier. Alternatively, the necessary degree of trust may break down or perhaps the risk is no longer commensurate with the reward. On such occasions, however rare, the financier needs an exit strategy. In this chapter, we have looked at how to assess the circumstances leading up to this situation, the options open to the financier and the actions required to achieve a satisfactory exit. Finally, we looked at the legal implications when a business becomes insolvent.

Epilogue

The concept of tailoring finance to specific assets is not new. Mortgages for property and hire purchase for large capital items are prime examples of products which help fulfil long term funding requirements and have been around for many years. However, the provision of cashflow by directly financing specific current assets is relatively new in the UK.

Factoring came to the UK in 1960 and its reputation in those early days was chequered as the fledgling factoring companies, enthused by a great concept, signed up new business without adequate checks to the underlying strength of the client or the probity of its management. The resulting bad debts, massive by today's standards, quickly taught these factoring companies the importance of risk assessment prior to offering their services and sound risk management thereafter. This led to stability within the industry and the start of impressive growth both in new business and profitability. It was this latter aspect that no doubt attracted the major banks to invest in the factoring sector either by acquisition or "growing their own".

It was not until the broadening of the range of products in the following decade to include export factoring and then invoice discounting, that real growth took hold. The managers of these invoice finance companies tended to have come up "through the ranks" or have had experience working for larger competitors. Thus experience was retained within the industry and new recruits were trained by the more experienced staff. So in the first twenty year's of the invoice finance industry's history, this passing down of experience was the only form of training available.

By 1977, the industry realised that to cope with its huge growth, it had to invest in education specifically designed to develop the skills necessary to manage that growth. Thus the major players formed their own association which provided such training. This training, the forerunner of today's diploma course provided by the ABFA, was supplemented by external courses provided by lawyers and accountants who had gained experience in various aspects of the invoice finance sector.

The industry broadened even further in the 1980s and 1990s with the increase of foreign ownership which brought both a different perspective and additional products. New American owners in particular brought in the concept of offering a package of solutions to cashflow needs rather than just invoice finance. Thus stock finance and floor planning were combined with the more traditional trade finance to broaden the market for what we now call the cashflow finance sector.

Along with the huge growth over five decades has come a commensurate change in the perception of this group of products. Invoice finance is now accepted as a mainstream financial product, aimed mainly at the SME market and as a credible alternative to traditional bank lending.

When I joined this industry in 1974, International Factors, the then market leader, had 100 staff looking after 100 clients, turning over £100 million of sales. They were figures that were easy to remember but reflect the modest size of the industry in those days and the poor productivity in those early years of computerisation. More than thirty years later, this industry has more than 6,000 staff looking after over 40,000 clients whose combined turnover is in excess of £132 billion. Huge leaps in client numbers and turnover, larger client sizes and of course more productive staff. It is these staff members that possess the skills required to help 40,000 small and medium sized businesses fund their growth. Training is even more important now in the ever more sophisticated world of cashflow finance.

The cashflow industry is a vibrant and important part of our economy and thus, for those with the skills and motivation, an exciting business to be in. For it to remain so, it needs just two things: growth and the retention of highly trained staff.

The aim of this book has been to enable students to gain an in depth understanding of the technical and practical aspects of the cashflow finance sector. The range of products offered by this sector has helped tens of thousands of small and medium sized enterprises to achieve levels of growth that they may not otherwise have achieved. For as long as the players in this sector continue to adapt to the changing needs of their client base, we can reasonably expect to see the continuing profitable growth of the cashflow sector in the foreseeable future.

The Author

Appendix 1

WAIVER BY A BANK (OR OTHER SECURED LENDER) WITH A PRIOR CHARGE OVER BOOK DEBTS (FLOATING OR FIXED)

With the letter heading of Prime Bank Ltd

TO: Top Finance Limited ("TFL")

AND

TO: Client Co Limited (the "Company")

Date:

Dear Sirs,

As you are aware, we have a charge over the present and future book debts of the Company ("Charge").

We have been informed that the Company proposes to enter into or has entered into (a) Factoring Agreement(s) ("Agreement") with TFL substantially in TFL's standard form, (such form having been supplied to us) whereby all or some of the Company's Debts together with their Related Rights (together referred to herein as "Debts") as defined therein vest in TFL.

We consent to the assignment by the Company to TFL of its Debts pursuant to the Agreement or in accordance with the procedures set out therein.

Further we agree that in relation to any of the Debts vesting or intended to vest in TFL prior to the time when you receive notice from us of an appointment of an administrative receiver under our said Charge we will not challenge TFL's title thereto. To that extent, we hereby waive any priority which we might otherwise be able to claim against TFL in respect of such Debts.

Provided that:

(i) if at any time we give TFL three months' notice of the cancellation of this letter then the provisions of this letter shall not apply to and shall have no effect in respect of any Debts created by the Company after the expiry of that notice; and

(ii) any amounts payable by TFL to the Company in respect of the purchase price of Debts or in respect of any Debts reassigned by TFL or otherwise shall not be included within this waiver, and shall form part of our security whether by way of charge, assignment or otherwise.

In arriving at the amounts so payable by TFL to the Company, TFL shall be entitled to exercise all defences, rights of set-off or combination of accounts or otherwise which TFL may have against the Company, whether arising before or after TFL's receipt of notice of our security.

We certify that to the best of our knowledge no event has occurred as a result of which our security has crystallised.

Yours faithfully,

for and on behalf of Prime Bank Limited

Notes:

1. Alternatives in brackets to be used as appropriate.

2. If the charge is subsequent to the Factoring Agreement(s) this letter should be dated the same day as the charge.

3. If the Factoring Agreement(s) is subsequent to the charge, this letter should be obtained prior to the signing of the Agreement(s). If the letter has not been so obtained the following additional paragraph should be inserted: "This release and consent shall be deemed effective on and since the ...." (date of the Factoring Agreement(s)).

4. This form applies only to charges under English law. It does not apply to Scottish charges.

Appendix 2

EXAMPLE OF PRIORITY DEED AND CONSENT TO FACTORING

THIS DEED is made the   day of   200 **BETWEEN:**

(1)   **TOP FINANCIERS LIMITED** Company Number 0000001 ("TFL").

(2)   **PRIME BANK PLC**
        Company Number 0000002 (the "Lender").

(3)   LIMITED
        Company Number (the "Company").

AND WITNESSES as follows:

1.   **Definitions and Interpretation**

1.1   Words and phrases defined or referred to in TFL's Security (as defined below) shall have the same meanings, unless the context otherwise requires, where used in this deed.

1.2   In this deed, except where the context otherwise requires, the following expressions shall have the meanings set out against each of them:

"Administrator"	has the same meaning as in Schedule B1 to the Insolvency Act 1986 as introduced by the Enterprise Act 2002;
"Agreement"	the agreement for the purchase of Debts between TFL and the Company and any extension of, amendment to or replacement of such agreement;
"Debts"	has the same meaning as in the Agreement;
"Lender's Security"	the debenture containing fixed and floating charges over all the Company's assets dated given by the Company to the Lender and all other present and future mortgages, charges, pledges, liens and other encumbrances or security granted by the Company to the Lender;
"Non-Vesting Debts"	any Debts or their Related Rights purchased or purported to be purchased by TFL pursuant to the Agreement which fail to vest absolutely and effectively in TFL for any reason;

"TFL's Security"   the fixed and floating charges over all the Company's assets dated given by the Company to TFL and all other present and future mortgages, charges, pledges, liens and other encumbrances granted by the Company to TFL;

"Receiver"   includes a receiver or a manager or a receiver and manager or an administrative receiver as defined in Section 29(2) of the Insolvency Act 1986 or a receiver of part only of the property of the Company or a receive only of the income arising from any part of the Company's property;

"Related Rights"   has the same meaning as in the Agreement;

"Securities"   the Lender's Security and TFL's Security together and "Security" means any one of them;

"Security Holders"   the Lender and TFL and "Security Holder" means either of them.

1.3   In the deed, unless the context otherwise requires:

Here would be set out rules of construction

1.4   If there shall be any conflict or inconsistency between any provision of this deed and any provision contained within a Security, the provisions of this deed shall prevail.

2.   **Consents**

2.1   Insofar as consent is required under the terms of any of the Securities or otherwise each of the Security Holders consents to the creation and continuance of each Security.

2.2   The Lender acknowledges the terms of the Agreement and consents to the Company entering or having entered into the Agreement (and such consent shall apply to any extension or variation thereto or replacement thereof) and agrees that all Debts and their Related Rights which are or shall be vested in TFL by virtue of the Agreement shall be free from the Lender's Security. The Lender will not challenge TFL's title to the Debts and their Related Rights. However if at any time the Lender gives TFL at least 30 days' notice of the cancellation of this deed, then the provisions of this deed shall not apply to and shall have no effect in respect of any Debts created by the Company after the expiry of such notice but shall remain in full force and effect in respect of any Debts created by the Company prior to the expiry of such notice.

2.3   For the avoidance of doubt, subject to Clause 2.2 the Lender's Security shall remain in full force and effect and any fixed charge on Debts and their Related Rights created by the Lender's Security shall apply to all Debts and their Related Rights which may at any time be re-assigned by TFL to the Company and shall also apply to any sums due from TFL to the Company from time to time.

2.4   In arriving at the amounts so payable by TFL to the Company pursuant to clause 2.3 above, TFL shall be entitled to exercise all defences, rights of set-off or combination of accounts or otherwise and whether actual or contingent which TFL may have against the Company and whether arising before or after TFL's receipt of any notice of cancellation under clause 2.2.

3.   **Priorities**

3.1   All receipts, recoveries and realisations pursuant to the enforcement of the Securities shall rank so that:

(a) in respect of the realisations of the Non-Vesting Debts they shall be applied:

(i) firstly in discharging the Company's obligations to TFL without limit; and thereafter
(ii) secondly in discharging the Company's obligations to the Lender;

(b) in respect of the realisation of assets (if any) listed in the Schedule hereto they shall be applied:

(i) firstly in discharging the Company's obligations to TFL without limit; and thereafter
(ii) secondly in discharging the Company's obligations to the Lender;

(c) in respect of the realisations of all the remaining assets (if any) of the Company, other than the Non-Vesting Debts and the assets listed in the Schedule hereto they shall be applied:

(i) firstly, in discharging the Company's obligations to the Lender, without limit; and thereafter
(ii) secondly, in discharging the Company's obligations to TFL.

3.2   The amount of any Receiver's remuneration and all outgoings, costs, charges, expenses, liabilities and payments ranking by statute for payment in priority to the amount secured by the Securities shall be deducted from all receipts and recoveries under the relevant Security prior to their application towards the discharge or satisfaction of the amounts secured by the Securities.

3.3   For the avoidance of doubt, each of the parties hereto agrees that the proceeds of any Debt whether created before or after the enforcement of any Security, and whether an asset of TFL or the Company shall constitute solely a realisation of a Debt (and as such shall be payable solely to TFL) and no part of any Debt shall be attributable to a realisation of any other asset of the Company.

3.4   Notwithstanding the provisions of clause 3.1 above, if all or any of the Securities shall be released or are or become wholly or partly invalid or unenforceable or shall not extend to particular assets of the Company then in such case each Security Holder shall rank as an unsecured creditor provided that each Security Holder shall not challenge the validity or enforceability of the Securities.

4.   **Continuing Security**

The Securities shall be continuing securities for repayment to the Security Holders of the money and liabilities thereby secured and the priority arrangements herein contained shall not be affected by any fluctuations in the amount from time to time due owing or incurred by the Company on any account to any of the Security Holders or by the existence at any time of a credit or nil balance on any such account of the Company with any Security Holder.

5.   **Enforcement of Security**

5.1   The Security Holders shall consult and co-operate with each other to the intent (without any requirement) that:

(a) the Securities shall so far as practicable be enforced by the same method and at the same time;

(b) in the case of an appointment of a Receiver or an Administrator by a Security Holder under its Security the same person shall be appointed Receiver or Administrator by the other Security Holder (if that other Security Holder shall also make such an appointment).

5.2   The provisions of clause 5.1 shall not affect clause 3.1 nor prevent any Security Holder from appointing a Receiver or an Administrator under its Security or from the exercise or enforcement of its Security or any rights thereunder or at law without any consultation if it considers it expedient to do so.

5.3   If any Security Holder shall appoint a Receiver or an Administrator under its Security or shall otherwise enforce or exercise its Security it shall promptly give written notice thereof to the other Security Holder.

6.   **Operation of Accounts**

6.1   Nothing in this deed or in TFL' Security or the Agreement shall prevent the Lender operating the bank accounts of the Company in the ordinary course of banking business including, without limitation, collecting cheques and other payment orders or accepting monies for credit of the Company's bank accounts and allowing the Company to draw cheques and other payments and generally to withdraw funds from its bank accounts or from exercising the Lender's rights to continue to set-off any credit balances against any liabilities the Company may have to the Lender.

6.2   TFL shall make no claim against the Lender in connection with any Debt and/or Related Rights the proceeds of which are credited to any account of the Company with the Lender and which proceeds are withdrawn, transferred or dealt with in any other way the Company may direct (other than any account in the name of the Company designated as in trust for TFL) unless:

(a) prior to Lender's receipt of such monies the Lender has received notice in writing from TFL that a specified sum of money belongs or will belong to TFL; such notice shall contain such information as the Lender may reasonably require to identify such monies in the day to day operation of the relative account in accordance with normal banking practice; or

(b) the Lender has procured the payment to the Lender of a sum which to the actual knowledge of the Lender should have been paid to TFL (and for the avoidance of doubt the Lenders awareness of the existence of the Agreement shall not be deemed to be actual knowledge that any payment or credit represents the proceeds of a specific Debt purchased by TFL).

In respect of (a) and (b) above, all monies received by the Lender in respect of such Debts shall be held by the Lender in trust for TFL subject to any law, regulation or court order.

7.   Floating Charges

7.1   For the avoidance of doubt, nothing contained within this deed operates to rank any floating charge contained within the Securities before any fixed charge contained within the Securities.

7.2   The Lender hereby confirms that it has taken no direct action to crystallise any floating charge contained within the Lender's Security nor is the Lender aware (without imposing any obligation of the Lender to make any positive enquiries or securities) that any such floating charge has crystallised.

8.   Continuing Effect

The priorities set forth above shall apply even though a liquidator or Receiver or an Administrator shall be appointed under the Insolvency Act 1986 in relation to the Company.

9.   Assignment

Neither of the Security Holders shall assign, transfer, charge or otherwise dispose of its Security or any of its rights or obligations under them to any person (a "Transferee") or agree or attempt to do so unless the Transferee shall first have agreed with the other Security Holder to adhere to and be bound by all the provisions of this deed affecting the other Security Holder including this clause 20.

10.   Law and Jurisdiction

10.1   This deed is governed by and shall be construed in accordance with English law.

10.2   The parties to this deed irrevocably submit to the exclusive jurisdiction of the English courts to settle any disputes which may arise out of or in connection with this deed.

Other clauses would deal with such matters as:

- *Mutual exchange of information about the client*
- *Client's acknowledgment of the priorities agreed between the financier and the bank*
- *Further rules of interpretation*
- *Service of notice*
- *Absence of rights for third parties*
- *Mutual access to records*

THE SCHEDULE

(Clause 3.1(b) – Other Assets for Priority to TFL)

Signed on behalf of all parties

Appendix 3

GUARANTEE AND INDEMNITY

TO: Top Financiers Ltd
        Percentage House
        Discount Street
        Moneytown
        Bankshire
        FAC1 1D

THE PARTICULARS

A.   **My Details:**
      Dell Bouy   (Full Names)
      Mon Repos   (Address)
      Hopetown
      Debtshire

B.   **Details of the Client:**
      Best Client Ltd   (Name)
      Dreamland Works   (Address)
      Hopetown
      Debtshire
      England and Wales   (Country of Registration)
      2000000   (Companies Registry Number)

C.   **Date of this Deed:** 1 January 200x

1.   I hereby:

      1.1   guarantee the due performance of all the obligations to you of the Client under the
             Agreement or any other agreement with you or any other form of obligation to you; and

      1.2   undertake immediately upon demand to pay to you all amounts now payable or which may
             at any time hereafter become payable to you by the Client, whether they arise under the
             Agreement or otherwise so that my obligations to you under this provision may be enforced
             against me at any time, without any prior demand on the Client; and

      1.3   undertake to pay you all costs and expenses (including legal costs on the basis of a full
             indemnity) incurred in enforcing or attempting to enforce either the terms hereof against me
             or the terms of any other guarantee and indemnity given by any other party in respect of the
             obligations of the Client to you.

2.   Without affecting Clause 1 above I will also indemnify you and hold you harmless against all Losses you may suffer or incur by reason of any failure of the Client to comply with any term or condition of the Agreement or of any other agreement with you or any other form of obligation to you.

3.   The guarantees and indemnities given herein shall be continuing obligations which shall apply to the ultimate amount payable by the Client. They shall not be discharged by any intermediate payment or satisfaction by the Client or the occurrence of a nil balance on any account.

4.   My liability under this guarantee and indemnity shall not be affected by:

       4.1   any indulgence granted or made by you to or with the Client, or any Customer; or

       4.2   any variation in the Agreement or in any other agreement between the Client and you (even if my liability to you is increased as a result) or by any defect therein or in their execution; or

       4.3   any failure by you to take or perfect any security from the Client or any other person or keep it unencumbered; or

       4.4   any change in the constitution of the Client;

       4.5   the absence of any intended guarantor or indemnifier for the Client's obligations to you

5.   I shall be liable to you in every respect as a principal debtor.

6.   If at any time there is a Co-Surety then my liability to you shall be joint and several and shall not be affected by:

       6.1   any Indulgence granted or made by you to or with any Co-Surety;

       6.2   any defect in the execution of any deed or document by any Co-Surety; or

       6.3   any defect in any other guarantee or indemnity or other security held by you in respect of the Client's obligations to you or in the execution thereof; or

       6.4   any notice of termination or the termination of any guarantee and/or indemnity given to you by any Co-Surety; or

       6.5   any limitation (whether or not I am aware of it) attached to the liability of any Co-Surety.

7.   I shall be liable to pay you interest on all sums demanded by you hereunder from me. Such interest shall accrue from day to day and be calculated at same rate as the discounting charge referred to in the Agreement. It shall run, from the date of your demand to the date when payment is received by you, both before and after any judgment. Interest will be compounded on the last day of each month.

8.   As security for the due performance of my obligations hereunder:

   8.1   I hereby assign to you the Client's present and future indebtedness to me;

   8.2   I irrevocably appoint you, your directors, Company Secretary and officers for the time being jointly and each of them severally to be my attorneys to execute in my name such documents and to do such other things as you or they may consider requisite in order to perfect your ownership of and to collect any such indebtedness or to collect any dividend or to vote in respect of such right of proof.

9.   In the event of the winding up or other form of insolvency of the Client, any monies received by you by virtue of or in connection with this guarantee and indemnity may be placed by you to the credit of a suspense account with a view to your preserving your right to prove or vote for the whole of your claim against the Client.

10.   For the purpose of determining my liability under this guarantee and indemnity (which shall be additional to and not in substitution for any other security taken or to be taken by you in respect of the Client's obligations to you) I shall be bound by any acknowledgement or admission by the Client and by any judgment in your favour against the Client. For such purpose and for determining either the amount payable to you by the Client or the amount of any Losses I shall accept and be bound by a certificate signed by any of your directors. In any proceedings such certificate shall be treated as conclusive evidence (except for manifest error) of the amounts so payable or of any Losses. In arriving at the amount payable to you by the Client or of any Losses you shall be entitled to take into account all liabilities (whether actual or contingent) and to make a reasonable estimate of any liability where its amount cannot immediately be ascertained.

11.   Any discharge given by you to me in respect of my obligations under this guarantee and indemnity shall be treated as being void and of no effect if any security taken from or payment made by the Client or any other person, which had been taken into account by you in giving the discharge, is subsequently avoided or reduced by or in pursuance of any provision of law or legal process. This deed shall remain your property even though my obligations to you are discharged.

12.   This guarantee and indemnity shall remain in full force and effect until the expiry of not less than three months written notice, from me to you of its termination delivered to your registered office (and acknowledged by you) no earlier than the ending of the Agreement (and if the Agreement comprises more than one agreement the last such ending). However the termination of this guarantee and indemnity shall not affect my liability for any obligation of the Client arising out of any transaction having its inception before the expiry of my notice.

13.   Any notice or demand on me shall be validly given or made if handed to me or, if delivered to or sent by post, to the address stated in section A of the Particulars or my address last known to you. If sent by post it can be treated as being received by me within seventy-two hours of posting.

14.   I shall not be entitled to be subrogated to any securities held by you for the performance of the Client's obligations to you until I have discharged my obligations to you nor will you be obliged to enforce such securities for my benefit.

15.   You may disclose this and other information supplied by me to any member or associated company of the Primel Bank plc's group of companies ("Group") or to any person acting on my behalf for any purpose connected with the Group's business. You and the Group may also use my name and address to mail me about services which may be of interest to me. I may advise you that I do not wish to be included in such mailings.

16.   This guarantee and indemnity is governed by English law. I accept the non-exclusive jurisdiction of the English Courts. If any provision hereof shall be invalid or unenforceable no other provisions hereof shall be affected. All such other provisions shall remain in full force and effect. This document contains all terms agreed as to my liability to you as a guarantor and indemnifier of the Client's obligations to you. All prior negotiations, warranties, offers and representations shall be of no effect unless set out in this document.

17.   In this deed except where the context otherwise requires:

(1) the singular includes the plural and vice versa and any gender includes any other; and

(2) any words or phrases which are defined in the Agreement have the same meaning assigned to them herein and any form of construction used in the Agreement is to be used herein; and

(3) the following words and expressions have the meanings given to them below:

"Agreement"

any agreement between the Client and you for the sale and purchase of debts or other financial accommodation as amended, varied, replaced or added from time to time and whether before or after the date of this deed;

"Client"

the company whose name and address appears in section B of the above particulars;

"Co-Surety"

any person (other than myself) giving a guarantee and/or indemnity for any obligations of the Client to you;

"Indulgence"

the grant of any time or indulgence or the conclusion of any agreement not to sue or of any compromise or composition or the release of any charge lien or other security or any part thereof;

"Losses"

losses, costs, damages, claims, interest and expenses;

"Particulars"

the particulars at paragraphs A to C above.

IN WITNESS whereof the Guarantor and Indemnifier has executed this document as a deed and delivered it on the date stated in paragraph C of the Particulars.

Declaration on behalf of Guarantor and Indemnifier

I confirm that before I signed this document and in relation to its nature, meaning, effect and risks:

(1) I was recommended to take independent legal advice; and

(2) I have taken or have had the opportunity to take independent legal advice.

I confirm that I fully understand the obligations placed upon me following my signature **(and in particular that my liability to you has no financial limit). I have signed this deed of my own free will without duress or undue influence.

I declare that in deciding to sign this guarantee and indemnity I have not placed any reliance upon any advice, opinion or representation of (i) any person having any interest in the Client whether by reason of directorship, shareholding or employment, or (ii) any other representative or agent of the Client, or (iii) you or any representative or agent of yours or of any company in the Prime Bank plc's group of companies.

SIGNED and DELIVERED by ***DELL A. BOUY**)
in the presence of:-

_____ (signature of witness)   )

_____ (full name of witness)   )   Signature of

_____ (address of witness)   )   Guarantor

_____   )   and Indemnifier

_____   )

_____ (occupation of witness)   )

*   insert name of Guarantor and Indemnifier
**   N.B. delete words in brackets if there is a limit

Appendix 4

BASIC CONTRACT LAW FOR FINANCIERS

WHAT IS A CONTRACT ?

A contract is an agreement made between two or more parties that is binding in law.

Such an agreement gives rise to rights and obligations that may be enforced in the courts. The normal method of enforcement is an action for damages for breach of contract, although in some cases the court may compel performance of the contract by the party who is in default ("an action for specific performance").

TYPES OF CONTRACT

Contracts can be classified as either:-

"Contracts By Deed"

This must be written, signed, witnessed and delivered. No "consideration" *(see later)* is necessary in order for the contract to be enforceable.

"Simple Contracts"

All other contracts, whether written, oral or arising out of conduct of the parties. *e.g. Taking your seat on a bus enters you into an implied contract to pay your fare.*

The rest of these notes will deal only with simple contracts. A separate section will deal with the special features of contracts involving the sale of goods.

SKELETAL OUTLINE OF A SIMPLE CONTRACT

In order to form a valid simple contract:

1.   the parties must have reached an agreement by means of an offer by one party and acceptance of such offer by the other party;

2.   they must intend to be legally bound;

3.   both parties must have provided valuable consideration; and

4.   the parties must have a legal capacity/ability to contract (e.g. not insane or infants);

In some cases, there must be compliance with certain formalities, particularly as to documentation, (e.g. contracts subject to Consumer Credit Act 1974). A contract consists of various terms, both those expressly set out in the contract and those implied by law or conduct. The most commonly found implied terms are those set out in the Sale of Goods Act 1979. (see separate notes). A term may be inserted into the contract to exclude or restrict one party's liability but only to the extent permitted by law. i.e. some exclusions are prohibited in certain contracts. *(see later about Unfair Contract Terms Act 1977).*

A contract may be invalidated by:

    (a) mistake
    (b) illegality
    (c) misrepresentation
    (d) duress
    (e) undue influence

Offer and Acceptance

A simple contract comprises an offer and an unqualified acceptance of the offer:

e.g. a bus company sends its buses along an advertised route to stop at advertised points – this is an implied offer to take you along the route. If you get on the bus at a stop – this is the implied acceptance of the offer obliging you to pay the fare.

The offer:

- must be communicated to the other party before it can be accepted;
- can usually only be accepted by the person to whom it is made;
- must be unequivocal and not vague.

The following are not "offers":

1.   Invitation to treat, i.e. where a person merely invites offers which he is then free to accept or reject, e.g.:

    (a) Display of goods in a shop window with prices marked upon them. (This is not an offer to sell the goods at that or any other price).

    (b) Advertisements/circulars/catalogues and price lists.

    (c) Invitations to tender. The party submitting the most favourable tender does not thereby enter into a contract.

2.   A statement of intention:

e.g. if a person goes to a concert venue having seen an advertisement with an intention of buying his ticket on arrival then if the concert is cancelled, there can be no action for breach of contract.

3.   A communication of information:

e.g. a statement of the minimum price at which one is prepared to consider negotiating the sale of a piece of land.

Termination of Offer

An offer can be withdrawn before acceptance, or be treated as being withdrawn if not accepted within a reasonable time.

Acceptance

Until it is accepted, an offer has no legal effect. An acceptance may be by word of mouth, in writing or implied from conduct. If a particular form of acceptance is required by the offer, then the acceptance must be in that form:

e.g. if the contract states that acceptance must be "by post to our registered offices not later than 12 noon on Monday 25 September 2007" this does not allow the contract to be accepted orally or in writing on 29 September 2007.

An acceptance must be unqualified and must correspond with the terms of the offer. A conditional acceptance or counter offer rejects the original offer and causes it to fail.

e.g. "I will buy at your price but subject to an engineer's inspection" is not a valid acceptance.

There must be active acceptance. i.e. a positive communication of acceptance.

e.g. a person cannot be deemed to have accepted an offer merely by his inactivity.

So, when unrequested goods are sent to a private individual, they will belong to him after six months, provided he remains silent. (Unsolicited Goods and Services Acts 1972 and 1975.).

Normally, an acceptance is valid only when communicated to the person making offer ("offeror"). There are exceptions to this as follows:

1.   Where the offeror waives communication either expressly or impliedly:

       e.g. when a general offer only requires conduct as acceptance, such as the acceptance of offer for sale of a debt under factoring agreement by crediting the debt to the debts purchased ledger.

2.   Where the contract is made by post, or post is envisaged as the means of communication, then acceptance is complete as soon as it is posted, provided that it is properly stamped and addressed. i.e. The other party will be bound even though he has no knowledge that the acceptance has been posted to him.

CONSIDERATION

In addition to offer and acceptance, and an intention to be legally bound, a further essential element for a simple contract (i.e. not by deed) is "consideration" (which is often money or the promise to pay money). English law will not enforce a "bare" promise not supported by consideration.

       e.g. if 'A' ("promisor") promises to repair the car of 'B' this promise can only be enforceable by B as a contract if B provides some form of "consideration". Such consideration would normally take the form of a promise by B to pay money to A. However, it could consist of some other service provided by B to which A might agree. Accordingly, 'B' as the recipient of the promise has to give something in return in order to convert a bare promise made in his favour into a binding contract.

FORMALITIES

It is often thought that contracts must be in writing. This is wrong. As a general rule, no specific written formality is required to render a contract valid and enforceable. However, there are exceptions:

1.   Certain contracts which must be by deed (until 1990 with a seal but now merely declared to be by deed and signed and witnessed). The most important for financiers is a power of attorney. Because factoring agreements contain a power of attorney from the Client this is the reason that they are signed as deeds.

2.   Certain contracts must be in writing, including contracts of guarantee. (Statute of Frauds 1677).

CERTAINTY NEEDED

A contract must be clear in intention. A so called contract is ineffective and unenforceable if:

*   it only agrees to contract to the future ("an agreement to agree"); or
*   it only agrees to negotiate a price later; or
*   it contains vague terms, such as "on credit terms".

However a contract will be enforceable:

1.   where both parties to the contract have agreed a formula for resolving uncertainties:

        e.g. they agree to be bound by an arbitrator's or expert's decision

2.   where terms are implied, either by previous usage between the parties or in the specific trade or by statute which are known as "implied terms":

        e.g. where a contract for the sale of goods does not state a price, the Sale of Goods Act 1979 provides that a "reasonable price" must be paid

3.   even if it has some meaningless terms, provided that the main thrust of the contract is clear.

CONDITIONS AND WARRANTIES

A "condition" is an important term of the contract, breach of which entitles the party injured to consider himself no longer bound to perform his side together with a right for damages.

A "warranty" is a less important contractual term, breach of which does not discharge the contract and gives a right only to a claim for damages.

Merely describing a term as a condition is not conclusive if, in fact, it is a warranty and vice versa. As to whether a term is a condition or warranty, depends upon the intention of the parties.

EXCLUSION CLAUSES

It is essential that any exclusion of liability must be written in clearly understandable words. The "Contra Proferentum Rule" has been developed by the courts. i.e. any lack of clarity in an exclusion clause will be construed as narrowly as possible against the party trying to rely on the clause.

Exclusion clauses must not attack the purpose of the contract. The courts will also strike down any exclusion clause which appears to defeat the main purpose of the contract.

Unfair Contract Terms Act 1977

There are also statutory restrictions on the use of some exclusion clauses e.g there can be no exclusion of liability for death or personal injury resulting from negligence. e.g. from defective goods sold.

This Act does not apply to the contracts for:
(a) property transactions
(b) insurance contracts
(c) transactions of a private nature

Where a party either:

(a)   "deals as a consumer"; or
(b)   in whatever capacity (including a business capacity) ***deals on the other party's written standard terms of business***

then the other party cannot exclude or restrict his liability for breach of contract except to the extent that such exclusion satisfies the requirement of "reasonableness". ***Remember that a factoring agreement would be considered as being on written standard terms.*** Any terms restricting the financier's liability for failing to perform the agreement must be reasonable.

A person "deals as a consumer" if he does not contract in the course of a business and the other party does contract in the course of a business. Where a person deals as a consumer, the following implied terms in the Sale of Goods Act *(see later)* cannot be excluded:

(a)   description
(b)   suitability for purpose
(c)   satisfactory quality

Where a person does not deal as a consumer, exclusion of the three above implied terms has to satisfy the test of "reasonableness". Guidelines as to reasonableness are set out in of the Act and include:

(a)   The strength of the bargaining positions of the party relevant to each other taking into account the availability of another source of supply.
(b)   Any inducement to agree to the terms.
(c)   Whether the customer ought to have known of the existence and extent of the terms.
(d)   Whether the goods were manufactured, processed or adapted to the special order of the customer.

In contracts for the sale of goods implied terms as to title cannot be excluded or restricted by contract *(whether the buyer is a consumer or business purchaser)*.

If a contract attempts to restrict the liability of a party for pre-contract misrepresentations or restrict the remedies available to the other party for misrepresentation then such terms shall be effective only to the extent that they are considered reasonable under the Unfair Contract Terms Act 1977. Whilst most factoring and ID agreements attempt to avoid liability for statements made during negotiations they may not be effective if the exclusion is unfair under the above rules. Salesmen should be careful with their promises.

DURESS AND UNDUE INFLUENCE

If an agreement has been entered into as a result of improper pressure (either duress or undue influence) which one party has exerted over the other the contract will be set aside. However, duress need not be the only or main reason for entering into the contract. Duress has been defined as "coercion of the will" such that there was no consent. Any pressure or coercion, falling short of the very strict rules of duress, such as threats against property, moral pressure or any other improper pressure, may be considered as "undue influence". It must be remembered that where a contract is tainted with duress or undue influence, it is merely a voidable contract (i.e. it continues as a valid contract until the injured party asks for it to be rescinded).

Guarantors sometimes allege that co-guarantors coerced them into signing guarantees in favour of a Financier.

DISCHARGE OF CONTRACTS

The discharge of a contract relieves a party wholly or in part from further performing his side of the bargain. Contracts can be discharged by:

> (a) performance
> (b) agreement
> (c) operation of law
> (d) under the doctrine of frustration
> (e) breach

Discharge by Performance of Contract

A contract is most usually discharged when performed exactly in accordance with the terms and conditions of the contract. But what amounts to full performance? This is an important question because the price of goods often does not become payable until the contract is fully performed.

A part performance, even if it is of the bulk of the contract, will not constitute a discharge, except:-

> (a) where performance is prevented by the other party; or
> (b) where partial performance is freely accepted by the other party; or
> (c) where the contract is divided into instalments and the parties agree that each delivery is to be separately paid for; or
> (d) where the performance has been substantial, i.e. where the contract is as complete as any reasonable man could expect, despite being not strictly in accord with the agreement. This is a matter of fact, not opinion.

Discharge by Agreement

A contract may be discharged or varied by agreement. If, however, one of the parties makes an alteration to what he does under the contract without the permission of the other, then the contract is discharged automatically and an action for damages may arise.

Discharge under Doctrine of Frustration

A contract will be discharged automatically if, without fault of either party, some event occurs rendering performance an impossibility or the contract becomes illegal or there is a radical change in the circumstances so that the contract becomes totally different from that which was originally undertaken. Examples:-

(a) *Impossibility e.g. the subject matter is destroyed or becomes unavailable.*

(b) *Illegality e.g. trading with the enemy on outbreak of war.*

(c) *Radical change in the circumstances e.g. letting a room solely to view the Coronation, which was then cancelled.*

The doctrine of frustration cannot be relied upon if:-

(a) the frustration is self induced; or

(b) there is express provision in the contract to this effect; or

(c) the event is foreseen or should have been foreseen by one of the parties.

Discharge by Breach of Contract

Breach of contract happens when one of the parties:

(a) denies his obligations; or

(b) fails to perform his part of the contract; or

(c) disables himself from fulfilling the contract.

Such breach can be a breach of warranty or condition. Where there is a breach of warranty (a less important term), the contract continues and the injured party can only sue for damages. Where there is a breach of condition (an important term), the innocent party, in addition to claiming damages, may treat himself as discharged from the contact. This is described as a "repudiatory breach". i.e. he is not bound to complete the contract. However, the innocent party does not have to treat the contract as discharged and may rely solely on his right to damages.

Anticipatory Breach

This is where one party shows that he does not intend to perform his part of the contract, in which case the other party can either sue for breach of contract at once ("accept the repudiation") or may await the due date for performance and hold the other party to the contract, thereby preserving his rights as the innocent party.

DAMAGES

Calculation. Damages are intended to put the injured party into the same position as if the contract had been properly performed and this can include pre-contractual expenses.

Remoteness. However, the plaintiff cannot recover all damages if the court considers that some would be too "remote". i.e. not in the contemplation of the parties at the time of contract.

Mitigation. The loss is not too remote, the injured party must take all reasonable steps to minimise any loss caused by the breach of contract.

Penalty Clauses. If a contract contains a clause providing for payment of a specific sum upon breach (e.g. cancellation charges in a holiday contract), this is only recoverable if it represents a genuine "pre-estimate of the loss". If it is not a genuine pre-estimate, but is more in the nature of a penalty to compel performance, then it will be treated as invalid and the plaintiff may only recover his actual damages.

Appendix 5

BASIC LAW OF THE SALE OF GOODS and SERVICES FOR FINANCIERS

INTRODUCTION

Statutory Provisions

People constantly buy and sell goods or services and rarely think through the consequences of what they are doing. Accordingly the Common Law relating to sale of goods and services has mostly been codified in:

(a) Sale of Goods Act 1979. ("SGA 1979").
(b) Supply of Goods and Services Act 1982. ("SGSA 1982").These provide a raft of presumptions about the transfer of ownership, delivery, payment of the price etc. to cover the absence of express agreement between the parties. The SGA 1979 covers the "sale of goods" which is defined as a contract under which the seller transfers or agrees to transfer the ownership of goods to a buyer for a monetary consideration called the price.

The SGSA 1982 applies when a contract is for "work done and the supply of materials".

Tests

The test as to which Act applies is whether the essential object of the agreement is the provision of goods or the exercise of skill. If skill, then SGSA 1982 applies. eg. if a plasterer is employed to plaster a wall, the contract is for work and materials and is covered by the SGSA 1982.

Contracts of barter are also covered by the SGSA 1982 as no money changes hands.

Contrary Intent

The SGA 1979 allows parties to contract contrary to its terms, either:

(a) by express agreement; or
(b) by a prior course of dealing between the parties; or
(c) by trade custom and usage.

But under the Unfair Contract Terms Act 1977, the right to contract out of the implied terms as to title/fitness for purpose/satisfactory quality/sale by description has been severely cut down.

The SGSA 1982 contains similar implied terms in relation to goods supplied under contracts for work and materials/barter/or hire as to title, fitness and purpose, merchantable quality and description as under the SGA 1979. *(see later)*. Likewise, contractual terms seeking to exclude liability for breach of implied terms under SGSA 1982 are subject to the provisions of the Unfair Contract Terms Act 1977.

TERMS IMPLIED INTO A CONTRACT BY SGA 1979

Time

Unless a different intention appears from the terms of the contract, stipulations as to time of payment are not deemed to be "of the essence" in a contract of sale of goods. Whether any other stipulation as to time (e.g. as to delivery) is of the essence in the contract depends upon the terms of the contract. In business transactions, stipulations as to the time of delivery are usually held to be of the essence.

Title (i.e. ownership)

In every contract for the sale of goods, whether commercial or private, there is implied:

(a) a condition on the part of the seller that he has the right to sell or that he will have such a right at the time that property (i.e. ownership) in the goods has to pass to the buyer;
(b) a warranty that the goods will remain free from any undisclosed encumbrances (such as liens, pledges or mortgages); and
(c) a warranty that the buyer will enjoy quiet possession of the goods, except as to encumbrances made known to the buyer before the making of the contract.

e.g. if the vendor buys a car from a thief and the car has to be restored to the true owner, the purchaser is entitled to reclaim the entire purchase price from the thieving vendor.

Description

Where the contract, whether commercial or private, is for sale of "goods by description", then a condition is implied that the goods will correspond with the description.

e.g. If a car is sold after being advertised as a "2001 BMW Convertible" but comprises the rear half of such a vehicle welded to the front half of an earlier model, then damages for breach of the implied term in the contract as to description would be available.

A sale by description includes cases where the buyer:

(a) has not seen the goods *(e.g. newspaper advertisement or a catalogue)*;
(b) has seen them but buys them by reference to description which he relies upon.

If the sale is by sample, as well as by description, then the bulk of the goods must correspond with both the sample and with the description. The "description" may include such matters as measurements, methods of packing or quantity.

The vendor may ensure that transaction is not a sale by description by including phrases such as *"bought as seen"*.

Quality and Suitability

The general rule of law is "let the buyer beware". There is no implied warranty or condition as to the quality or fitness for any particular purpose for goods supplied unless either:-

(a) there is a trade usage to this effect; or
(b) such a term is implied by Sale of Goods Act 1977 as below:-.

Satisfactory Quality

Where the seller sells goods in the course of a business, there is an implied condition that the goods shall be of "satisfactory quality" except:-

(a) for defects specifically drawn to the buyer's attention before the contract is made; or
(b) where the buyer examines the goods before the contract, in which case there is no condition implied as to defects which that examination ought to have revealed.

"Satisfactory quality" is defined by the Act as meeting "the standard that a reasonable person would regard as satisfactory taking account of any description of the goods, the price (if relevant) and all other relevant circumstances.

> *e.g. a brand new washing machine should wash your clothes properly, new shoes should not fall apart on first outing, a meat pie purchased for lunch should not make you ill, a second hand "enthusiasts car" should not have previously been written off after having been submerged in water for 24 hours.*

Goods must remain of satisfactory quality for a reasonable time. Where perishable goods are sent to the buyer, they must generally remain satisfactory throughout a normal journey and for a reasonable time thereafter.

SGA 1979 says that the quality of goods includes their state and condition and then gives a list of some relevant aspects. These are:

(a) fitness for purpose
(b) appearance and finish
(c) freedom from minor defects
(d) safety
(e) durability

We shall now examine the effect of these quality aspects.

Fitness For Purpose

Where the seller sells goods *in the course of a business,* there is an implied condition that the goods are reasonably fit for any purpose made known to the seller by the buyer (except where the circumstances show that the buyer does not rely, or that it is unreasonable for him to rely, on the seller's skill and judgment) whether or not it is a purpose for which such goods are commonly supplied. This also applies to second hand goods.

Disputes mostly arise as to whether the buyer made the purpose known to the seller. This condition does not apply if the buyer did not rely on the seller's skill and judgment, nor if it was unreasonable for the buyer to so rely.

> *N.B. If buyer asks for an item under its brand name or lays down detailed specification of requirements, this would make it difficult to prove he relied upon the seller's skill.*

These provisions impose a strict liability on the seller who is liable even if someone else, such as the manufacturer, is at fault.

Terms implied in a Sale By Sample

A sale by sample occurs where there is a term in the contract to that effect. The mere exhibition of a sample, during the negotiation of a contract, does not of itself constitute the contract as one for sale by sample.

In both business and private sales, where there is a sale by sample then the following conditions are implied:

   (a) the bulk will correspond with the sample in quality; and
   (b) the buyer will have a reasonable opportunity of comparing the bulk with a sample; and
   (c) that the goods will be free from any defect causing them not to be of satisfactory quality which
         would not be apparent on reasonable examination of the sample.

If the goods do not correspond with the sample, it is no defence to the seller that by a simple process, they can be made to do so.

WHO BEARS THE RISK OF LOSS OR DAMAGE TO GOODS?

Prima facie, the risk of accidental loss or damage passes when ownership passes. This is important where goods are in transit from the seller to the buyer. The buyer bears the risk of damage during the journey. He cannot complain if the goods arrive damaged. This rule may be varied by agreement or by trade usage so that the seller then has to replace the goods or provide compensation.

However, if delivery is delayed by the fault of either party *(e.g. if buyer wrongfully refuses to give delivery instructions)* then the goods remain at the risk of the defaulting party as regards any loss caused by delay even if ownership has not passed e.g. because of a reservation of title clause.

RESERVATION OF TITLE ("ROT")

ROT is a contractual device which takes advantage of s.19 SGA 1979. This section provides that where the seller has reserved the right of disposal of the goods by the buyer until some condition is fulfilled then ownership of the goods will not pass to the buyer until that condition is met. This is so despite delivery to the buyer or to a carrier or to anyone else for the purpose of transporting them to the buyer. ***The most common condition which is imposed is that ownership does not pass until the goods are paid for.***

The result is that a seller can retrieve his goods and resell them if the buyer defaults in paying for them e.g. because of the buyer's insolvency. A retention of title clause was held to be valid in the case of Aluminium Industrie Vaassen v Romalpa Aluminium Ltd (1976) and since then retention of title clauses have also been known as "Romalpa clauses".

Insolvency practitioners acting for insolvent buyers never accept at face value claims to repossess goods by unpaid sellers. They:

(a) look at the ROT clause in the contract and analyse its scope;
(b) question whether it is incorporated in the parties' contract; and
(c) consider whether the goods held by the buyer are the ones covered by ROT.

Simplest clause:

"Full legal title to the goods shall not pass to the customer until they have been paid for in full".

However, if goods are onward sold by a buyer who has possession of the goods, the original seller loses his rights to repossess goods under an ROT clause. This is because SGA 1979 entitles a buyer with possession of goods with the consent of the seller to effect an onward sale to a bona fide purchaser without notice of the ROT. But if the buyer with possession of the goods onward sells under the buyer's own ROT provisions then the original seller can repossess from the end customer if he has not paid the insolvent buyer. This is the "Highway Foods Principle" of double ROT. It puts a Financier at risk of an uncollectable debt, if it has factored the debt due by the end customer from an insolvent Client selling on such double ROT terms. The original seller can collect the goods from the end debtor who does not have to pay the factor.

ROT is best effected on goods with serial numbers or bar codes. Otherwise if the buyer obtains goods of the same type from a variety of different sources the seller will be unable to tell which are the ones he delivered and will lose his claim.

ROT can be drafted with an "all monies clause" i.e. ownership of any goods sold and paid for will not pass to the buyer until all other goods supplied by the same seller have been paid for. Sample wording:

"Title in the goods shall not pass to the customer until all sums due from the customer to the supplier on any account have been paid".

Attempts to trace and reclaim the goods into which the sale goods are converted *(e.g. raw materials into a carpet)* or to trace the proceeds of sale are likely to be struck down by courts because:

    (a) where the buyer is a company, by determining that it creates a security charge over goods or proceeds of sale, which is therefore unenforceable for non-registration at Companies House; or

    (b) that the tracing remedy is unavailable either because:
        (i) the necessary fiduciary relationship is lacking; or
        (ii) where sale goods have been reprocessed, the goods originally supplied have lost their specific identity.

The courts are unhappy about a seller trying to assert ownership over something which he has not owned before (i.e. the newly produced goods).

In order for the seller to reclaim goods under ROT it is important that the seller writes into the contract that he has the right to enter the buyer's premises in order to collect.

Financiers take care that under their factoring agreements their clients' rights as unpaid sellers are also transferred to them. If a debtor becomes insolvent, the factor can then claim the return of identifiable goods sold on ROT.

PERFORMANCE OF THE CONTRACT

It is the duty of the seller to deliver the goods and of the buyer to accept and pay for them. The parties are free to make their own specific arrangements as to delivery and payment. If they do not specify the arrangements then SGA 1979 sets out their obligations, which are summarised below:

Delivery

It is the duty of the seller to deliver the goods and of the buyer to accept and pay for them in accordance with the terms of the contract. *Payment of the price and delivery of the goods must take place at the same time unless otherwise agreed. i.e. the seller can hold onto goods until they are paid for unless credit terms have agreed.*

Credit is a negotiated privilege, not a right.

"Delivery" in the context of the SGA 1979 means *"the voluntary transfer of possession from one person to another"*. Delivery may consist of:

    (a) physically handing over the goods; or
    (b) handing over the means of control of the goods, e.g. keys to warehouse where stored; or
    (c) transferring documents of title; or
    (d) where goods are in possession of a third party, an acknowledgment by the third party that he is holding goods on behalf of the buyer.

If nothing else has been agreed then *the place of delivery is the seller's place of business, if he has one, otherwise his residence.*

A seller who has agreed to deliver to the buyer's premises will discharge his obligations by delivering at those premises to a person apparently having authority to receive the goods, (even though such person is not actually authorised).

If the contract is for specific goods, which to the knowledge of the parties at the time of making the contract are in some place other than the above, then such place shall be the place of delivery. If the goods are in the possession of a third person, there is no delivery until such third person acknowledges to the buyer that he holds the goods on his behalf.

Where the seller delivers to the buyer a quantity of goods less than he contracted to sell, the buyer may reject them. If the buyer accepts the goods so delivered, he must pay for them at the contract rate.

The courts will not take into account trivial or microscopic variations. The seller can always protect himself by incorporating into the contract the expressions "about" or "more or less".

In the absence of a specific agreement no buyer need accept delivery of goods by instalments. Where, however, there is an agreement for instalment deliveries, it is important to know whether it is an indivisible or severable contract. It will only be a severable contract if it is agreed that each delivery is treated as a separate contract and each instalment is to be separately paid for. i.e. part delivery of an indivisible contract gives no right to payment.

Acceptance by the Buyer

If the buyer accepts the goods, he forfeits his right to reject them as not in accordance with the contract. He accepts them:

(a) when he informs the seller that he has accepted them; or
(b) when he does any act in relation to the goods inconsistent with the seller's ownership, (e.g. sub-selling goods or using the raw materials); or
(c) when, after the lapse of a reasonable time, he retains the goods without telling the seller that he has rejected the goods.

What is a "reasonable time" as a question of fact?

Where goods are delivered which the buyer has not previously examined, he cannot be treated as having accepted them until he has had a reasonable opportunity of examining them to find out whether they are in accordance with the contract.

Where the buyer lawfully refuses to accept goods, e.g. because of short delivery he is not bound, in the absence of contrary agreement, to return them to the seller. It is sufficient to tell the seller that he refuses to accept them and the seller must then pick them up.

If the buyer refuses to take delivery within a reasonable time when requested to do so, he is liable to the seller for any loss and any reasonable charge for looking after the goods.

REMEDIES FOR BREACH OF CONTRACT FOR SALE OF GOODS

A seller who is not paid has these "personal" remedies against the buyer:
> (a) he can sue for the price provided ownership has passed or the date for payment has passed; or
> (b) he can sue for damages for non-acceptance where the buyer wrongfully neglects or refuses to accept and pay for goods; the seller is expected to mitigate his loss by selling elsewhere.

The unpaid seller has these "real" remedies against the goods:

> (a) he can exercise a lien i.e. right to retain possession (but not to sell them) until payment;
> (b) he can stop the goods in transit to the buyer, regain possession and retain them until paid;
> (c) he can exercise a right of resale if:
>   (i)   the goods are perishable; or
>   (ii) the seller gives the buyer notice of his intention to resell and the buyer does not pay within a reasonable time; or
>   (iii) the right of resale has been expressly reserved by the contract in the event of the buyer's default.

After resale, damages for loss can also be obtained.

Buyer's remedies for breach of contract

The first question to ask is whether the express term that has been broken is a warranty or a condition:

> (a) if it is a condition – the buyer can treat the contract as discharged, reject the goods and claim damages or affirm the contract and claim damages only.
> (b) if it is a warranty – the buyer can only claim damages.

If it is a term implied by SGA, then it is a condition that has been broken,

Rejection of goods

The buyer may repudiate the contract and reject the goods where the seller is in breach of a condition. The right to reject is lost as soon as goods have been accepted *(see above)* and he must then limit his claim only to damages.

Damages

An action for damages is available:

(a) where the seller wrongfully neglects or refuses to deliver goods - any deposits are recoverable; or
(b) where the seller is in breach of a warranty; or
(c) where the seller is in breach of a condition but the buyer has chosen to carry on with the contract and claim damages instead; or
(d) where the right to reject the goods has been lost.

Damages for breach of the condition of satisfactory quality could include:

- cost of repairs or
- extra cost of having to buy goods elsewhere
- damages for personal injury

Action for "Specific Performance"

In an action for breach of contract to deliver specific or ascertained goods the court may, if it thinks fit, order specific performance of the contract either unconditionally or subject to such conditions as to damages, payment of the price or otherwise as the court may seem just. Specific performance will only be granted where damages would be an inadequate remedy. Usually only granted where similar goods are not available elsewhere.

IMPLIED TERMS IN A SERVICE CONTRACT

Where services are supplied under a contract, to which the SGSA 1982 applies, then the supplier must:

(a) provide the service with reasonable skill and care, *(e.g. dry cleaners will not damage your clothes)*.
(b) carry out the service in a reasonable time, if none is fixed by the contract, *(e.g. your car will be serviced by a garage within days, not months)*;
(c) make a reasonable charge if the cost is not fixed by the contract.

Breach gives rise to a claim for damages.

SALE OR SUPPLY OF GOODS – OTHER CLAIMS

The above notes explain the rights under contract law if the goods are defective goods or services are sub-standard. So how does an injured party otherwise obtain recompense from a manufacturer from whom he did not buy the goods. The law is clear that a person putting defective goods into circulation will incur liability to non contracting parties for his products:

(a) in the tort of negligence; or
(b) strict liability under the Consumer Protection Act 1987 (CPA); or
(c) for breach of statutory duty under the Consumer Protection Act 1987.

NEGLIGENCE

Under the principles established in Donoghue -v- Stevenson (1932) - ("Snail in ginger beer bottle case") the plaintiff who suffers damages must prove:

    (a) the defendant owed a legal "duty of care" to the plaintiff;
    (b) the defendant was in breach of this duty;
    (c) as a result of which the plaintiff suffered injury or loss.

A manufacturer may defeat a claim or secure a reduction in damages by showing an accident was caused wholly or partly by the consumer's own negligence – called, "contributory negligence".

STRICT LIABILITY – CIVIL

Consumer Protection Act 1987 – introduces strict liability for personal injury and damage to private property caused by defective products. If proven then damages are payable. Negligence is not necessary. This overcomes the difficulties of "thalidomide" type cases. The "producer" is usually the defendant and is:-

    (a) the manufacturer of the product; or
    (b) the person who obtained or abstracted the product *(e.g. mining company);* or
    (c) the processor *(e.g. canning company).*

Persons responsible for paying damages are:

    (a) "producer" of the product; or
    (b) any person putting their name on the product e.g. *own branders;* or
    (c) any person who imports the product into EU in course of business; or
    (d) where the producer cannot be identified then any person who supplied the product *e.g. retailers or wholesalers who cannot identify the manufacturer, importer or own branders.*

Thus, factors who sell repossessed goods should be safe so long as they keep records identifying the source of the goods.

Defences to a claim include any of the following:

    (a) defect attributable to compliance with UK or EEC legislation (but not British Standards);
    (b) product never supplied;
    (c) product not supplied in course of a business or for profit;
    (d) defect did not exist in product at relevant time;
    (e) state of scientific and technical knowledge at the time was such that producer could not have been expected to discover the defect;
    (f) contributory negligence by plaintiff.

N.B.   *Liability cannot be excluded by contract.*

Strict Liability – Criminal

Consumer Protection Act 1987

It is a criminal offence to supply consumer goods which fail to comply with general safety requirements. The Secretary of State can take action in respect of unsafe goods already in the market. The Act also provides a civil remedy for a consumer who has suffered loss or damage as a result of a trader's failure to comply with safety regulations.

TRADE DESCRIPTIONS AND PRICES

Under Trade Description Act 1968 it is a criminal offence for a person in the course of trade or a business:

(a) to apply a false trade description to any goods or supplying goods to which a false trade description is applied; or
(b) knowingly or recklessly to make a false statement in respect of the provision of services, accommodation or facilities.

Consumer Protection Act 1987

It is an offence in the course of a business to give a misleading price indication. Compensation orders can be made following a conviction.

REMEDIES AGAINST THE SELLER OF GOODS OR SERVICES FOR MISREPRESENTATION

A seller may be held liable for misrepresentation, i.e. a false statement of fact by one party to a contract, which induces the other party to enter into the contract.

A misrepresentation must be distinguished from a mere "puff" (e.g. extravagantly worded advertising - not actionable).

If there is a misrepresentation the buyer's remedies are:

(a) if the misrepresentation was fraudulent – damages for deceit.
(b) if the misrepresentation was negligent – damages under the Misrepresentation Act 1967 unless the maker proves that he had reasonable grounds for believing, and did believe, that the statement was true.
(c) totally innocent – no damages.
(d) in all cases – rescission of the contract provided it is still available. In non-fraudulent cases the court may refuse rescission and award damages instead.

Appendix 6

EXAMPLE OF NON-RECOURSE FACTORING AGREEMENT

THIS AGREEMENT IS MADE ON: the last date shown for the signatures of the parties at the end of this document.

BETWEEN:

(1)   **TOP FINANCIERS** ("We/Us")

and

(2)   **THE CLIENT** NAMED IN THE CLIENT PARTICULARS ("You")

1.   **INTRODUCTION**

1.1   This Agreement applies only to those Debts specified in the Schedule at the end of this document created by you under whatever trading name or style you may ever carry on business. We may later extend or reduce the scope of this Agreement to such Debts as we agree in writing signed by both you and us. Certain words used in this document have special meanings which are explained in the Annexe of Definitions. Their first letter is in capitals.

1.2   You will sell to us with full title guarantee and we will purchase from you all Debts to which this Agreement applies which are created after the date of this Agreement and until its termination. You will also Offer to us all Debts to which this Agreement applies which are Outstanding on the date this Agreement is made.

2.   **START AND LENGTH OF RELATIONSHIP BETWEEN US**

2.1   This Agreement shall start on the date it is made and it will run for the minimum period shown in the Schedule. After the end of the minimum period our relationship with you will then continue until ended by either you or us giving to the other notice of at least the minimum shown in the Schedule. Such notice may be given at any time, even during the minimum period, provided it runs out on or after the end of the minimum period. During any period of notice you will continue to comply with all your obligations to us.

2.2   Should this Agreement end within the minimum period shown in the Schedule you must pay us a sum equal to the shortfall between the amount of the minimum service charge that would have been earned had this Agreement continued for the minimum period, and the service charges actually earned.

2.3   Should you wish to end this Agreement but give us notice of less than the minimum shown in the Schedule we may still agree to your request, subject to an additional fee. For each month or part of a month that your notice falls short of the minimum notice period the fee will be the higher of:

2.3.1   the monthly average of the service charges earned in the six calendar months before we agree to accept your request; or

2.3.2   one twelfth of the minimum service charge for the twelve calendar months before we agree to accept your request.

2.4   We can also immediately end this Agreement by giving you written notice at any time after a Termination Event.

3.   OUR OWNERSHIP OF DEBTS, OFFERS AND NOTIFICATIONS

3.1   As soon as possible on or after the date of this Agreement you will deliver an Offer in respect of each Initial Debt Outstanding together with its Related Rights. If we wish to accept an Offer, this will be done by crediting the Notified Value of each accepted Debt to the Debts Purchased Control Account. Upon doing so our ownership of such accepted Debt shall be complete and the Debt thereby assigned to us.

3.2   You hereby transfer to us the ownership of all Debts and in addition you hereby assign to us all Scottish Debts (in each case together with their Related Rights) created after the date of this Agreement until the ending of this Agreement. Our ownership of such Debts shall be complete and they shall vest in us the moment they are created even though such Debts may not yet be Notified to us.

3.3   During the life of this Agreement you will send us a Notification of each Debt and any relative credits following Delivery of the Goods, unless it is a Non-Notifiable Debt.

4.   PURCHASE PRICE OF DEBTS

4.1   The Purchase Price of the Debts covered by this Agreement is to be the amount received by us towards the discharge of the Debts but less:

4.1.1   Customers' prompt settlement discounts later claimed; and

4.1.2   any other later claimed Customers' deductions, abatements or set-offs; and

4.1.3   the discounting charges and service charges; and

4.1.4   all other sums due to us.

4.2   In respect of each Approved Debt for which no Remittance is received by us the Purchase Price shall be calculated and paid by us in accordance with clauses 7.1 and 7.2.

5.   **FUNDING LIMITS**

5.1   We may also set up a Funding Limit for each Customer.

5.2   No Prepayments will be available against Debts in excess of a Funding Limit. If, following a reduction of a Funding Limit, the amount of Prepayments already made exceeds your Availability, the excess must be paid back immediately to us.

6.   **APPROVAL OF DEBTS**

6.1   At our discretion we may establish or decline to establish Credit Limits. Debts within Credit Limits will be treated as Approved Debts in the order in which they are Notified. No Initial Debt can be an Approved Debt. The establishment of Credit Limits, changes and withdrawals will take place in accordance with the procedures set out in this section 6. Failure by you to comply with any term, obligation or procedure in this Agreement will change the status of an Approved Debt to an Unapproved Debt without notice.

6.2   You will submit to us a request for a Credit Limit if at any time you have any of the following:

        • a Customer who was not indebted to you at the date of the Agreement;

        • a Customer for whom you consider our existing Credit Limit is less than the expected Outstanding Debts of that Customer;

        • a Customer for whom a Credit Limit has been withdrawn;

        • a Customer in respect of whom you have been required by us to apply for a revised Credit Limit.

6.3   Information given to us or in a request for a Credit Limit must be true and accurate. If you later become aware of any change to the information given or you have knowledge of any financial difficulty or the threatened Insolvency of any Customer, you must immediately tell us. You must also inform us in writing and obtain our prior approval if you change your credit or discount terms to any Customer.

6.4   Any Credit Limit will only be valid for as long as the particulars submitted by you in seeking such Credit Limit remain unchanged. Any alteration by you without our prior approval will automatically cancel the relative Credit Limit given and the Debts within such cancelled Credit Limit shall rank as Unapproved Debts.

6.5   We may at any time establish, change, suspend or remove a Credit Limit with immediate effect. Any Debts subsequently created or Notified will be so affected.

6.6   A Credit Limit previously given shall automatically be withdrawn without notice to you, if:

6.6.1   the Customer prohibits the assignment of any Debt; or

6.6.2   the Customer will not accept our ownership of Debts; or

6.6.3   you request us not to pursue our collection procedures against the Customer; or

6.6.4   you are in breach of any of your obligations to us in respect of the Customer; or

6.6.5   at any time you trade with the Customer on cash or proforma terms without our prior written consent.

Upon such withdrawal all Outstanding Approved Debts and all future Debts of that Customer shall be treated as Unapproved Debts.

6.7   Once we have issued legal proceedings for any Debt Outstanding, then the Credit Limit for that Customer shall be withdrawn and you must not Deliver any further Goods on any terms (including on a cash or proforma basis) without our prior written consent.

6.8   Upon or at any time after a Termination Event we can withdraw any Credit Limits and treat any previously Approved Debts as Unapproved Debts. The exercise of this entitlement shall be at our discretion. If this Agreement ends all Credit Limits previously given shall automatically be withdrawn without notice.

7.   **INSOLVENCY OF CUSTOMERS**

7.1   If we decide that a Debt is uncollectable or if we are advised of both the Insolvency of a Customer and that the Debts of that Customer have been accepted by the Customer's Insolvency Practitioner as undisputed Debts then we shall remove them from the sales ledger and debit the Debts Purchased Control Account.

7.2   If the Debts referred to in clause 7.1 are Approved Debts, we will credit the Purchase Price of them to you. This will be calculated by taking the value of such Outstanding Approved Debts and then deducting:

7.2.1   firstly the VAT included in such Debts;

7.2.2   secondly the First Loss; and

7.2.3   finally the recourse percentage shown in the Schedule of the Notified Value of the Outstanding Debts.

Any surplus remaining shall be credited to the Client Account. If you have complied with all your obligations to us we may at any time thereafter reassign such Debts to you.

7.3   If a Customer due to pay an Unapproved Debt, including a Debt outside a Credit Limit or included in a First Loss, becomes Insolvent such Debt shall forthwith become an Ineligible Debt.

7.4   If an Approved Debt has been reassigned to you following the Insolvency of a Customer:

   7.4.1   you will use your best endeavours to recover payment of the Debt (including any dividend from the estate of the Customer);

   7.4.2   we may complete and lodge in your name any claim, proof or statement of Debt in the Insolvency of the Customer; and

   7.4.3   you will pay to us any future sums (after deduction of the relevant VAT) which you recover in respect of such Approved Debt. You will hold such sums in trust for us until paid to us.

8.   **DISPUTES**

8.1   If any Customer disputes a Debt or his liability to pay us by its due date or asserts any counterclaim or claim for reduction of or retention or set-off against a Debt (except for a settlement discount not exceeding 7.5%), then:

   8.1.1   you must promptly give us full details; and

   8.1.2   you must do your best to settle all such disputes and claims promptly and directly with your Customers; but

   8.1.3   we may also settle or compromise (or require that you should settle or compromise) disputes on such terms as we may decide in our absolute discretion and you will be bound by such compromise.

8.2   If we become aware that a Customer is disputing a Debt or his liability to pay by its due date, we will normally, but need not, send you a notice called a "dispute notice". You must resolve the dispute within the period which we will tell you in such notice. The Debt will be an Ineligible Debt and an Unapproved Debt whilst we await evidence satisfactory to us that the dispute has been resolved.

8.3.   You must promptly raise a credit note if a customer is entitled to one. Unless we have brought clause 8.4 into effect you must immediately deliver the credit note to the Customer and include its details on your next Notification. You will put such notice on the credit note as we specify and it will be debited to the Debts Purchased Control Account.

8.4   We may at any time write and tell you either that no credit notes can be despatched to your Customers without our prior consent or that any credit notes must be sent to us for our consent before we then despatch them.

9.   **OUR ACCOUNTS**

9.1   The Notified Value of all Debts will be credited to our account known as the"Debts Purchased Control Account". If the information sent with your Offer or Notification is incomplete or is missing we may reverse or refuse to make the entry. The balance on this account is our record of the prospective Purchase Price of Debts before any of the deductions used under clause 4.1 to calculate the Purchase Price. The Notified Value of Debts will also be debited to the sales ledger, which shows the amounts owing by your Customers.

9.2   You may also take Prepayments from us in respect of Debts credited to the Debts Purchased Control Account. These payments will be debited to the Client Account. The amount taken must not exceed the lesser of either your Availability or the Prepayment review level set by us from time to time. Your Availability will immediately be affected if any Debt later becomes an Ineligible Debt.

9.3   We may debit the Client Account with all other sums you owe us. If the debit balance on the Client Account results in a negative Availability you must immediately pay the excess to us without our having to ask you.

9.4   The value of any Remittance will be debited to the Debts Purchased Control Account and credited to the sales ledger and to the Client Account with an effective date for calculating discounting charges as the next working day after we receive funds cleared for value at our bank.

9.5   The balance on the Client Account will reflect:

9.5.1   payments taken by you;

9.5.2   any sums owed by you to us; and

9.5.3   any Remittances received by us.

9.6   If the Client Account shows a credit balance we will normally pay this to you without your asking us but, at our discretion, we may withhold amounts equal to:

9.6.1   any credit balances on Customers' accounts; and

9.6.2   the amount of Your Responsibility.

9.7   We will provide you with statements of the Debts Purchased Control Account and the Client Account. These shall be treated as correct and binding upon you, except for those errors which shall be obvious or contrary to law or where we receive your written notice within 10 days of our despatch of such statements to you.

9.8   You will accept a certificate signed by our Company Secretary or a director of ours as to all or any of the following on the date referred to in the certificate:

9.8.1   the balance on the Client Account;

9.8.2   the balance on the Debts Purchased Control Account;

9.8.3   any balance on a Customer's account or the sales ledger;

9.8.4   any loss or damage suffered by us;

9.8.5   the amount of Your Responsibility;

9.8.6   any other amount payable to us.

In any proceedings such certificate shall be conclusive evidence as to the balance, loss, damage or amount on the date so certified.

10.   CHARGES AND INDEMNITIES

10.1   You will pay us the discounting charge which shall accrue from day to day. It will be worked out at the rate shown in the Schedule on the debit balance on the Client Account. Any payment to you will be debited to the Client Account on the day that we initiate the transfer.

10.2   The discounting charge shall be debited monthly to the Client Account. Any debit to the Client Account shall be treated as a Prepayment for the purpose of working out the discounting charge.

10.3   We shall be entitled to a service charge at the rate shown in the Schedule for each Notified Debt. We shall debit the service charge to the Client Account when we receive your Offer or Notification. No refund of any service charges can be made either if a credit note is issued or if this Agreement ends.

10.4   If the total of all service charges in each period shown in the Schedule falls short of the sum needed during that period to reach the minimum service charge you will pay us the shortfall. If we consider such shortfall likely then we may debit it to the Client Account.

10.5   If our bankers charge us, you will repay to us their charges for

10.5.   10.5.1   dealing with dishonoured Remittances;

10.5.2   collecting any Remittances in a currency other than Sterling;

10.5.3   collecting Remittances in Sterling drawn on a bank outside the United Kingdom.

10.6   You will pay us a facility fee at the rate shown in the Schedule on each anniversary of this Agreement. You will also pay us an arrangement fee for any variation of this Agreement requested by you or any additional service provided outside its scope. If we permit payments in excess of your Availability, we may also make an additional facility charge until the excess is repaid.

10.7   You will fully indemnify us against all losses, costs, demands, disbursements, fees and expenses of:

    10.7.1   obtaining the release of Debts from charges, trusts or other encumbrances or enforcing such release;

    10.7.2   assignments or reassignments of Debts or Related Rights or giving notices of assignment or reassignment;

    10.7.3   taking guarantees or indemnities from any person, including a receiver;

    10.7.4   enforcing either this Agreement or any guarantee or indemnity given in respect of it;

    10.7.5   all matters arising from any breach by you of this Agreement or the occurrence of a Termination Event;

    10.7.6   dealing with disputes by Customers;

    10.7.7   any Customer failing to pay a Debt to us at its full Notified Value, other than an Approved Debt solely for reason of the Customer's Insolvency;

              collecting or attempting to collect any Debt from the moment that we threaten legal proceedings, except in respect of Approved Debts, including the costs of any solicitor and costs payable to any other party to the proceedings.

10.8   On a pro rata basis we will share with you the above charges, costs, expenses and fees:

    10.8.1   where the claim involves both Approved and Unapproved Debts; or

    10.8.2   if you are responsible to us for a First Loss in respect of the Approved Debts of that Customer.

10.9   VAT, if applicable, will be added to all fees and charges quoted by us.

10.10   You will pay us immediately on demand any amount which we have to pay to any Customer by way of refund claimed under a direct debit guarantee given by us.

11.   **REPURCHASE**

11.1   We may at any time require you to Repurchase an Ineligible Debt from us.

11.2   Should we require you to Repurchase Debts from us we will continue to own all such Debts until we receive the price for all Repurchases. At this point we shall transfer them back to you. We shall then account to you for any further sums received by us from your Customers in respect of such Debts.

12.   **NOTICES TO CUSTOMERS**

12.1   Notice to each Customer that we are the owner of the Debts must appear on each invoice and all copies. If we ask you, you will also give a general notice to each Customer that we own all your present and future Debts. We will tell you the wording of the notice which we can also give on your behalf.

13.   **CUSTOMERS' ACCOUNTS AND DEBT COLLECTIONS**

13.1   We will maintain your Customers' accounts in the form of a sales ledger.

13.2   We alone shall be entitled to collect and enforce payment of Debts in whatever way we see fit, and you must ensure that Customers pay all their Debts to us or as we direct, including by direct debits.

13.3   In our absolute discretion we can at any time grant time or other indulgence to any Customer and compromise claims with Customers or accept payment from a Customer which is less than the Notified Value of the Debt without discharging you from your obligations to us.

13.4   Where a Customer sends a Remittance to us, without allocating it to specific invoices either before or at the time of its receipt by us, we shall be entitled to apply the unallocated portion in satisfaction of such Debts as we may decide. We may likewise apply any payment made generally on account.

13.5   Upon request you will help us to collect Debts, whether or not we shall issue legal proceedings. In our absolute discretion we may start, defend or compromise any legal proceedings and you will be bound by our actions and decisions. The proceedings may be in our or your name. You will give us all evidence we may at any time need, whether before during or after any proceedings. You will make sure that those witnesses we need will attend court. We may use an alternative dispute resolution procedure involving mediation or arbitration.

13.6   If you request us not to issue or continue with proceedings for a Debt, we may agree to your request but shall not be obliged to do so. If we do agree then the Debt will immediately become an Ineligible Debt.

14.   **TRUSTS AND OTHER RIGHTS**

14.1   If you receive any Remittance, from that moment you will hold it absolutely in trust for us. We may give notice to anyone that such trust exists.

14.2   When you receive a Remittance you must:

14.2.1   immediately hand over to us the identical Remittance or pay it into such bank account as we tell you;

14.2.2   not pay it into any other account or deal with or negotiate it;

14.2.3   give us any advice received with it.

14.3   If we do not become the owner of any Debt or its Related Rights covered by this Agreement for any reason then you will be treated as holding such Debt or its Related Rights on trust for us free from all encumbrances.

14.4   You must promptly tell us about all Returned Goods. We may require you to set these aside marked with our name as the owner. You will then deliver them to us, or deal with them as we direct. We can sell any Returned Goods on such terms and at such prices as we consider appropriate. We shall credit the net proceeds towards the discharge of the relative Debts.

15.   YOUR UNDERTAKINGS TO US

15.1   Whilst this Agreement is in force and then until you have paid all monies owing to us you undertake:

15.1.1   to make sure the payment and settlement discount terms for each Debt and any rights of retention, abatement or rebate are not more generous than those appearing in the Schedule and that these appear on every invoice and all copies;

15.1.2   not to cancel or vary any Sale Contract or any payment terms or settlement discounts after Delivery unless you have our written consent;

15.1.3   to make sure that every Sale Contract shall:

• only be made in the ordinary course of your business stated in the Client Particulars;

• not include any prohibition against assignment of the Debt;

15.1.4   to make sure that neither you nor any Associate enters into any other agreement for the factoring, charging, declaring in trust or discounting of Debts with any other party or into any arrangement prejudicial to our outright ownership of Debts;

15.1.5   immediately we ask:

• to provide information about your Customers;

• to give evidence satisfactory to us of any order and the completion of any Sale Contract;

• to exercise any reservation of title to Goods in the Sale Contract;

• to deliver to us and not to your Customer the originals of any of the items comprised in the Related Rights, together with as many copies as we may require; we may forward these to the Customer or other persons or organisations as appropriate at your expense;

15.1.6   immediately to cease and desist from any contra accounting arrangements with your Customers;

15.1.7   not to include in an Offer or Notification any Debt until the Goods have been Delivered;

15.1.8   promptly to perform all your further and continuing obligations to a Customer and, if we ask, to give evidence of such performance;

15.1.9   to sign any additional documents and do anything we may need to exercise or enforce our rights, to sign assignments of Debts or Related Rights or endorse or Assign any instrument or security included in the Related Rights; any such assignment of a Scottish Debt or any of its Related Rights will support the assignments given in clauses 3.1 and 3.2 but will not prejudice the earlier assignments;

15.1.10   to take all steps we may require for the protection of our interests under or arising out of this Agreement and in mitigating any loss we may suffer;

15.1.11   to make sure that in relation to your sole trader and unlimited partnership Customers your processing of information about them (including any transfers to us) complies in all respects with the Data Acts, and is accurate;

15.1.12   to advise us promptly should you receive any notice or allegation of non-compliance with the Data Acts;

15.1.13   to advise us promptly of all changes made to information transferred to us if you receive a correction request from a Data Subject;

15.1.14   to permit us to advise your sole trader and unlimited partnership Customers about your disclosure of information about them to us and the use we will make of such information, including supplying it to and making searches with our credit reference and fraud prevention agencies;

16.   **WARRANTIES**

16.1   By including a Debt in an Offer or Notification you will be treated as having given all of the following warranties to us:

16.1.1   all the particulars contained in the Offer or Notification are correct and complete and the Debt has not been previously Notified to us;

16.1.2   each Debt relates to an actual and bona fide sale and Delivery in accordance with the Sale Contract;

16.1.3   the Debt is payable in the U.K. without any retention, set-off or counterclaim by a Customer with an established place of business in the U.K.;

16.1.4   you have the absolute right to transfer the Debt to us and, except in our favour, it shall remain free from any security, charge, trust, option, pledge, hypothecation, encumbrance, lien or any tracing rights adversely affecting the Debt, the Goods or the proceeds;

16.1.5   our ownership of the Debt will not violate any laws or agreement affecting you;

16.1.6   the Notified Value of the Debt is the same as its Contracted Value;

16.1.7   all sums due or obligations by you to the Customer have been paid or performed and you will have no other obligations towards the Customer which could reduce the amount payable to us for the Debt;

16.1.8   no right or claim of rescission, defence, adjustment or other right or claim exists or will arise to reduce or extinguish the Notified Value of the Debt or affect our ability to collect the Debt;

16.1.9   the Debt is one to which this Agreement applies.

16.2   You warrant that prior to entering into this Agreement you have disclosed to us every fact or matter known to you or which you should have reasonably known might influence us in our decision whether or not:

16.2.1   to enter into this Agreement on these terms; or

16.2.2   to accept any person as a guarantor or indemnifier of your obligations to us.

17.   **INFORMATION FOR US**

17.1   You must give us a signed copy of your full set of accounts, including your directors' or partners' (as the case may be) and auditor's report or such other financial reports as we request, for each of your accounting reference periods (as defined in the Companies Act 1985). You must give us these items as soon as you have them, which must be no later than six months from the end of each accounting period.

17.2   You must give us your management profit and loss account and balance sheet at such intervals as we tell you. You will also give us such other financial reports that we may ask for and you will ensure that your auditors or external accountants report to us directly any information we require. If we ask you will provide us with a copy of your partnership agreement and any amendments if you are a limited liability partnership.

17.3   You will let any employee, representative or agent of ours enter any of your business premises or locations under your control in order to:

17.3.1   inspect Goods, stocks, Sale Contracts and evidence of their performance;

17.3.2   verify, check, remove or be provided with copies of all Accounting Records.

17.4   We may at all times rely upon any signature, act or communication of any person purporting to act on your behalf and the same shall be binding upon you.

18.   **TERMINATION EVENTS**

18.1   In addition to the right of either you or us to give notice to the other to end this Agreement under clause 2.1, we may immediately end it at any time after any of the following events:

18.1.1   any breach or threatened breach by you of this Agreement;

18.1.2   the breach or threatened breach or the termination of any contract between us and any of your Associates;

18.1.3   any application by any creditor of yours for a court order that we must pay money to your creditor or must stop paying any monies to you;

18.1.4   if you have an obligation to a third party for repayment of borrowed money which is declared due prior to its stated maturity date or you do not pay it when due;

18.1.5   any change in your directors or partners (as the case may be), ownership, control, constitution or composition reasonably considered by us to prejudice our position;

18.1.6   breach or termination by you or a third party of any representation, warranty or undertaking given to us;

18.1.7   the termination of any waiver, consent, ranking or priority arrangement in our favour;

18.1.8   your ceasing or threatening to cease to carry on your business referred to in the Schedule;

18.1.9   your Insolvency including but not limited to the appointment of, or the giving of notice of intention to appoint, an administrator under the Insolvency Act 1986 or the coming into effect of a moratorium under the Insolvency Act 2000 or taking any steps towards such moratorium;

18.1.10   the Insolvency or death of any person who has given a guarantee or indemnity for your obligations to us, or the service of a notice of intention to end such guarantee or indemnity or the legal disability of that person;

18.1.11   if any Associate factors or discounts its debts with another party or is threatened with Insolvency proceedings or becomes Insolvent;

18.1.12   your failure to comply with the minimum notification requirements shown in the Schedule.

18.2   Upon your Insolvency, ceasing to trade or failure to repay the entire Repurchase price under clause 18.4.2, we may:

18.2.1   immediately debit your Client Account with an additional service charge at the percentage shown in the Schedule of the Notified Value of the Debts then Outstanding or Notified to us thereafter in order to cover our additional administrative work; and

18.2.2   immediately increase the discounting charge by the percentage shown in the Schedule.

18.3   Upon or at any time after a Termination Event, which in good faith we reasonably and honestly consider prejudices our position (whether or not we use our right immediately to end this Agreement), we may do any or all of the following:

18.3.1   upon making the information available through our screen based system (whether or not you access your screen):

• reduce the Prepayment percentage to zero or such other figure as we may decide;

• designate all or any Outstanding Debts as Unapproved Debts and / or Ineligible Debts;

• create a special reserve against your Availability to cover Your Responsibility;

• consolidate the balances on all accounts recording transactions between you and us;

18.3.2   demand that you pay us immediately any debit balance on the Client Account that exceeds the lesser of either your Availability or the Prepayment review level set by us from time to time or any balance due to us after such consolidation plus in each case service charges and discounting charges accrued but not yet debited and an amount equal to all credit balances on Customers' accounts;

18.3.3   require you to Repurchase any Debts then Outstanding;

18.3.4   delay at least ten calendar days, to allow for cheque clearances, before paying to you any credit balance on the Client Account.

In connection with a Termination Event set out in clause 18.1.1 we want you to be aware that the following matters will usually be considered as prejudicing our position:

• your breach of sub-clauses *(here cross refer to clauses that Top Financiers consider important to them)*;

• your failure duly to honour any payment obligation to us;

• your breach of any undertaking in clause 15 or any warranty in clause 16;

• your breach of clause 17.

However this list is not exhaustive and there may well be other situations where a Termination Event prejudices our position.

Within 30 days of our exercising our rights under sub-clause 20.3.1 (points 1 and 2) or taking action under clause 18.3.2 or 18.3.3 you may give notice to us immediately to end this Agreement.

18.4   Upon the ending of this Agreement, for whatever reason:

18.4.1   all Approved Debts shall forthwith become Unapproved Debts and Ineligible Debts;

18.4.2   you must Repurchase all Outstanding Debts from us at a price equivalent to the debit balance on the Client Account and all other sums due to us;

18.4.3   you will not attempt to cancel any notices of assignment given to Customers or attempt to collect Debts until you have paid the Repurchase price under clause 18.4.2 and we shall continue to own all Debts until so paid;

18.4.4   you will be responsible for all credit balances on Customers' accounts and indemnify us in respect of all claims for them;

18.4.5   you will not Notify us of any Debts arising after the date on which this Agreement ends; and

18.4.6   we shall pay you any credit balance on the Client Account less the amount of Your Responsibility but allowing at least ten calendar days for cheque clearances.

18.5   Except as otherwise provided, the ending of this Agreement shall not affect our respective rights and obligations in respect of:

18.5.1   any Debts which shall have come into existence prior to such termination; and

18.5.2   all transactions or events having their inception prior to such termination, including the continued running of the discounting charge and our rights to set-off monies or combine accounts.

Such rights and obligations shall remain in full force and effect until all monies due from you shall have been received by us and all monies due from us to you shall have been paid.

18.6   Any discharge of your obligations to us shall be of no effect to the extent that any receipt by us shall later be set aside under insolvency law.

19.   **POWER TO ACT IN YOUR NAME**

19.1   To ensure that you carry out your obligations to us and as security for all sums which shall become due to us, you irrevocably appoint us and our directors, Company Secretary and officers, at any time, jointly and each of them severally to act as your attorneys as we or they think fit in order to do any of the following:

19.1.1   complete and perfect our title to or deal with any Debt, Related Rights or Returned Goods;

19.1.2   obtain payment of and give valid discharges for any Debt;

19.1.3   secure performance of any of your obligations to us or to any Customer.

9.2   For these purposes, your attorneys may do any of the following:

19.2.1   sign all documents;

19.2.2   endorse and/or negotiate all Remittances;

19.2.3   conduct, defend or compromise any legal proceedings and settle any indebtedness;

19.2.4   take all other steps they consider necessary.

19.3   These powers shall continue both during and after the ending of this Agreement and during any disability on your part until all sums due to us have been paid. You will ratify and confirm whatever shall be lawfully done under these powers.

19.4   You also irrevocably appoint any assignee of ours or any person to whom we may novate this Agreement to perform any of the acts set out above. We may also appoint or remove a substitute attorney.

20   **LAW AND JURISDICTION**

Our relationship with you is to be governed and interpreted by English law. You submit to the jurisdiction of the English courts. We may, however, use the courts of any other jurisdiction.

21.   **GENERAL**

21.1   The whole agreement between you and us consists of only this document, including any annexes referred to in the Schedule (and any document referred to in such annexes). References to "the Agreement" or "this Agreement" include all the annexes and all subsequent amendments, variations or extensions. Except as provided in any special conditions all earlier agreements, prior negotiations, quotations, warranties, advertisements and representations shall be of no effect. You have not relied upon any representation made to you by us or on our behalf or been influenced, induced or persuaded to enter into this Agreement by any representation.

21.2   This Agreement is considered by both you and us to be reasonable. Should any part of it be valid only if some other part were deleted then the Agreement will apply as if it were so deleted. The remainder of this Agreement will not be affected by such deletion.

21.3   This Agreement is not intended to confer any right or benefit on any person who is not a party hereto. No term of this Agreement is enforceable pursuant to the Contracts (Rights of Third Parties) Act 1999 by any person who is not a party to this Agreement.

ANNEXE OF DEFINITIONS

In the attached Agreement the following expressions have the meanings set out against each of them.

"Accounting Records"

Any of the following:

(1) accounting books, records and ledgers, financial and management accounts;

(2) computer data or materials about your financial position, purchases and sales;

(3) all invoices, credit notes or documents evidencing entries in such books of accounts, records and computer data and any other documents we require.

"Approved Debt"

A Debt (except an Initial Debt) within a Credit Limit in respect of which:

(1) you are not in breach of any warranty or undertaking to us;

(2) the value does not comprise discount wrongly claimed by the Customer; and

(3) there is no dispute.

"Associate"

(1) Any subsidiary or holding company of yours as defined in sections 736 and 736A of the Companies Acts 1985 to 1989 or Articles 4 or 4A of the Companies (No. 2) (Northern Ireland) Order 1990; or

(2) any other form of associate of yours as defined in section 184 of the Consumer Credit Act 1974; or

(3) a director, partner, shareholder or employee of yours or the spouse of any of them; or

(4) any company in which you or any of them have an interest other than purely for investment purposes in a publicly quoted company.

"Availability"

Your entitlement to Prepayments calculated by:

(1) taking the credit balance on the Debts Purchased Control Account and deducting the amount of all Ineligible Debts; and

(2) multiplying the resultant sum in (1) by the Prepayment percentage; and

(3) from the resultant sum in (2) deducting:

- any existing debit balance on the Client Account;
- the amount of Your Responsibility;
- any special reserves created at our discretion.

"Client Account" An account operated by us to calculate discounting charges.

"Concentration Limit Percentage" Initially the percentage shown in the Schedule of the balance of all Outstanding Notified Debts.

"Contracted Value" The amount of a Debt payable by a Customer in accordance with the Sale Contract after taking into account any deduction, discount, claim or allowance.

"Credit Limit" The maximum value decided by us of the Debts due by a Customer which we are prepared to designate as Approved Debts, including the amount of the first invoice cover referred to in the Schedule.

"Customer" A person who incurs or may incur any indebtedness under a Sale Contract.

"Debt" Any present, future or contingent obligation of a Customer to make payment under a Sale Contract together with its Related Rights or where the context allows a part of such obligation or its Related Rights, including:

(1) the future right to recover sums due following the determination, assessment or agreement of the amount of the obligation; and

(2) VAT; and

(3) all duties and charges.

"Debts Purchased Control Account" An account reflecting the prospective Purchase Price of Debts.

"Delivered" In relation to Goods:

(1) their removal from your control and from your premises, carriers and agents; and

(2) their physical delivery to the Customer in the United Kingdom or to the Customer's order; and

(3) the assumption of risk therein by the Customer; and

(4) complete performance of the Sale Contract.

In relation to services: fully performed.

"Deliver" and "Delivery" are to be similarly construed.

"First Loss" The higher of either the amount or the percentage initially shown in the Schedule as the First Loss up to which Debts within a Credit Limit shall be Unapproved Debts.

"Funding Limit"	A monetary limit established by us in respect of each Customer against which the Prepayment percentage will be applied.
"Goods"	Any merchandise or services the subject of a Sale Contract.
"Ineligible Debt"	A Debt:

(1) which is disputed or in respect of which the Customer shall dispute their liability to pay or pay it by its due date for payment; or

(2) in respect of which you shall be in breach of any undertaking or warranty given to us about it or any other obligations of yours to us arising from it; or

(3) which is an Initial Debt Outstanding beyond 3 months from the date of this Agreement; or

(4) in excess of our Funding Limit; or

(5) owing by any Customer in excess of the Concentration Limit Percentage; or

(6) which is an Unapproved Debt Outstanding beyond the end of the Recourse Period or in respect of which we have threatened legal proceedings; or

(7) where the Customer is Insolvent; or

(8) specified by us at any other time.

"Initial Debt"	A Debt Outstanding at the date of this Agreement.
"Notification"	Your notification to us, in such way as we may specify, of Debts and credit notes which have not previously been Notified to us together with such evidence of the performance of the Sale Contract or reasons for a credit note as we may specify.
"Notified/Notify/ Notifying"	Inclusion of a Debt in an Offer or Notification.
"Notified Value"	The amount of the Debt as shown in an Offer or Notification.
"Offer"	An unconditional offer to sell us a Debt with full title guarantee to be made in such form and with such evidence of the performance of the Sale Contract as we may specify. Where more than one Debt is at the same time subject to an Offer it shall be treated as an independent offer to sell us each Debt so offered which may be accepted or rejected by us entirely at our discretion.
"Outstanding"	A Debt unpaid to us by the Customer or a third party.

"Prepayment"   A payment on account of the Purchase Price of Debts based on the Prepayment percentage initially as specified in the Schedule and arrived at in accordance with the definition of Availability.

"Purchase Price"   The price payable by us for a Debt calculated in accordance with clauses 4.1 and 4.2.

"Recourse Period"   The period initially as specified in the Schedule after which Unapproved Debts will rank as Ineligible Debts.

"Related Rights"   Any of the following in relation to any Debt or Returned Goods:

(1) all your rights by law as an unpaid vendor or under the Sale Contract but without any obligation on us to complete the Sale Contract;

(2) all evidence of the Sale Contract or its performance or any disputes arising;

(3) documents of title to goods, warehouse keepers receipts, bills of lading, shipping documents, airway bills, certificates of origin, customs forms, commercial and consular invoices, insurance documents or similar;

(4) the benefit of all insurances;

(5) all Remittances, securities, bonds, guarantees and indemnities;

(6) all Accounting Records to do with the Debt;

(7) the ownership of all Returned Goods;

(8) interest.

"Repurchase"   Our right to require you to buy back and in respect of a Scottish Debt to take a reassignment from us of an Outstanding Debt at a price equivalent to its Notified Value or the Prepayment paid in respect of it.

"Returned Goods"   Any Goods relating to or purporting to comply with a Sale Contract which any Customer shall for any reason:

(1) reject or give notice of rejection; or

(2) return or attempt to or wish to return to you or us; or

(3) which you or we recover from a Customer.

"Sale Contract"   A contract in any form, including a purchase order, between you and a Customer for the sale or hire of Goods or the provision of services or work done and materials supplied.

"Schedule"   The Schedule to this Agreement.

"Scottish Debts"   Debts arising under Sale Contracts where either those Sale Contracts are governed by Scots law or the invoices for the Debts are addressed to Customers in Scotland.

"Termination Event" Any event listed in clause 18.1.

"Unapproved Debt"   A Debt which is not an Approved Debt.

"Your Responsibility" Monies payable or possibly payable to us in the future including liability:

(1) arising from debts transferred to us by any of your suppliers; or

(2) as a guarantor or indemnifier of another client of ours; or

(3) for the breach of your obligations to us; or

(4) for legal costs and expenses;

and our reasonable estimate of such monies where the amount cannot be immediately found out.

Non-Recourse Domestic Factoring Agreement

THE SCHEDULE

1.	**Annexe(s) incorporated in this Agreement:** (clause 21.1)	Definitions
2.	**(a) Minimum Period of this Agreement:** (clause 2.1)	12 months from the date this Agreement is made.
	(b) Minimum Notice Period: (clause 2.1)	6 months.
3.	**Debts to which this Agreement applies:** (clause 1.1)	All UK Debts.

N.B.   In paragraphs 4 to 18 below:
• if we keep the Debts Purchased Control Account, Client Account and the sales ledger in respect of Debts in currencies other than Sterling then any sum expressed in Sterling shall be treated as if the words "or its currency equivalent" were also added.

UK DEBTS

4.	**Minimum Notification Requirements:** (clause 18.1.12)	We must receive a Notification from you at least once every 4 weeks.
5.	**Prepayment Percentage:** (definition of "Prepayment" and "Availability")	%.
6.	**Concentration Limit Percentage:** (definition of "Ineligible Debt" and "Concentration Limit Percentage")	%.
7.	**Prepayment Review Level:** (clause 9.2)	To be determined by us.
8.	**Recourse Period:** (definition of "Ineligible Debt" and "Recourse Period")	60 days from due date.
9.	**Discounting Charge:** (clause 10.1)	% above Base Rate.

10. **Service Charge:**   % of the Notified Value of each
     (clause 10.3)   Debt.

                                                U.K. DEBTS

11. **Minimum Service Charge:**   In any period of   month(s) £   .
     (clause 10.4)

12. **Additional Service Charge:**   %.
     (clause 18.2.1)

13. **Discount Charge Increase:**   £   per annum or part thereof.
     (clause 18.2.2)

14. **Your Payment and Settlement Discount Terms:**   days from   with a settlement
     (clause 15.1.1)   discount not exceeding   %.

15. **First Loss:**   The higher of either £   or   % of
     (clause 7.2.2)   Approved Debts.

16. **Recourse Percentage:**   %.
     (clause 7.2.3)

17. **CONDITIONS TO BE COMPLIED WITH BEFORE WE START MAKING PREPAYMENTS:**

18. **SPECIAL CONDITIONS:**

CLIENT PARTICULARS
CORPORATE CLIENT

NAME: _____

COMPANIES REGISTRY NO: _____

ADDRESS: _____

_____

_____

NATURE OF YOUR BUSINESS: _____

EXECUTION _____

To confirm the respective consent of each party to this Agreement and to acknowledge having had the opportunity to take independent legal advice both parties have executed and delivered this agreement as indicated below on the   day of   200 .

SIGNED and DELIVERED as a deed on
behalf of **TOP FINANCIERS**
by *_____   _____
duly appointed Attorney in the presence   Attorney for TOP FINANCIERS
of this Witness:

Witness' Signature: _____

Witness' Full Names: _____

Witness' Address: _____

_____

_____

Witness' Occupation: _____

CORPORATE CLIENT

SIGNED and DELIVERED as a deed on behalf of _____ LIMITED)

by *_____   _____
Director   Signature of Director

and *_____   _____
        **Director/Company Secretary   Signature of **Director/
          Company Secretary

Key
*   Insert full names.
**   Delete as applicable.

Appendix 7

BASIC INSOLVENCY PROCEDURES

The most common descriptions of insolvency are that the company cannot pay its debts when they become due or that the value of its assets is less than the amount of its liabilities, or both. "Insolvency" is also used to describe the various formal procedures which may apply to an individual or business. The Act of Parliament under which most formal procedures are administered is the Insolvency Act 1986. Insolvency law provides a system for dealing fairly with the assets of the insolvent individual or company and the claims of creditors. The law also deals with what happens to the individual or company following the insolvency.

Corporate Insolvency

If a company appears to be insolvent, there may, depending on the circumstances, be the following options open (Insolvency Act 1986):
- a voluntary arrangement
- administration
- administrative receivership
- liquidation

Liquidation may also take place even when the company is insolvent because the members just want to wind it up and realise the assets.

Company Voluntary Arrangement (CVA) (as revised by Insolvency Act 2000)

Purpose

The theory behind voluntary arrangements for companies is very similar to that for individual voluntary arrangements – to arrive at a composition in satisfaction of debts or a scheme of arrangement, so that the business may continue trading thereafter. It is therefore not surprising to find that there is a fair degree of commonality about the two procedures.

Procedure

Company voluntary arrangements start off with a proposal for a composition in satisfaction of the company's debts, the proposal being made by one of:

- the liquidator (where the company is in liquidation)
- the administrator (where an administration is in force)
- the directors (in other cases)

A proposal is drawn up explaining why a voluntary arrangement is desirable, and this goes to the nominee, an insolvency practitioner who will have helped in drafting the proposal. The proposal gives details of the assets and liabilities, the proposed duration of the arrangement, and details of the proposed distribution. For example an offer to all unsecured creditors to pay 50p for every £1 owed over a specified period of time.

Small Companies (Moratorium) If the company is eligible it has the option of obtaining a moratorium to keep the creditors at bay for up to 28 days to allow for a meeting of creditors to be held without fear of a winding-up petition being presented or an existing petition being progressed. To be eligible for protection under a moratorium, the company is required to be defined as small in accordance with the definition set out in S.247(3) Companies Act 1985. This requires that at least two of the following apply:

- Turnover not more than £5.6m
- Balance sheet total not more than £2.8m
- Number of employees not more than 50 (average over last 12 months)

The general procedure for making a CVA proposal without a moratorium, is similar for a company that does not meet the above criteria. However, the impact of not having the initial protection of a moratorium prior to approval of the proposal may be a major consideration for the directors and for the insolvency practitioner advising the company. Until such time as the proposal is approved, a creditor can bring or continue proceedings.

Report and Meetings

The nominee (an insolvency practitioner) files with the court his opinion of the proposed arrangement and if he is satisfied that it has a reasonable prospect of being achieved, then calls meetings of the creditors and members of the company. A minimum of 14 clear days' notice should be given and both meetings are normally held on the same day at the same place, the members' meeting being held after that of the creditors. The creditors can vote to approve the proposal (with or without modifications).

A resolution to approve the proposal, or any modification of it, must be passed by a three-quarters majority; any other resolution, by a simple majority (greater than 50%).

If the meetings of creditors and shareholders come to different conclusions, the result of the meeting of creditors will prevail, unless the court orders otherwise. Once approved, the arrangement is binding on all creditors, whether or not they voted in favour of it (or at all).

The meetings must be chaired by the nominee or a nominated substitute, who is an insolvency practitioner or an employee of the nominee. A report as to the outcome must be made to the court within four days.

Challenge

A decision taken at a meeting may be challenged within 28 days by:

- a person entitled to vote at either meeting;
- the nominee or any person who has replaced him; or
- the liquidator or administrator if the company is being wound up or is in administration.

The grounds for a challenge may be that:

- the composition or scheme unfairly prejudices the interests of a creditor, member or contributory of the company; and/or
- there was some material irregularity at or in relation to either meeting.

If it agrees with the challenge the court may:

- revoke or suspend the approvals; and/or
- direct that further meetings be held to consider any revised proposals that the original proposer may make.

Insolvency Practitioner's Role/Supervisor

The role is to implement the approved arrangement acting as "supervisor".

He acts under the authority of the arrangement, but may apply to the court for directions.

Assets

The supervisor takes charge of the assets included in the arrangement and starts agreeing creditors' claims so that distributions can be made In due course.

If the company continues to trade subsequent to an arrangement being approved, "new" creditors are not bound by the arrangement and are able to present a winding-up/administration petition should they not be paid.

Summary

Individual voluntary arrangements are very much a mirror of company voluntary arrangements, but note these differences:

- In a company voluntary arrangement, in addition to the creditors' meeting, the nominee must hold a meeting of shareholders of the company.

- In a company voluntary arrangement there is no initial report of the proposal to the court if the nominee is the same person as the liquidator or administrator.

In the case of either a company or individual voluntary arrangement, if the arrangement is approved, then, so far as is relevant, any proceedings in the winding-up of the company, or bankruptcy of the individual, are stayed and any administration may be discharged.

Fixed and Floating Charges

Where possible the chargee will seek to show that the charge is fixed, since this gives better security. The question is essentially a matter of control. If a chargeholder is able to demonstrate that he exercises control over the assets, then a fixed charge may be valid. In the absence of control, the charge is likely to take effect as a floating charge. This is a question of fact in each case.

Floating charges generally give security over assets not otherwise secured by fixed charges and become payable after the claims of the preferential creditors have been satisfied. It is appropriate for assets which are subject to change on a day to day basis, such as stock. Individual items move into and out of the charge as they are bought and sold in the ordinary course of business. The floating charge crystallises if there is a default or similar event (see below).

Crystallisation

Crystallisation is the term used to indicate that a floating charge has become a fixed charge. This happens upon the occurrence of an event specified in the charge, e.g. presentation of a petition for winding-up. The failure of a borrower to pay interest when it falls due is a breach of the repayment terms. Following the breach, the lender may take appropriate action such as appointing a receiver, and then the charge crystallises. The effect of crystallisation is that the charge becomes a fixed charge on those assets owned by the company on that date.

G.E. Tunbridge Ltd (1994) (a company in administration)

In this case a debenture over office furniture, typewriters, electronic equipment and tools, expressed to be a fixed charge, was held by the court to be a floating charge because the goods concerned were of a type which changed frequently.

Spectrum Plus Limited

Since the case of Siebe Gorman vs Barclays Bank (1979) it has been possible to take a fixed charge over book debts, provided that the security holder controls the asset. In a series of subsequent and conflicting cases, including New Bullas (1994), Agnew (2000) and Brumark (2002) the degree of control needed over the collection proceeds by the charge holder has been examined, to determine whether the charge is fixed rather than floating. The House of Lords in June 2005 gave their judgment in the case of Spectrum Plus. This confirmed that book debts could be subject to a fixed charge but not if the collections proceeds are paid into a bank account which the borrower is free to draw against. The court gave little guidance on what control would be effective other than to emphasise that the collection account must be a "blocked account" against which the borrower could not draw. This would then preserve the proceeds for the benefit of the bank. Clearly this will be very unattractive to most customers.

It is expected that banks will increasing transfer their funding against book debts to their factoring and invoice discounting subsidiaries. This should substantially increase the business handled through debt purchase arrangements.

Administration

Purpose

The administration is a concept introduced by the Insolvency Act 1986 and subsequently amended by the Enterprise Act 2002. It can be compared with an administrative receivership and has proven to be an effective means of rehabilitating businesses in difficulty. Administration is an alternative to an administrative receivership where:

- administrative receivership cannot apply because there is no floating charge or the floating charge was created on or after 15 September 2003; or
- the floating charge holder does not wish to appoint an administrative receiver.

Procedure

Appointment can be made by:

- the company (or its directors);
- by the holder of a qualifying floating charge (essentially a holder of all-embracing security); or the court on the petition of the company, or of its directors, or of a creditor.

Once notice of intention to appoint an administrator has been lodged at court, a moratorium commences and the court's permission must be sought before a third party can:

- take action to enforce any security over the company's assets;
- repossess goods under the terms of a hire-purchase, conditional sale, chattel leasing or retention of title agreement; or

- take steps in relation to any other proceedings, execution or other legal process including distraint and peaceful re-entry by a landlord.

An administrator must pursue one of the of the following objectives:

- rescue of the company as a going concern;
- a better result for creditors as a whole than in a winding-up; or, if neither of the above is reasonably practicable,
- the realisation of property for distribution to secured or preferential creditors.

Prior to appointment, the intended administrator must state that the purpose of the administration is reasonably likely to be achieved.

Administrator's Role

To manage the affairs, business and property of the company until a meeting of creditors is held (which must be as soon as reasonably practicable, but no later than ten weeks after the appointment of the administrator). After that time, he must act in accordance with his proposals.

Administrators have wide powers. They may do whatever is necessary to manage the affairs, business and property of the company. They also have many specific powers, including:

- to sell property,
- to borrow money and charge the company's property as security,
- to insure the company's property,
- to use the company's seal,
- to establish subsidiaries.

Some of their powers are very important to the finance industry:

- to sell assets which are subject to a floating charge,
- to sell assets subject to a fixed charge if their disposal is likely to promote the purpose of the administrator's appointment and if a court order is obtained,
- to sell assets subject to hire-purchase, leasing or similar agreements, if their disposal is likely to promote the purpose of the administrator's appointment and if a court order is obtained.

Employees

An administrator is taken to have adopted a contract of employment by allowing it to continue beyond fourteen days after his appointment. Adoption does not result in any personal liability for the administrator. However, payments of continuing wages/salary, accruing holiday pay and continuing pension contributions will rank ahead of the administrator's remuneration. Liability does not extend to payment in lieu of notice or redundancy claims.

Tax

Any tax liability incurred in the period of the administration, including tax on chargeable gains on the sale of assets, is an expense of the administration. However, in a receivership the tax is the liability of the company and ranks as an unsecured claim in a subsequent liquidation or as a liquidation expense, should one be running concurrently with the receivership.

Administrative Receivership

The option to appoint an administrative receiver was effectively abolished by the Enterprise Act 2002. An administrative receiver may now only be appointed by the holder of a floating charge created prior to 15 September 2003 or in limited other cases.

Purpose

Administrative receiverships are often confused with administrations and liquidations.

The principal objective of an administration is to rehabilitate a stricken company or improve the return to creditors, whereas the sole purpose of a liquidation is to finalise the affairs of the company. In contrast an administrative receivership is a means of enabling a secured creditor to realise its security, though it is by no means unknown for an administrative receivership to result in the survival of the business concerned.

An administrative receiver is in a very special position, because he can effectively take over and run the business of the company. For this purpose, he is given the same basic powers as an administrator (but for the special powers to sell assets subject to hire-purchase or leasing agreements and without the protection against the landlord).

Procedure

An administrative receiver is appointed by the holder of a floating charge which covers the whole (or substantially the whole) of the company's assets. Where appropriate, he will wish to keep the company in business with a view to the business being sold as a going concern, thus maximising the proceeds.

However, a floating charge created within 12 months of liquidation or administration is void except to the value of money, goods or services supplied at or after the time, unless the company was solvent immediately after creating the charge. In addition, it could be a voidable preference if the company was influenced by an intention to prefer the lender over other creditors.

The administrative receiver is required to:

- convene a meeting of creditors,
- give information to a committee of creditors as reasonably required.

Upon appointment, an administrative receiver must send notice of that appointment to the company; and within 28 days, unless the court says otherwise, must notify all creditors. When he is appointed, the directors lose their executive powers, although they retain their fiduciary duties.

Administrative Receiver

The administrative receiver is an agent of the company, but is personally liable on contracts he enters into in that capacity. However, he may contract out of such liability and is indemnified out of the company's assets.

The administrative receiver's powers are conferred upon him in the charge under which he was appointed, and will enable him to:

- carry on the business of the company,
- take possession of the company's property,
- raise or borrow money, and grant security,
- refer issues affecting the company to arbitration,
- appoint a solicitor, accountant or other professional,
- present or defend a petition for the winding-up of the company; call up uncalled capital; change the registered office; use the company seal; execute documents and deeds; draw, accept, make or endorse bills of exchange or promissory notes,
- rank and claim in bankruptcy, insolvency, sequestration or liquidation proceedings against a debtor,
- establish subsidiaries,
- grant or accept a surrender of a lease or tenancy,
- employ or dismiss employees,
- do anything else incidental to these powers.

Assets

Under the Insolvency Act 1986, an administrative receiver may apply to the court for an order to sell property, which is subject to another charge. However this does not apply in the case of any security held by the person by or on whose behalf the administrative receiver was appointed, or of any security to which a security so held has priority. An order will be granted if the court is satisfied that this would result in a more advantageous realisation of the assets of the company than would otherwise be the case. But, if a sale does take place, the receiver cannot just use the proceeds without more ado. Instead, he must pay them to the other charge holder up to the amount of the claim.

The proceeds are used to discharge previous charges in order of priority. One important point to note is that, unlike an administrator, an administrative receiver cannot seek a court order allowing him to sell assets which are subject to hire-purchase and leasing agreements and so on.

Creditors

Creditors must be notified of the administrative receiver's appointment within 28 days, and must receive a report within three months. The latter is presented normally at a meeting of creditors, at which point they may appoint a committee. The report must include:

- the events leading up to the administrative receiver's appointment,
- the disposal or proposed disposal of any property of the company, and the carrying on or proposed carrying on of any business,
- the amounts of principal and interest payable to the debenture holder(s) by whom or on whose behalf he was appointed, and the amounts payable to preferential creditors,
- the amount likely to be available for other creditors,.
- a summary of the statement of affairs submitted to him with his comments.

Liquidation

One of the functions of the personal insolvency procedures is to enable the debtor to make a fresh start. The same is not necessarily true in relation to corporate insolvency. Although it is desirable for a company to be rehabilitated if possible, where there is no hope of this the company will merely go into liquidation. This contrasts with the law on bankruptcy, which involves a discharge of the debtor within one year.

There are essentially two main categories, one of which can be subdivided giving us three methods of liquidation:

- voluntary winding-up, which can be subdivided into:
  – members' voluntary winding-up
  – creditors' voluntary winding-up
- compulsory winding-up

Members' Voluntary Liquidation

The term "liquidation" is in this context interchangeable with the term "winding-up". Here we are concerned with solvent companies. A declaration of solvency, which includes a statement of assets and liabilities, must be made for this purpose and accompanied by a sworn affidavit. The liquidation is commenced by special resolution.

The special resolution and the declaration of solvency must be filed with the Registrar of Companies, notice of the resolution and the liquidator's appointment advertised in the Gazette and all creditors notified.

The liquidator's functions, as with all liquidations, are to wind-up the affairs of the company and distribute the assets.

It may become a creditors' voluntary liquidation if the liquidator believes that the company will not, after all, be able to pay its debts in full. In that case, he must:

- summon a creditors' meeting within 28 days of forming that opinion,
- give creditors seven days' notice by post,
- gazette that notice and advertise it in two newspapers circulating in the locality in which the company had its principal place of business,
- provide creditors with information as required prepare a statement of affairs for the creditors' meeting,
- preside at the creditors' meeting.

Creditors' Voluntary Liquidation

This can be initiated if the company is insolvent and the interests of the creditors must be protected. An extraordinary resolution must be passed and the date of the resolution is the commencement of liquidation. In addition:

- the creditors must be given at least seven days' notice of a meeting,which must be held within 14 days of the resolution, and notice of the meeting must be published;
- the notice must give for enquiry purposes the name and address of an insolvency practitioner who can provide information, or an address where a list of creditors may be inspected;
- the directors must make out a statement of affairs, which goes before the meeting and then to the appointed liquidator;
- a director must chair the meeting;
- the liquidator must attend the meeting, if appointed at that stage;
- resolutions are passed by a simple majority;
- the winding-up resolution is filed with the Registrar of Companies, and notice of the resolution gazetted;
- the powers of the directors cease when the liquidator is appointed. The liquidator:
  - must notify the liquidation committee of disposals of assets to any party connected with the company,
  - can disclaim onerous property,
  - can apply to the court for directions,
  - must call an annual meeting and make annual returns.

When the company is fully wound up, he calls creditors' and contributories' meetings and puts the final result before them.

Compulsory Liquidation

This involves the presentation of a petition to the court for winding-up. The petition may be presented by the company, its directors, a creditor or a shareholder. It can occur when a company will not admit its insolvency and carries on trading, at risk to its creditors. The ground for a creditor's petition for compulsory winding-up will be that the company is unable to pay its debts as they fall due which may be proved by the company failing to comply with a statutory demand within 21 days.

There is no requirement for a statutory demand, provided there is a clear undisputed debt which the company after demand has failed to pay.

Any creditor whose debts are over a certain figure and who has served a written demand on the company may present a petition, which is filed in court and verified by affidavit. The petition is served on the company, and advertised in the Gazette.

Once a petition is presented:

- any disposition of property may be invalid,
- status of members and share ownership may not be changed,
- any pending action or proceedings are stayed,
- a provisional liquidator may be appointed.

When the court makes a winding-up order:

- the Official Receiver becomes liquidator and continues as such until another person is appointed,
- all actions and proceedings against the company are stayed (other than with leave of the court),
- the Official Receiver may require a statement of affairs to be made out
- a first meeting of creditors is normally convened, and a liquidation committee appointed if required,
- directors' duties and powers cease,
- the business of the company may be carried out only so far as it is beneficial to the liquidation, and then it requires committee or court sanction.

A liquidation committee may be set up, and if one-tenth of the creditors (by value) request it, the liquidator must convene a meeting of creditors.

Liquidator's Powers

The liquidator's powers in any type of liquidation are to:

- pay any class of creditors in full,
- make any compromise or arrangement with creditors,
- compromise any debt,
- compromise any question relating to the assets or the liquidation,

- take security in respect of previous two,
- bring legal proceedings peculiar to liquidations (e.g. wrongful trading, preference, transactions at undervalue).

These powers are given him:

- in a members' voluntary liquidation by extraordinary resolution;
- in a creditors' voluntary liquidation with the sanction of the court or the liquidation committee or a meeting of creditors; and
- in a compulsory liquidation with the sanction of the court, or the liquidation committee.

Additionally, the following powers may be exercised with sanction in a compulsory liquidation and without sanction in any voluntary liquidation:

- to bring or defend any action or other legal proceedings,
- to carry on the business of the company so far as may be necessary for the winding-up.

The following powers may be exercised by any liquidator without sanction:

- to sell any assets privately or by public auction (but see below),
- to do all acts and execute all deeds, etc. using the company's seal if necessary,
- to prove, rank, claim and receive dividends in the insolvency of any contributory,
- to draw, accept, make or endorse bills of exchange or promissory notes,
- to raise money on security,
- to appoint agents,
- to do all other things necessary.

A liquidator may not prevent a hire-purchase creditor from repossessing its goods. A liquidator has no power to sell goods subject to a hire purchase agreement, nor can the court authorise this.

Distribution of Assets in Insolvency

When considering the distribution of assets, particular care needs to be taken to ensure that they have been categorised correctly. There are three classes of assets, namely fixed charge, floating charge and uncharged. In each type of procedure the order of distribution of the floating and uncharged assets differs.

Distribution of Fixed Charge Assets

In all cases, an asset subject to a fixed charge is available to the holder of the fixed charge over that asset.

Distribution of Floating Charge Assets

Liquidation

1. The costs of realisation and, to the extent that uncharged assets are insufficient, the costs of dealing with preferential creditors
2. Preferential creditors (to the extent not paid in full from uncharged assets)
3. Floating charge holder

Any remaining funds to be treated as uncharged (see below)

Administrative Receivership

1. Costs
2. Preferential creditors (to the extent not paid in full from uncharged assets)
3. Floating charge holder
4. The company (probably by this stage in liquidation; the floating charge holder having been paid in full, the liquidator will receive these funds as uncharged assets)

Administration

1. Costs
2. Preferential creditors (to the extent not paid in full from uncharged assets)
3. Floating charge holder
4. Unsecured non preferential creditors (with court approval only, otherwise the administration will be converted to a liquidation and the distribution will continue from categories 3 to 6 under Liquidation below)

Distribution of Uncharged Assets

Liquidation

1. The costs of the liquidation not payable from floating charge
2. Preferential creditors
3. Unsecured non preferential creditors
4. Post-liquidation interest on claims in 2 and 3 above
5. Debts to members as members (e.g. an unpaid dividend)
6. Repayment of capital and distribution of surplus in accordance with the Articles of Association

Administration

1. Costs
2. Preferential creditors
3. Unsecured non preferential creditors (with court approval only, otherwise the administration will be converted to a liquidation and the distribution will be continued by the liquidator from categories 3 to 6 under Liquidation above).

Administrative Receivership

An administrative receiver has no power to deal with uncharged assets.

Company Voluntary Arrangement

The distribution in a company voluntary arrangement will depend on the terms of the proposal, but the secured and preferential creditors will retain their priority as in a liquidation (unless voluntarily surrendered). The supervisor cannot be empowered to return capital or surplus to shareholders.

Administration – survival of the company

If the company is restored to solvency and returned to the control of its directors the creditors may be paid in the ordinary course of business, so the concept of distribution is not relevant.

Glossary of Insolvency Terms

Authorised (or licensed) Insolvency Practitioner	A person authorised by the Department of Trade & Industry (DTI) or a professional body to act as trustee in bankruptcy, nominee, supervisor, liquidator, administrative receiver or administrator
Contributory	Shareholder
Fixed charge	A specific charge on a definite or specific property of a permanent nature e.g. land or heavy machinery (legal or equitable charge)
Floating charge	An equitable charge over assets turned over in the course of trade (e.g. stocks), allowing a company to carry on its business in the normal way
Official Receiver	The civil servant employed by the Insolvency Service (an Executive Agency of the

BERR) to head the regional offices whose responsibilities cover bankruptcies and compulsory liquidations. There are currently 33 regional offices in England and Wales. In Scotland, the Accountant in Bankruptcy has similar responsibilities as regards personal insolvency

Preferential Creditors	Certain employment claims defined in Schedule 6 to the Insolvency Act 1986
Winding up	The procedure whereby the assets of a company are gathered in and realised, the liabilities met, and the surplus, if any, distributed to shareholders

Administration and Administrative Receivership

A Comparison

	Administration	Administrative Receivership
Appointment	By company/directors; or By holder of qualifying floating charge; or By court on petition of company/ directors, creditor, or supervisor of CVA	By holder of floating charge secured on whole or substantially whole of the assets
Role	To achieve one or more of: rescuing the company as a going concern, achieving a better result for creditors than in a liquidation, realising property to make a distribution to secured or preferential creditors	To realise assets for the benefit of the chargeholder (in practice achieved where possible by selling the business assets as a going concern)
Duty of care	Balances interests of all classes of creditor and other stakeholders	Primary duty to chargeholder. Duty to other creditors to obtain a proper price and may be other duties depending on circumstances
Choice of insolvency practitioner	By appointer/petitioner, but holder of floating charge able to over-rule choice of company/directors or of petitioner	By chargeholder
Status	Officer of the court and agent of the company	Agent of the company
Liability	No personal liability	Personal liability on contracts entered into (but may contract out of liability), and on employment contracts retained for more than 14 days

	Administration	**Administrative Receivership**
Disposal of assets	Power to sell company assets, subject to need for consent (or permission of court) where there is a prior fixed chargeholder. Also power to sell third party assets (hire purchase or reservation of title) with permission of court	Power to sell company assets, subject to need for consent (or permission of court) where there is a prior fixed chargeholder

Protection from creditor action

	Administration	**Administrative Receivership**
Winding up	Prohibited	Permitted (although the receiver has a weak power to oppose the making of a winding up order)
Landlord **- Distraint** **- Forfeiture**	Only with consent of administrator or permission of court	No protection
HP / lease / RoT	Repossession only with consent of administrator or permission of court	No protection
Execution by judgment creditor	Only with consent of administrator or permission of court	Not possible
Antecedent transactions	Can challenge transactions at undervalue and preferences	No power to challenge
Meeting of creditors	Within 10 weeks to vote on administrator's proposals	Within three months to receive a report
Funding of continuing trade	If appointment by holder of floating charge, chargeholder likely to be willing. Otherwise may be problematic	Chargeholder almost always willing
Directors	Directors remain in office. May expect active role if administrator appointed by company and objective is rescue of the company. Administrator may appoint or remove	Directors remain in office, but have no active role

Power to pay creditors

	Administration	Administrative Receivership
Fixed charge	Yes	Yes
Preferential	Yes	Yes
Floating charge	Yes	Yes
Unsecured	With permission of court, or to assist achievement of objective	No
Exit routes	Hand back to directors (with or without CVA to restore solvency)	Liquidation
	Liquidation	Dissolution
	Dissolution	Hand back to directors
Public perception of process	Positive through association with the rescue culture	Adverse – seen as foreclosure by lender and as a terminal procedure as the company does not survive, even though the business frequently does